BINGE CRAZY

M000197507

If you or someone you know su~~gg~~
ing-related issues, *Binge Crazy* is a compelling read. It offers both an experiential and professional view of what does and doesn't work in the treatment of binge eating and overeating, along with valid insight into the disorder's psychological and sociological origins.

The story moves from a Toronto mental hospital to a taping of the David Frost show in London, England, spanning more than fifty years on two continents. *"Binge Crazy* is a true story of how I lost my mind and ultimately came to my senses," says Gold, who has a private practice in Toronto and has led workshops on eating-related issues for more than ten years. "I now know I blamed binge eating and my mother for my misery. But really, my compulsion to overeat was just the symptom of a deeper unrest."

Gold, a Registered Psychotherapist, is a graduate of Ryerson University, Toronto, holds a graduate certificate in Addiction and Mental Health, a post-graduate certificate in Gestalt Therapy, and is a member of the Ontario Association of Consultants, Counsellors, Psychometrists and Psychotherapists (OACCPP), and the Association for the Advancement of Gestalt Therapy (AAGT).

WHAT IS BINGE EATING DISORDER (BED)?

"Recurring episodes of eating significantly more food in a short period of time than most people would eat under similar circumstances, with episodes marked by feelings of lack of control. Someone with binge eating disorder may eat too quickly, even when he or she is not hungry. The person may have feelings of guilt, embarrassment, or disgust and may binge eat alone to hide the behavior. This disorder is associated with marked distress and occurs, on average, at least once a week over three months."

— *Diagnostic and Statistical Manual of Mental Disorders, Fifth Edition (DSM-5)*

Binge Crazy

A psychotherapist's memoir of food addiction,

mental illness, obesity and recovery

Natalie Gold

ISBN: 978-1-934675-99-1

Arrow Publications, LLC
20411 Sawgrass Drive
Montgomery Village, MD 20886 USA

arrow_info@arrowpub.com
www.arrowpub.com
www.myromancestory.com

Author recognizes that all trademarked items mentioned in the book belong to the trademark holders of said items.

Because of the dynamic nature of the Internet, any web addresses contained in this book may have changed since publication and may no longer be valid.

DEDICATION

For the people out there who still suffer,

and those who are in their lives

TABLE OF CONTENTS

INTRODUCTION i
  Everybody's Got a Story i
  In My Life ii

CHAPTER 1: APPOINTMENT WITH GILDA 1
  Has Anyone Got a Chair? 1
  The Greatest Role of My Life 4
  I Am Not the Walrus, or Am I? 7

CHAPTER 2: THE GIBBLE-GABBLE 12
  Dealing with Crazy 12
  The Unrelenting Tenth Degree 13

CHAPTER 3: ALL IN THE FAMILY 20
  Shirley 20
  Robert/Bob 23
  Shirley and Bob 27
  Rosemarie 29
  Me 30
  My Sister 33
  The Shadow 38

CHAPTER 4: OPENING NIGHT 45
  Noelle 45
  Brown Camps 49

CHAPTER 5: CONNECTS AND DISCONNECTS 55
  The Source 55
  The System 56
  The Great Pretender 59
  Mealtime at Our House 63
  Gabby Girdle Gold 66
  Splits 72

CHAPTER 6: EARLY IN THE NINTH 74
  A Teensy Bit about the Clarke Institute of Psychiatry 74
  The Original April Fool 75
  Jagged Little Pills 80

Food, Glorious Food 82
Gilda's First Take 83

CHAPTER 7: O-BLAH-DEE-O-BLAH-DAH 87
Location, Location, Location 87
May I Help You Out? 94
Ms. Personality 97
Dotter 105

CHAPTER 8: MEASURING THE MARIGOLDS 113
Family Therapy 113
Drugged Tests, Part 1 115
Alarming 116
Drugged Tests, Part 2 120
Bob and Shirley at the Clarke, Take 1 124

CHAPTER 9: THE UNWINDING 128
Who Are You? 128
Not a Rape 130
Basement Daze 133

CHAPTER 10: CHEZ CLARKE 138
On the Move 138
Guitar 141
Other Peeps 144
Remnants 150
Sex Ed 156
Bob and Shirley at the Clarke, Take 2 161

CHAPTER 11: PLAN B 164
The Second *Mauritania* 165
Cold Fish and Chocolate 167
Nellie and the Stain 168
Insincerity Times Two 172
Don't Ask, Never Tell 173

CHAPTER 12: REALITY ORIENTATION 179
Don't Wear Red 179
Shift that Paradigm 181
Potential 183
Whose Reality? 185
External Validity 188

Mudville 189
Future Tense 196
A Mind of My Own.. 199

CHAPTER 13: LEAVINGS 203
Falling Through.. 203
You Can Go Home Again, but 205
Toronto-Bound.. 207

CHAPTER 14: OUTPATIENT 209
Out of the Frying Pan.. 209
Into the Fire... 213
Farewell Gilda, Hello Jack... 220

CHAPTER 15: UP TO THE BOTTOM 222
Yorkville Revisited... 222
Sitcom Anyone? 223
London Revisited 226
Fat Acceptance 227
The Parking Lot 230
Does It Look like a Duck? 233

CHAPTER 16: A NEW DIRECTION........................ 239
The Turning Point.. 239
Goal Weight at Last... 240
The Myth of Thin... 243
Fathead... 245
Food First.. 247
The Power to Choose 260
Relapse... 264
Archeology... 270
Here's the Thing 282

APPENDIX: UNDERLYING TRIGGER ISSUES.................. 289

ACKNOWLEDGMENTS 295

BIBLIOGRAPHY 296

ENDNOTES 305

INTRODUCTION

Everybody's Got a Story

Neediness. It's a word I've had a lot of trouble with over the years. A word I've used to judge and evaluate people, especially myself, in a less-than-flattering way. You're not enough if you need to the point of neediness. It's a state, a gimme-gimme state that oozes out through the pores and asks others for their souls.

When I was a kid, I had two parents who were needy. Very needy, emotionally. They couldn't help it. It wasn't conscious. But they fed off me, because they needed me so much. They needed me to fill them up and give them a reason to go to work and to clean and shop and cook and manage. And somehow in all this, I got lost. And it has taken a very long time to get un-lost. Un-lost and found in the big city.

So when I sensed that someone was too needy the way my parents were, I made a run for it, buckled up and sped away as fast as I could. Afraid I'd have the life sucked out of me. Very sad. No wonder I turned to a substance like food to fill myself up. I was a kid then and didn't know how to look after myself. Didn't fully realize what was happening to me. But I did keep trying to get away. I'd hide in the back room, pretending to do my homework. But I'd really be daydreaming, listening to music or reading a book, and mostly trying to figure out the world.

But it didn't matter how much I figured things out. By the time I was twenty-one, I needed a mental hospital to help me get away. And to stop the life from being sucked out of me.

This is the story of how that came to be. And what happened during and after. This is also the story of a pernicious and chronic affliction – binge eating disorder[1], or BED – and how it develops and progresses over time, how it can contribute to obesity, how it can influence and affect every aspect of your life until you get the appropriate treatment and start on the long, often gruelling path to healing.

i

In My Life

I began writing this book in 2000, more than thirty years after my stay in a mental hospital, and stopped shortly after I bumped into Vivian at the discount grocery store. I'd first met her at Toronto's Clarke Institute of Psychiatry, where we were both inpatients. She told me she'd been back there recently, as had happened to her from time to time over the years. After some chitchat in the produce section, we parted company once again. Afterwards, I realized my good fortune. All my personal growth work had paid off. Despite the various ups and downs, I'd managed to avoid returning to the Clarke. Except that the sticky cobwebs from my time there were still woven into my dreams and fears.

I didn't resume writing until 2005, when some pieces were added and a coherent form began to take shape. By then, I'd returned to the Gestalt Institute of Toronto to train as a psychotherapist (I'd spent two years there in the mid-1980s, but never dealt with being crazy. Too much else going on). Gestalt requires self-awareness and completing "unfinished business" from the past. I suspect this is what made me return to the story. I worked at it for a few months, but put it aside again when life interfered.

In May 2006, almost forty years after my time at the Clarke, I acquired a photocopy of my medical records,[2] at the prompting of a colleague. Despite the passage of time, I'd become keenly aware of the shame I still carried, and decided it was time to cough up this hairball from my past. Confront the stigma. Not surprisingly, I couldn't wait to skim through the hospital records, fascinated to learn how the Clarke staff perceived my parents and me. After highlighting particular passages in bright yellow, I put them away for later, when I could give them the attention they deserved. Later came after I spent five years as a full-time university and grad student.

Since 2013, I've been back at it. But this time is different. This time I feel the need to finish telling the story. This time I'm writing because I want to help others and share some of what

I've learned over the years, especially about binge eating disorder and how to cope with being crazy. Because I want to warn mothers of overweight teens to take note and avoid following my own mother's path. And to warn people about family secrets and the havoc they can wreak. I want to encourage people to become more conscious and self-aware, especially those in the medical profession and the mental health field. And to underline the value and importance of finding a spiritual path to follow.

On a more personal level, I'm writing because I can't *not* write. Because I can't put it off anymore. Because I want to acknowledge how much resistance and difficulty I've had with change – from formerly obese, formerly crazy, formerly undisciplined and formerly lazy – to who I am today. Unlike others who overcome enormous obstacles in a relatively short time, I've taken so very long to get my act together. And I'm still not finished.

Because I want to honour all the people who've helped me along the way, and they are legion. From the famous authors and celebrities I've never met, who showed me that a woman could be brave and live differently than society's limited female roles. To personal therapists and guides, whose patience and wisdom helped me see what I didn't want to see. To my friends, who've hung in there with me over the years. And to my fellow addicts who trudged with me through the program I joined in June 1981. Because reclaiming a soul and getting a life onto a hopeful and positive track is not a solitary journey.

This time I need to put the past, finally, into the past. To own it, acknowledge it, honour it, process it, let it go, finish with the residual shame and move on with my life. Or, as author and teacher Carolyn Myss[3] would say, to call my spirit back. To gather up all the missing fragments from other time zones and reclaim them, bring them into the present, so that my energies aren't scattered, and so I can live more fully in the here and now.

And finally, because I need to honour my mother, Shirley – this woman who brought me into the world, who without a doubt has been my most difficult, my most troublesome relationship, and has therefore been one of my greatest teachers. As for my father, Robert, after many years, I've opened my heart and made peace with this kind but troubled man. Yet my learning is less clear. These were good people, Shirley and Bob. Well-meaning and big-hearted. I didn't know it then, but I loved both parents deeply, truly and profoundly. It seems ridiculous I didn't know how much I loved them.

I also didn't know how scared I was all the time. Scared of them, scared of living, and scared of myself. But mostly, scared of my feelings, which is partly why I ate over them, muddying their meaning, obscuring their truths.

If my parents were still alive, I wouldn't be writing this. Too much guilt. Revealing dirty laundry in public is a no-no for many people. But in our family, even saying things out loud was taboo. The implication: what you don't say can't hurt you. Absurd, and not true. Our secrets can hurt us the most. All the unspoken and unacknowledged thoughts, feelings, words and deeds. They fester inside. Infecting our bodies, affecting our spirits. Until we express them, let them go. I'm doing that now.

This time I've had the benefit of the Clarke records,[4] full of long-forgotten facts about my life before and after my two-year involvement at the Clarke – ten months as an inpatient and fifteen as an outpatient.[5] With a more thorough reading, the notes evoked many different feelings: laughter, sadness, surprise, embarrassment, and a weird sense of eavesdropping on private and sometimes highly unflattering conversations.

The richness of the information brought home how disturbed I really was at twenty-one, and how blessed to have found help at the Clarke Institute, considered the finest mental health treatment centre in Canada at the time.

The notes also contained an unexpected document – a three-page letter dated March 1979 from staff psychiatrist Dr. Paul Garfinkel, who ultimately became head of the hospital, now known as CAMH.[6]

BINGE CRAZY

Most of this narrative has been written from memory. And while the medical records corroborate certain events, add some rich detail, offer a glimpse into my family's reaction, and provide an accurate timeline, they also tell more than just my side of the story. I've let the psychiatrists, doctors, and social workers speak for themselves.

I've decided to use real names for most of the Clarke staff, initials only for those I disliked, and aliases for my fellow inpatients, personal friends, and acquaintances. My sister Tsiporah, my dear aunt Hannah, and my friend Dorothy didn't want aliases. I refer to my mother as Shirley (something I'd never do when she was alive) and to my father as Robert or Bob – he was Bob to my mother and his friends. You'll also notice a few men named David, distinguished by their last initial. David X is the one I obsessed over.

One more thing: my story is not unique. Nothing, absolutely nothing that happened to me is one- of-a-kind. Each life incident has happened to others, sometimes in more dramatic, traumatic, funny, or exciting ways. Sometimes less. While the combination of factors, their timing, and some details may be specific to me, sadly, similar events have happened to others in far greater numbers than any of us would like to admit. Here's to my fellow travellers.

CHAPTER 1: APPOINTMENT WITH GILDA

Has Anyone Got a Chair?

Late in the afternoon of March 31, 1967, at the ripe old age of twenty-one, my body slowly slid down the wall as I waited in the basement hallway at the Clarke Institute of Psychiatry. This unplanned downwards descent, surprisingly pleasant, initially struck me as amusing. Gilda had told me to wait outside her office for a few minutes while she conferred with some other folks who worked with her there at the Clarke.

Gilda was the social worker I'd come to see. She'd asked me a few questions, and then sent me into the hall to wait while she chatted to these other people. I had no idea why. All I knew was that they were taking way too much time in there, with me outside in the hallway and no chair in sight. I was exhausted. It had taken most of my energy to get myself there that Friday afternoon. At least the wall felt comforting against my back – strong and solid.

The trip downtown had called for my best Anne Klein Junior Sophisticate camel-hair suit (a straight skirt, with matching three-quarter-length jacket featuring a detachable lynx collar). And spiked, high-heeled shoes. The outfit also came with a matching lynx hat and muff, which I might have given away en route. Like most of my clothes up until that time, the suit was not something I picked out for myself. My father chose it for me. A furrier who was also in the rag trade, he sold sophisticated ready-made women's clothing to complement the furs he fashioned. The lynx collar was his creation, which I'd hung on to for many years. My sole politically incorrect fur memento.

As I leaned against the wall, waiting, waiting, interminably waiting, I took off my shoes. Might as well get comfortable. The floor felt refreshingly cool on the soles of my nylon-stockinged feet. Then I began to slide further. Slowly, slowly, feet steadily slipping out and away from the wall. Back and hips gliding down. Inch by inch, my bum gradually sinking towards the cold

1

tiled floor. Until *thump!* I hit bottom. Surprisingly, it didn't hurt. And it felt much more comfortable than standing or even leaning. So I figured I'd stay there on the floor, in the hallway outside Gilda's office. My back straight against the wall, my legs and feet out in front. I wiggled my toes, stretched my neck from side to side, and contemplated what could be taking so long in there. Didn't they know I was waiting?

I realized I probably looked a bit absurd sitting on the floor in the fancy getup I was wearing. But I decided I just didn't care. I was tired, and I was waiting. So if anyone had any complaints, too bad. As I looked up and to my left, I could see the knob on the door to Gilda's office. Was there a keyhole I could peek through? Curious to see what was taking so long, and already down on the floor, I rolled over onto my hands and knees to get a closer look. I cannot tell you now if there was a keyhole or not. Because just as I began to move my face close to the door, it opened.

There I was, on all fours, kneeling on the floor in my camelhair suit. I recognized how ridiculous I must look. How funny, like a dog waiting to be let in or out. And so I barked – "Arf, arf!" – to show the people in the room that I knew this situation was silly and that I knew what I was doing. "Arf, arf!" Then I crawled into the centre of the room. Everyone filed out past me, except Gilda.

Let me tell you right now that a dog's-eye view of the universe is quite strange. If you crawl around on your hands and knees for a while, you'll understand. On all fours, you see a lot of adult legs. So you have to look up to see faces. Faces are what tell you the most about people.

Gilda's face was smiling as I crawled into her office. She asked me to sit on the chair. Asked me – that's key. She didn't tell me to, she *asked* me. Would I mind sitting on the chair? I didn't mind. So I got up from my hands and knees and sat on the chair.

Before she'd banished me to the hall, Gilda had wanted to know some details about me. I'd only wanted to talk about David

X – a tall, dark, handsome guy I'd become infatuated with about a year earlier, ever since I volunteered at the youth centre he ran in downtown Toronto. I obsessed about him constantly. So Gilda would ask for my address, and I'd prattle on about David X.

Eventually this incredibly smart woman told me we could talk about David if I gave her some information first. That was a promise I've never forgotten. Because up until then, no adult had *ever* tried to make a deal with me. No adult had ever given me a choice, tried to negotiate, or offered me one thing in exchange for another. How profound! Despite the agitated, anxious state I was in, I still remember that moment. Of course I agreed, and told Gilda at least some of what she wanted to know.

To be honest, I found most of Gilda's questions annoying, even idiotic. She wanted to find out where I lived, whom to contact in case of emergency, and so on. Where I lived? What kind of question was that? I didn't live. I existed. I survived. What did it matter where? I was in her office now, so that's where I lived now. Wherever I was, there I would be. Emergency? Was there an emergency? Did someone die? If so, it wasn't me, because I was right there, living, in her office. These are the sorts of answers I gave Gilda. That's probably why I was sent into the hall, so she could consult with her colleagues.

After my doggie-like return, I began to feel sleepier and sleepier during Gilda's questions, and also quite warm. I needed to take off my jacket. Soon, someone else arrived. A woman. A doctor – a psychiatrist, Dr. B. Her full name reminded me of someone I disliked from my childhood. So I was immediately suspicious when Gilda introduced us. Dr. B had another strike against her. She was quite heavy, probably weighed two hundred pounds, maybe more. Now you'd think that with my trunk-load of painful experiences about being fat, I would not unfairly judge another overweight woman. If you thought that, you'd be wrong. My mistrust of Dr. B solidified due to her obvious professional success, despite being fat. She thereby contradicted one of my cherished beliefs that success only comes to those who are thin, or at least not fat.

Dr. B was there to sign me in, to give me the official psychiatric seal of approval. They weren't going to let me go. They were going to keep me there for a few days. Gilda asked me if I'd like to go to sleep. Sure, I said, but I hadn't brought my pyjamas.

The Greatest Role of My Life

Strange how I remember much of what I was thinking while I crawled into Gilda's office that day at the Clarke.

It had taken me a long time to get the help I so desperately needed. Yet getting help was the farthest thing from my mind. I didn't realize I'd arranged to see someone at a mental hospital, or that I was there as an outpatient. My thinking wasn't that clear.

It had taken all my energy, intuition, and instinct for self-preservation to get to the building at College and Spadina in downtown Toronto. That morning when I awoke, doing anything at all seemed to take a monumental effort. Washing, moving, standing up, sitting down, and getting dressed. They all took forever in my extremely anxious state. The air felt too thick and too heavy to budge, and I lacked the strength to push through it.

In the week leading up to my appointment with Gilda, I must have called the Clarke dozens of times. I'd decide not to go, and then change my mind. Then I'd call to tell them I'd changed my mind. Each time I changed my mind I'd call and say just that: "I've changed my mind." To clarify the situation, the receptionist (what a job that must have been!) would repeat that I was or was not coming. It usually sounded totally wrong. I was frustrated having to continually explain things to her, and I'd get huffier and more irritated each time I tried to clarify so simple a concept. I thought I was doing a good thing – calling to let them know the status of my pending visit. But my efforts went unappreciated.

I'd also phoned the Toronto Transit Commission (TTC) several times to find the best way down to the Clarke from my little

4

basement room in a small family home near Bathurst and Lawrence (a few miles to the northeast). I'd have to take the bus to the subway, the subway south to College Street, then the streetcar west along College to the Clarke.

But these instructions were too difficult to remember in my agitated state. So I kept asking people, to make sure I'd get to my appointment on time.

The day itself was one of those beautiful end-of-winter days. Sun shining, blue sky, puffy white clouds, crisp clean air. After much angst, I decided not to wear an overcoat with my camel-hair suit, or boots. I recall standing on the subway platform waiting for the southbound train. Waiting. It was taking too long. For some reason I took off my watch, waved it about for a few moments, then smacked it against a pillar. "I'm killing time," I joked to myself, quite pleased with the cleverness of my pun. The handful of other people waiting pretended not to notice.

The transition from subway to streetcar at College and Yonge: nerve-racking. Even though I'd lived in Toronto for several years, this was my first streetcar ride. My anxiety grew. The car was packed. But the most vivid memory of that short trip west along College was of someone handing out cash to the passengers. It was me. As folks got on or off the streetcar, there I was, waving a fistful of paper money in the air, randomly peeling off one- and two-dollar bills (yes, we had them then) along with fives and tens. Maybe because I'd heard the best things in life were free, or that money was the root of all evil, or because I hated what money did to people. The reason escapes me now, but of this I am sure – it made perfect sense at the time.

Something else struck me as odd: my fellow streetcar riders seemed quite nervous. Suddenly, I felt someone from behind pawing my lynx collar. Very creepy. As I turned to see who, the petting stopped, amplifying my apprehension. Was this the way to the Clarke? I asked numerous times, and in case people wondered why I, of all people, was headed there, I told them I was an actress "trying out for the greatest role of my life." Just so they didn't get the wrong idea, you understand.

Someone said the Clarke was only a few stops from College and Yonge. Taking things literally, I counted – one, two, three, and got off the streetcar (at Queen's Park). Whoops! No Clarke Institute.

Several more passersby pointed west, said it was a few blocks away. Close enough to walk, but not in spike heels. Not enough time, anyway. How could I be late for the greatest role of my life? I hailed a cab, asked the driver if he knew where the Clarke Institute was, told him I was an actress trying out for the greatest role of my life, and that I didn't have much money. I'd given most of it away by then.

Whoever that kind cabbie was, I thank him from the bottom of my heart. He dutifully drove me to the Clarke, pulled into the quarter-moon-shaped driveway, and stopped at the spherical cement steps leading up to the front door, like a concrete womb. (Now, the Clarke's box-like front portal extends the building almost out to the street.) I handed my remaining change to the cabbie, who graciously accepted it without complaint. Then I rushed up the winding stairs into the building. Into my destiny.

The Clarke Institute of Psychiatry as officially opened in
June 1966, courtesy of the Centre for Addiction and
Mental Health (CAMH) Archives.

I Am Not the Walrus, or Am I?

My initial psychiatric diagnosis – a "psychotic episode of
a schizophrenic nature" – was based on several symptoms as
seen through the eyes of my beholders: Gilda, Dr. B, and Dr.
B's su-pervisor, staff psychiatrist Dr. Gerry Shugar. They
probably based this on the very first *Diagnostic and
Statistical Manual (DSM-I)*[7] used to classify mental illness.

Throughout the hospital records, certain terms and
phrases appeared to describe my manner and behaviour not
only during the admission process, but before my arrival at the
Clarke. Gilda and Dr. B clearly agreed that my behaviour was
inappropriate, erratic, bizarre, confused, incoherent, and
disoriented.

7

Dr. B added "uncontrolled" and "bossy," and that I'd had a "previous depressive illness with suicide attempt" two years earlier. While the timing was off by several years, I can't fault her for that. In the highly charged atmosphere of my intake session, the possibility of small errors was strong. I'm simply astonished I mentioned my suicide failure. I'd never told anyone before. Ever. But then again, no one had ever asked.

According to Dr. B, my "psychotic episode" classification was based on several symptoms: "loose associations, some flight of ideas, intellectualizing." [8] In other words, I didn't answer the questions asked, my thoughts didn't seem logically connected to one another (they were to me), I chattered continuously, quickly changing topics whenever distracted (which was often), and provided overly analytical responses. Clearly, my runaway thoughts were in full throttle and no longer just inside my head.

While these descriptions seem appropriate in hindsight, I remember feeling quite frustrated at the time. I was trying so hard to answer and to please my interviewers. But my racing thoughts got in the way. I couldn't talk as fast as I could think. I wanted so much to give them accurate information. But I was sidetracked because everybody seemed on edge. And once again, the questions they asked seemed idiotic, senseless.

They were probably conducting some version of the Mental Status Exam (MSE), a series of brief questions used to quickly assess someone's mental condition. [9] But asking me about the current month and year, for example, would have felt insulting and time-wasting. Especially with wristwatches and a calendar in plain sight. I had some inkling I was being tested, but was clueless about the tester's difficulties or perspectives. My normally hyper-vigilant state was in disarray.

No wonder I was disoriented. Without my usual externally focused compass, I was truly lost.

Here's the very first thing Gilda wrote on my intake form:

Patient hallucinating – feels she is Dr. F, myself, David V, an actress, etc. Wants to see a psychiatrist immediately. Calls me "Gilda" although I don't know her, I'm sure.

Hallucination, one of the key indicators of schizophrenia, is a perception of the senses (sight, touch, sound, smell, or taste) with "no basis in external stimulation."[10] Given the erratic circumstances of my arrival, I can see how Gilda might think I was hallucinating. But I wasn't. At least not then.

Looking back, the lyrics of the old Beatles' tune "I Am the Walrus"[11] come to mind: "I am he / as you are he / as you are me / and we are all together." These first few lines capture the essence of my interpretation, or misinterpretation. The concept, based on ancient spiritual or metaphysical teachings that "we are all one," blossomed in North America during the 1960s. In typical fashion, I'd spun it through a literal filter, and while clearly confused about what it meant, I did not think I was other people. I thought I was *like* them in some way. I was looking for similarities. I also quite liked saying the phrase "I am" out loud, which was undoubtedly perceived as odd.

Taken together with some of my other behaviour, it's easy to understand this first of several eventual diagnoses.

By the way, I always referred to Mrs. Gilda Katz as Gilda. From the moment we met, I liked this youngish-looking woman – she was probably in her mid-thirties. Average height. Average weight. Plenty of natural silver streaks in her short brown hair. Horn-rimmed glasses. A slight American accent. If I met her now, I'd ask where she was from.

The Clarke records show general agreement that I was young, stylishly dressed, 5' 4 ½" and obese at about 200 pounds. Dr. B usually wrote the word "obese" first on every document, along with my estimated weight. I guess it stuck out for her every time we met. It sticks out at me now, almost half a century later.

Understandably, Gilda and Dr. B recorded different details of my intake. In Dr. B's version, I pounded on various doors in the outpatient department, crawled on the floor, and removed my shoes and stockings. Of that, I only remember taking off my shoes, but the rest is quite possible. However, she also said I offered to remove my other clothes – something I would never have done under any circumstances. Regardless of my distress, I was not an exhibitionist when it came to my body, since I had far too much shame about it. Dr. B corrected this two weeks later, but then added a different note:

When asked if she would remove her coat, she volunteered to do so, despite the fact that she was wearing nothing underneath it.

Nothing underneath? What about the camel-hair skirt and the long-line bra? Nowadays not nothing, but back then, perhaps. Dr. B then tells how my constant shouting led to my hall expulsion. I'm guessing my shouts of anger and frustration were partly in reaction to the questions, but mainly because I was so desperate to be heard.

Dr. B noted that I'd stopped shouting by the time the security guard arrived. She stated that I "expiated" and stomped on my fur hat, and alternated between tears and "bizarre laughter." More importantly, she said that I was unclear as to why I'd come to the Clarke, other than to get "help of some sort." She added that due to the "sudden onset of this psychotic episode," I was admitted informally.

Gilda's version sounds less clinical and accusatory, and more humane:

When first seen, Natalie presented herself in a silly manner. She laughed or cried inappropriately, crawled on the floor, saying she was a "method actress" and was playing the role of a baby. She said she wanted our help in helping the children at Brown Camps. She spat on her fur collar, cried briefly when giving her father's name, saying it wasn't his real name, and spoke in rhymes, riddles, liberally sprinkled with free associations.

Two things stand out here. The first: I couldn't ask for help on my own behalf. The second: I was actually telling the truth about my father's name.

Reading the medical records, surprise and sadness greet me every time I encounter some aspect of my behaviour that shows the pain and anger I felt towards my father. We never explored any of these feelings at the Clarke. And I didn't face it for several decades afterwards. My spitting and stomping on the fur hat, designed and created by my father, had nothing to do with any anti-fur sentiment[12] and everything to do with Robert's actual identity and the emotional trauma he carried. And I carried.

CHAPTER 2: THE GIBBLE-GABBLE

Dealing with Crazy

When you've been crazy and have lived in a mental institution, it's not something you want other people to know. It's not something you can talk about freely and comfortably. But it *is* something that shapes the rest of your life. That is, if you're me. So I had a crazy spell when I was young. Nowadays, with books and movies being written about mental hospitalization, it's kind of "in" or "cool" to be a little loopy. I'm not talking about the kind of mental illness where you can't fully function in society or the kind of psychoses found in serial killers or the criminally insane.

I'm talking about ordinary, run-of-the-mill nutty behaviour, when you perform at a minimum to mediocre level and might need a hospital to contain you or to keep you safe.

Years ago, I managed to sit through the movie *One Flew over the Cuckoo's Nest*[13] without too many reminiscences of the Clarke and without over-identifying with the main character, played by the amazing Jack Nicholson. But I had to wait many years after the release of *Girl Interrupted*[14] before I could bear to watch two slender, stunning actresses play their inpatient roles. Seeing aspects of the shameful and secret part of your life up there on the big screen is bad enough. But having beautiful people portray the characters makes it seem glamorous, fashionable, almost enviable. And while I knew that my hospitalization was the beginning of my journey into awareness, self-discovery, consciousness, and hope, I still hid it.

Even after all these years of healing, I'm not finished yet with the shame. I'd still prefer not to have needed hospitalization, not to have been at the Clarke. Because it isn't glamorous or fashionable or enviable at all. Not one little bit. It *is* dramatic, though, which I suppose is something.

There's also the shock of seeing aspects of your own life as art, as a picture that someone else painted. And you, dear soul that you are, missed the boat, or palette. You weren't quick enough, determined enough, or brave enough to speak up and tell your story. So you continue being unheard. Until now. Because what happened to you was real. And you've learned to focus on what's real, inasmuch as you can identify it and sort it out from all the rest of the gibble-gabble in your mind and in the world around you. But I'm getting ahead of myself.

The Unrelenting Tenth Degree

If I had to pick one main cause of my hospital stay, it would be the gibble-gabble in my mind. Dangerous stuff, for sure.

We've all got gibble-gabble in our heads to a greater or lesser degree. Sometimes self-help gurus and psychologists refer to it as negative voices, critical self-talk, or even the voice of a very bossy conscience telling us we should do this and not do that. Cognitive psychology is based on a simplified version of gibble-gabble, referred to as irrational, automatic, or unwanted thoughts that need stopping.

I've heard it called noise, stream-of-consciousness, thought-patterns, self-reflection, ruminative thinking, and mindless chit-chat. Take your pick.

Gibble-gabble is all of the above to the tenth degree, plus an extra, urgent element, a darker dimension. Endless, unrelenting, circular threads of odd thoughts, sounds, and images, hovering ominously behind the scenes, obscuring the more meaningful strands swirling around in the mix. Some fragments break through the clutter. But the sinister, foreboding tone warns of imminent, ever-present danger.

When I started writing this book, I still had remnants of the gibble-gabble, but decibels lighter, fainter, less frequent, and less intense than when I was in my early twenties. It's faded now, because over the years I trained myself to identify the content. Once given voice and form, I believed it couldn't hurt me or make me crazy. And that turns out to be true.

13

The Who You Hallelujah Chorus

Some of my gibble-gabble was definitely significant. Like the who-you-hallelujah chorus, which stayed around for many years, always accompanied by pain.

The who-you-hallelujah chorus is similar to the choruses in ancient Greek tragedies and plays. Could be five people or twenty-five. A picture, a sound, or both. But the sound is the killer. The picture is relatively harmless: people in black veils and black draping robes standing together in a semi-circle, glaring at the central character – you. The sound: many deep voices together, droning in a low, slow, monotone dripping with disdain, repeating the rhyme "Who-ooo, you-ooo?" As if the idea that *you* could do or be anything other than a total loser was preposterous, absurd. Don't even think it. The who-you- hallelujah chorus had a hold on me for a very long time. It's a real party pooper, I assure you. The disdain makes me think it's the voice of my father, disguised.

The gibble-gabble's other main line was the rhetorical question "What will people think?" and the immediate response "I don't care what people think," which sounds like *bzzt!* It happens that fast – whatwillpeoplethinkIdon'tcarewhatpeoplethink – *bzzt!* Less than a split second. So fast you can hardly tell what's going on. Except that you stop dead in your tracks. Whatever you're doing or thinking comes to a sudden halt. Your mind is now a blank. Whatever you were saying is gone, thanks to the *bzzt!* The paralysis renders you helpless, stuck in your own mind. Going nowhere. I now recognize this as the voice of my mother, not so disguised.

The gibble-gabble has played a central role in my life, as a constant companion. In my early years, I heard it only as white noise, like the on-and-off hum of a refrigerator or furnace, unnoticeable unless you're deliberately listening. And I wanted to do anything but deliberately listen to what my thoughts were telling me. Too difficult. It's been only after years of unravelling the knots and tangles, of painstakingly picking the threads apart, that I discovered the contents.

If the gibble-gabble was a play, the who-you-hallelujah chorus and whatwillpeoplethink would be two central characters. They might not have the most lines or occupy centre stage, but they would affect all action, as well as the outcome of the play. But this is no play.

Choice-less, but Not in Seattle

Awareness of your thinking process is great if you're somewhat centred or have some control over your life. But back in my early days, neither of those conditions applied. A tightly bound collection of runaway thoughts and impulses had me at its mercy, leaving me unable to consciously choose what was good for me. Unable to consciously choose anything.

Unaware of choice, I couldn't understand how other people managed or accomplished anything. So I devoted much time to trying to figure this out. And all this why-think became part of the gibble- gabble. I assumed that such an understanding would help me influence people, maybe even change my own responses. Then people might like me more. That was the key. I wanted people to like me more. The notion that my people-pleasing was a subtle form of manipulation did not cross my mind. I assumed that the more people liked me, the better off I'd be and the happier I'd be.

Quite simple, really. Except that this load of wishful thinking wasn't true and didn't work. But it was all I knew. My struggle to find answers and reap some undefined psychological or social benefit had me living in my head, an increasingly busy place.

Navigating through my daily life was also fraught with questions that demanded answers. For example, when people said, "Hello, how are you?" I wondered what they meant. Because I took things so literally, I'd actually tell them how I was, and watch as they smiled politely while trying to get away. Or they'd say, "Hi, how are you?" as they walked by, not even stopping to give me a chance to answer. So what was going on here? Did they care? Did they really want to know how I was? If not, why did they ask? How could they be so insincere? After racking up many unbillable hours on these issues, I realized that people were making small talk and really just meant "Hello." But it took a long time to figure that out. And it always hurt that most folks didn't really care.

I, on the other hand, cared very much about everyone. Oh yes. That's what I told myself. After all, I spent an enormous amount of time focusing on others and what they said, inventing theories to explain their behaviour, which rarely met my hopes or expectations. You can see how much energy I spent on the most trivial encounters and how hard I tried to make sense of the universe I inhabited.

Living in your head is not a unique phenomenon. Not by a long shot. Thankfully, I've moved on. But it has taken me a very long time to learn to live in my body, to become aware of how I experience my emotions, sensations, and feelings, and to make decisions based on information from my heart *and* mind together.

But back then, I made few actual decisions. Instead, I kind of ricocheted through life, reacting to events and circumstances as they emerged, trying to sort it all out. At the same time, I was very busy looking for meaning and answers, wanting desperately to understand the world, so I could better understand myself. Whoops. I sure had that upside-down, or inside-out. But that was the best I could do. I knew no other way. I was constantly amazed at people who did things, who set and reached goals. At people who could discipline themselves, who knew what they wanted and went after it.

Most of us are taught what to want, by various elements of society -- cultural and religious institutions, the educational system, the media, our friends and families. I, however, was taught *not* to want. Nobody actually came out and made the pronouncement "Thou shalt not want." But they may as well have.

Because from a very early age, saying "I want" sparked a range of parental reactions. From simple eyeball-rolling disdain, "Humph!" or "Humph, she wants!" to the mocking "Don't be silly!" to direct contradiction, "No, you don't!" or the more frequent "You don't know *what* you want!" Now I can see this was how Shirley and Bob said no. But back then, and for many years afterwards, I believed I didn't know what I wanted.

So that by the time I reached adolescence, I operated under that conviction. Then it was me who repeatedly told myself I didn't know what I wanted. Not knowing what I really wanted meant I had very few anchors to ground me or arrows to point the way on the road ahead.

As a therapist, I equate trying not to want with trying not to breathe. As human beings, wanting is built right into us. Wanting moves us forward. Denying our wants, as I did for much of my younger life, can lead to all sorts of problems. Like binge eating. It wasn't as if I didn't try to move forward. I tried desperately, all the time. I tried so hard I was exhausted at the end of every day. But trying hard and obsessively figuring things out amidst the gibble-gabble weren't the only factors affecting my life. Far from it.

The Hunch

I also had to fight to keep a lid on my shame, lest it ooze out without my knowing. My shame and my guilt were carried in almost every cell of my body. That may be another reason I became fat. To help carry around all that psychic heaviness. I couldn't give these feelings a name, but they made me bow my head, turtle-like, when I walked, and hunch my shoulders, hoping you wouldn't notice my large breasts. Hunching over helped me feel invisible. So you wouldn't stare or make comments.

My hunched-over posture was the physical manifestation of the gibble-gabble, and a contributing factor to this inner cacophony. Try it. Slump your shoulders a little and notice what happens to your neck and head. Notice that your eyes automatically focus on the ground. Great for finding lost change and for block-ing out the world. But not so great for facing life head-on.

Out of the blue I'd hear my mother screech, "STAND UP STRAIGHT!!" But by the time I was fourteen, my spinal column and shoulder musculature had adjusted themselves to such a slouched-over posture that it became physically impossible for me to maintain a stand-up-straight stance for more than a few seconds.

Standing up straight was also psychologically impossible, as was following any of Shirley's countless commands. These were subject to automatic opposition on my part, as if the opposite was what I'd wanted to do my whole life.

I experienced constant embarrassment about my breasts, which had blossomed when I was in the sixth grade. I wasn't the first in my class to get them, but one of a small group of girls who had to wear bras. I hadn't wanted to wear a bra. Too con-stricting. But sweater sets, a.k.a. twin-sets, were the fashion in the late 1950s. So I agreed to a bra. I remember Shirley saying, "Don't be silly. Soon you'll never want to go anywhere without one." And she was right – I never did. And by the time I got to junior high (grades 7 and 8), I was grateful that bras existed.

One of Shirley's admonitions gave birth early on in my ex-istence to a life-saving gift. My sense of humour. Silliness, to be exact. Shirley used "Don't be silly" a lot. "Don't be silly, there's nothing to be afraid of," or, "Don't be silly, you've got to stand up straight." "Don't be silly, just do as you're told." "Don't be silly, of course we love you." "Don't be silly, what will people think?" This last one was usually about my obvious weight gain and expanding waistline.

So, given my literal interpretations and my penchant for do-ing the opposite, no wonder I got silly. And stayed silly. Silliness is the one constant I've always liked about myself. I liked it in my mother, too. Shirley's sense of the silly often carried a slight-ly risqué tone, especially when recounting stories from her work-ing days back in London, England, before she met Robert. For example, she told us, after one very cold night, that an unthinking office girl would say to the boss, "Ooo, wasn't it cold in bed last night, Mr. Jones?" This little faux pas always made Shirley laugh. Life was always better when my mother laughed.

Predictably, not everyone appreciated silliness the way I did. That's clear in the Clarke notes where my silly behaviour was noted, and not in a good way. Judged and frowned upon because it was inappropriate.

The hunched posture was a sure sign, of course, that I had very low self-esteem. But back then, self-esteem was not the buzzword it is today. In yesteryear, people didn't talk in public about themselves. And as far as I can make out, people didn't talk about themselves even in private, either. Self-awareness, living in consciousness, and other concepts from the early human-potential movement of the 1960s hadn't yet entered mainstream society, nor had the many self-help book and groups they spawned.

CHAPTER 3: ALL IN THE FAMILY

Shirley

My mother, Shirley, died in hospital in April 1993 of a heart attack, two weeks after suffering a paralyzing stroke. She was eighty-one. It was quite a jolt to my sister, my father, and me. We'd all pretty much expected my father would be the parent to die first. But Shirley surprised us. Perhaps it was merciful, her going first, because she probably wouldn't have lasted very long without my father. She was totally dependent on him: emotionally, psychologically, financially, and even physically (she couldn't drive, and in her later years had difficulty walking). Robert seemed to have somewhat more resilience, but succumbed to liver cancer a mere three years later, in March 1996. He was eighty-four. Robert and Shirley had been married for fifty-three years.

During the later years of my mother's life, I had finally reached a place of compassion for her. It had been a long time coming. I seem to have been a rather slow learner. But to be fair, I had a lot of confusion and resentment to work through, from all her abuse, plus tons of blame. Unable to accept who she really was, I hated her for not accepting me the way I was. It was, in retrospect, a tough task for both of us.

"You *hate* your mother!" she'd shriek at me during those awful teenage years. "Why don't you just *admit* it!" I'd instantly deny it. Silently to myself and out loud to her. But somewhere within I knew she'd got it right. And I felt plenty guilty about that. After years of therapy I gradually became able to own more of my negative feelings towards Shirley. And it took so long, so very, very long to acquire any kind of positive feelings for her.

It's been quite a shock for me to realize how deeply I loved this woman. And I did tell her that, especially during her last few years. I'd usually end phone conversations, no matter how frustrating, with an I-love-you. I don't know how much she was able to take in, because she didn't have that healthy place inside for positive comments or energies to land.

My maternal grandparents emigrated from Poland to England in the 1890s, to escape the usual, all-too-frequent anti-Semitic pogroms that have plagued the Jewish people for centuries. As did many, they took up residence in London's east end. Shirley was born in December 1912, the youngest of five girls, and the seventh of eight children. She liked to say she was the seventh child of a seventh child, to help explain her psychic and intuitive abilities.

My mother lived much of her young life within a few blocks of London General Hospital and the Whitechapel tube station. Grandpa Nathan, after whom I was named, worked close by as a tailor in one of the countless east-end factory sweatshops. As the family patriarch, he ruled the roost. My mother adored him, worshipped him, actually. This I know beyond a doubt because she told me often, and expected me to do the same. "You should worship your father," she'd say, whenever I said anything sounding remotely disrespectful.

I don't know much about my maternal grandmother at all. I can't even recall her name. My mother never talked about her. I've heard from others, though, that she was a bit of a cold fish. But who could blame her with eight children to look after? Apparently, she never taught my mother how to cook or clean or do any housework. But more importantly, she never taught my mother how to give and receive love, or that she was worth loving. It's no secret that people from previous generations didn't use terms like "worthwhile" or "self-esteem." But they did show love, warmth, caring, and compassion. My maternal grandmother didn't and maybe she didn't know how, either. Nowadays, the inter-generational passing down of familial emotional patterns is widely accepted in the psychotherapy community.

Growing up, my mother has been described by members of her family as a rather frivolous young woman. She loved getting all dolled up in new clothes and makeup and attending tea dances at the posh London hotels. To Shirley, the word "dance" conjured up elegant tables covered in crisp white linens, with live, full-piece orchestras playing the popular tunes of the day. This was during the late 1920s and early 1930s.

Shirley had two main influences in her household: her oldest sister, Freda, whom she loathed, and her second-oldest sister, Irene, who was one of her major role models. Freda lasted till she was ninety-six and was generally disliked by the rest of the clan. An independent woman, an opinionated know-it-all with an incredibly demanding and bossy streak. Sometimes when I expressed a point of view that differed from Shirley's – in my younger years, while still living at home, before being overweight became the main focus of our interaction – she'd shout that I was just like my auntie Freda. When I met Freda, at several points in my life, I found her somewhat eccentric, even peculiar. She often reminisced about travelling to Boston on a business trip when she worked as a secretary. This would have been quite a special honour in the 1930s. "They have good lettuce up in Boston," she'd say. I kid you not. That's what she remembered.

Irene, who smoked cigarettes like a trooper, hung in there till the age of ninety-nine. She had a rather brusque personality with mannerisms and phrasings that often reminded me of my mother, along with a sharp sense of humour. After my mother's death she took to phoning me periodically, perhaps as a way of connecting with her younger sister. She always asked me if I'd found a sugar daddy yet.

Shirley only ever talked about one of her girlfriends, someone named Sally. Apparently, Sally and my mother could be completely honest with one another. "That dress looks awful! Take it off right now!" That was how such honesty between friends should be, said Shirley. Not surprising, then, that Shirley directed the same type of rather brutal Sagittarian honesty at me.

Like countless other women of her generation, Shirley remained financially dependent on a man her whole life. She went from living under the care of her father to living under the care of her husband. Her secretarial earnings, before she married and during the war when my dad was away, were quickly spent. On clothes, makeup, and entertainment in her younger years. On clothes and shoes as she got older. And on charities. She had a generous heart and contributed to any and all requests. If she'd been Internet savvy, she'd undoubtedly have been quite vulnerable to heartfelt pleas for financial help by Nigerian princes and other such scammers.[15]

"Shirley" wasn't even her real name. She was born Sadie Rebecca. And, like many children of immigrants at that time, she adapted to the British culture by anglicizing her name. Her seven brothers and sisters went along with the change. My sister and I didn't discover her real name until we saw her death certificate. Surprise!

Robert/Bob

My mother wasn't the only one in the household with secrets. My father's name wasn't Robert at birth. Nor was he born in London, England, as we'd been told. In fact, his whole identity and history were false. But I didn't learn any of this till I was sixteen. When he died in 1996, he took many of his secrets with him to the grave.

What amazes me now is that while the pre- and post-Clarke history has been therapist fodder countless times, I wasn't ready to confront the truth about my father's influence for decades. Not until I'd resolved most of my issues with Shirley, which took some doing. But when I look back at some of my behaviour and reactions at the Clarke, and read the hospital records, my real feelings towards my father show up loud and clear. Evidence of forgetting and denial.

I've told you how I saw my father as almost godlike, an idea Shirley promoted. He lent a hand to a lot of people over his lifetime, but in a quiet way, helping them find work, get needed surgery, connecting them to others. Worshipping my father was one of the few indirect commands I could obey, with both parents' encouragement.

As a kid, I can remember visiting my dad at his store. First in Midland, a small Ontario town on the shore of Georgian Bay, and then in Niagara Falls, where we moved after he'd lost everything to a crooked business partner. Robert's Quality Furs became the locale for the second part of a pre-teen, Saturday-afternoon ritual. My friend Jenny and I would see an afternoon movie downtown, then wait for a ride home at my dad's store, where we'd watch him sell to a customer.

"Sell" isn't really the right word. "Lecture" would be more appropriate. For example, Robert (or Mr. Roberts, as some people called him) would proclaim that the customer should absolutely not wear a particular style or colour. No matter how much money she was willing to spend, no way would my father let her walk out of *his* store with that item. Because it was *wrong* for her. That's how convinced my father was of his superior judgment. If he couldn't persuade the customer to change her mind, she was welcome to go elsewhere. The other furrier down the street, well, he'd probably be happy to sell her what she wanted, even if it didn't suit her. But my father wasn't going to have *his* label on a coat that looked wrong. That's why the word "quality" was on the front of his store. Not just for effect. He meant it. The customer should trust him. He knew what was best. Jenny and I usually agreed with his opinion.

My father seemed to really enjoy his work. Running his own business, he'd say, was the only way. I simply couldn't imagine my father being told what to do by anyone. Except Shirley.

When we got home late Saturday afternoon, my father watched wrestling on our black-and-white TV. Wrestling was one of the few things that made him laugh. And that was a good feeling, when my dad laughed. It was important to see my dad happy, and important for me to try to make him happy.

Unfortunately, I failed at this assignment in a big way. I say "assignment" because somehow I got the idea that it was my responsibility to make my father happy. It was one of the things I was put on this earth to do. I was also supposed to make my mother happy. But it was so obvious that nothing would make her happy (except my weight loss and total surrender to everything she wanted) that my efforts didn't count. Making my father happy, however, seemed possible. He didn't appear to require weight loss in order to love me or care about me. This is an idea I clung to and came to believe.

I did, however, realize that like my mother, Bob was also embarrassed (a) to be seen with me in public, and (b) that I was his daughter. Imagine. He owned and operated a fur store. And also sold other high-priced sophisticated women's apparel, including exclusive women's suits, dresses, and coats. The labels were as familiar to my father as the TV wrestlers.

Robert would usually introduce me to his customers or acquaintances by saying, "And this is my big daughter." Very clever, because "big" could also mean his oldest daughter, which I was. So I told myself that's what he probably meant. And dropped it from my ruminative repertoire (the gibble-gabble). Or so I thought.

But my body knew. I automatically cringed every time I heard it, and I heard it a lot. A little mental cringe each time. A silent whammy, unacknowledged, then finally buried. That's how I coped with the huge verbal punch in the gut my father delivered. Evidence surely of hostility towards me and my weight, which were becoming fused into one shameful identity. My father's introductions hinted at truths I couldn't face. Not then. Not for a long time.

Couldn't I say something to him? You might wonder. Why didn't I just tell him how it hurt me, explain it to him? Because I didn't have the awareness. I denied the hurt. And I also lacked the words. In books on child-rearing, experts have coined a phrase to help the child cope with feelings, instead of acting out in destructive ways. Parents are encouraged to say "Use your words" to their errant two-year-olds.

And if the toddlers don't know what to say, the adults ideally help them define what they're feeling. This wasn't common knowledge back in the late '40s and '50s when I was a kid. I don't know how many parents practiced it. Probably only those who were exceptionally astute, which Shirley and Bob were not (may they rest in peace). They were, however, exceptional in their own ways.

And even if I'd had the awareness and the words, I didn't have the wherewithal to know that confronting my father was okay. How could you confront someone you worshipped? (Hint: you could not.) Oh, I could argue with him about political ideology. But even these discussions ended with one of his dismissive, hand-waving gestures, a scornful eyeball-roll, head shakes from side to side, and much tsk-tsking. These were accompanied by the stern declaration that I didn't know what I was talking about.

Some years ago, I wrote a poem that precisely described the set of criteria I used to relate to my father. It went something like this: "What you want, what you think, what you want, how you feel, what you want, how you feel, what you think" – and so on. When it came to my father, what *I* thought, felt, or wanted simply didn't count. I was totally co-opted to function according to what he wanted. More precisely, what I perceived he wanted.

One of the things I now know he wanted was to always be ahead of the game, ahead of you. No one could out-early Robert. For example, if you agreed to meet my father at 10:30 a.m. and you decided to show up twenty minutes early and sit quietly with a cup of coffee, he'd already be there when you arrived. If you decided to turn up forty-five minutes ahead of time, he'd be there. Robert never ever wanted *anyone* to have to wait for him. Once I figured that out, I showed up on time, but never early, so he didn't have to anticipate my earliness.

Robert was a man of few words. He was at his most loquacious and charming with his customers and with company. Then he could show off with jokes and funny stories. But at home, with just his family, most of the time he was tired and tuned out.

My father's suppressed silences counter-acted my mother's explosive reactions. Bob would arrive home after a day at the store, he'd receive a perfunctory welcome-home kiss on the cheek from Shirley, then he'd head straight for his La-Z-Boy reclining chair in the den. He'd park himself there, feet up, and stare at the TV in the corner. Shirley would call him for supper, which he'd gobble up compulsively. He'd then return to the den for the evening, unless he was going to one of his male-bonding, service club meetings (the Kiwanis, Optimists Club, or the Masons). Or to his weekly poker game.

I hated it when we had the poker game at our house. Mr. K's stinky cigars would poison the air for days afterwards. Not that we didn't smoke. My father's brand was Du Maurier. And by the time I was sixteen I was into menthol cigarettes. Cameo. One of my few permissible vices.

Jenny got me started smoking back behind Diamond Jubilee Public School during fifth grade.

Jenny's dad often brought American cigarettes back from business trips to the US. Winston was a glamorous brand at the time, advertised regularly on TV with a neat jingle. Jenny and I could perform it at a moment's notice. I remember the refrain and even the verse:

Winston tastes good like a – click, click – cigarette should.
Winston gives you real flavour, full rich tobacco flavour,
Winston's really flavoured too, the filter lets the flavour through.

Let's hear it for cultural influences!

Shirley and Bob

In 1939, petite and slender, five-foot-tall Shirley met broad-shouldered, six-foot-tall husband-to-be Bob on the street, not too far from where she lived. They'd pass one another as my mother walked to the bus stop and my father was en route to or from work. That's one version. Another is that my father kept a look-out for my mother from the second-floor window of the fur factory where he worked. And made sure he was on the street when he saw her coming. Either way, they began to say hello and make idle chit-chat, which eventually led to a date, which in turn led to my parents falling deeply in love. My father even had my mother's face tattooed on his upper right arm just beneath his shoulder with the caption "My Shirley."

On June 16, 1940, several days before my father was shipped out to fight in the Second World War, my parents got married. People did that in those days. Maybe to make sure the soldier had something to fight for, someone to return home to. My father would have needed this. Also, on my grandfather Nathan's deathbed, several months earlier, he had my father promise to look after my mother always – a promise Robert kept until my mother died. Sounds kind of romantic, and perhaps it was. I don't know, I wasn't there. But this promise certainly affected me and my life later on down the line.

During the war, with my father away, and London under the merciless blitz of the German Luftwaffe, my mother went to stay with my father's relatives in Sheffield, and later with some cousins in Northern Ireland. Like other war wives, she hated knowing her beloved husband was in danger.

**Bob and Shirley's wedding photo, June 1940,
just before he went off to war.**

28

**Bob in his British Army uniform
(1940), a photo always on display.**

Rosemarie

Sometime in the three years between 1941 and 1944, Shirley had a stillborn baby. Rosemarie was dead at birth, which was called "born blue." Back then, there was no remedy to counteract the RH negative factor in my mother's blood. Shirley was probably still living in London's east end. I don't know if my father was able to be there or if he was off in India, Bahrain, or elsewhere in the Middle East. It was something Shirley rarely talked about to me. When she did, it was usually in the form of scolding. "You would have had an older sister, you know," she'd say from time to time. As if I could forget an important piece of information like that. "Maybe she could have talked some sense into you, because *I* certainly can't."

Somehow, I was always under the impression that Rosemarie's death was my fault. I know now that as a child, I carried some of my mother's unexpressed guilt and blame for the loss of her firstborn. Young impressionable children are like sponges. They soak up every type of energy from their environment. Rosemarie was a devastating loss for my mother, to be sure, and for my father. A loss for me, as well. I feel sad when I think about the sister I might have had. Rosemarie would have been

29

the first and primary parental learning experience for Shirley and Bob. I wonder what my life would have been like with an older sister to look up to. Perhaps she'd have looked out for me and protected me, the way I did for my younger sister. I'll never know.

When my mother had Rosemarie, a blue baby was a non-event to hospital staff. Seen as sad and too bad, but no big deal. Women were expected to just suck it up. What with the war going on, there were worse horrors to contemplate.

Research over the years, however, has shown the strong impact of a stillborn on the mother, on her subsequent pregnancy, and on the child of that pregnancy. Researchers found that women unable to release guilt feelings about their stillborn child, women who didn't complete a grieving process, often suffered severe depression and/or post-traumatic stress disorder (PTSD). These women also showed a strong tendency to abuse children who did survive the birth process. This helped me understand another factor contributing to how Shirley treated me.

Me

I was born in London, England, at the end of November 1945, several months after the war ended. I weighed a mere five pounds at birth, perhaps the only time in my life I've been underweight. It became quite the challenge for almost thirty-three-year-old Shirley to fatten me up. In post-war London, she bought eggs for me on the black market, along with chocolate, which she doled out one square at a time to get me to go to sleep as an infant. My earliest sugar fix.[16]

A perfectionist and quite competitive, my mother was determined that I was going to be the best baby ever, perhaps in part to compensate for Rosemarie. She was also the type of woman who was insecure enough to take even an infant's facial expressions personally. Shirley probably interpreted any sign of distress on my little face, any frown or grimace, as rejection. In turn, the hurt from this perceived rejection probably made her angry and frustrated, feelings she then took out on the infant culprit – me. Recently, psychology research has shown the reciprocal relationship between mother and infant, how each impacts the other.

I have two stories my auntie Rae told me about how my mother carried out her parenting duties. Our family was visiting Auntie Rae and Uncle Jack, my mother's brother, at their suburban home in London's north end, where most of my mother's family had moved shortly after the war ended. At perhaps eighteen or twenty months old, I sat in a high chair in the kitchen while the women prepared the meal. My aunt gave me some sliced tomatoes to nibble on while waiting. *Whoops!* I dropped a piece of tomato on the floor. To my aunt's astonishment, my mother smacked me hard on the hands for making a mess. And then smacked me again several times for crying.

Then there's the curbside incident. I was probably two or three years old. According to Rae, I'd stepped off the sidewalk curb into the path of an oncoming car. It swerved in the nick of time and narrowly missed me. My mother yanked me back onto the curb and immediately gave me a "good spanking." The message: this was very dangerous, so never do it again. Never! I'd certainly given her a terrible fright! No hugs of relief, no holding. Just punishment. When we got home that evening, she spanked me again, apparently to make sure I'd gotten the message. The following morning, she remembered her fright, so she gave me a third spanking to drive the lesson home!

How did my aunt know this? My mother told her, even bragged about it. To what end, I don't know. I was a mere toddler. But for decades after, I was slightly anxious and extremely cautious when crossing the street.

Auntie Rae saw these incidents as evidence that Shirley wanted or needed to be a perfect mother. This meant it was up to me to be a perfect child. Sadly, neither my mother nor I came even remotely close to that ideal. The only perfection Shirley and

I achieved was in our excellent display of a bad, do-not- copy mother-daughter relationship.

Shirley's memories of me as a young child were more positive. Apparently I was the "Shirley Temple"[17] of the family. She and my father both enjoyed my spunkiness and my gregarious, talkative nature. They loved to reminisce about the good old days. The story goes that when people asked me how old I was, I'd tell them. Then I'd ask them the same question, to much laughter. I rarely got an answer.

Very confusing.

My mother taught me cute nursery rhymes, as well, which I'd perform for whoever asked. Or whoever happened to enter my mother's sphere.

There was an old woman who lived in a shoe
She had so many children, she didn't know what to do.
There was another old woman who lived in a shoe She
had no children. She knew what to do.

Shirley loved recalling this one. "You were a cheeky little devil," she'd say. As if I'd made the rhyme up myself. Imagine, teaching a two- or three-year old a verse about birth control. The mind boggles.

Me at age 4.   Me at 5.

My Sister

In May 1948, my parents and I immigrated to Canada and took up residence in a second-floor flat in one of those huge old houses that used to line Toronto's High Park Avenue – homes long since demolished and turned into pricey condos. My sister was born at the end of January 1950, about a year and a half after our arrival. I was four, and that's when my life got decidedly worse.

With my mother in labour at the Toronto General Hospital, my father brought me to work at his fur factory on Adelaide Street, just east of Spadina Avenue, in what was then Toronto's fur and *shmuttah* (Yiddish for garment business) district. He settled me in the reception area with my colouring book and crayons. I still remember the moment he returned to answer the phone, wearing his white lab coat, which protected his clothing while he cut, dyed, stretched, blocked, and stitched the fur skins. I looked up just as he put the phone back in its cradle. He then announced I had a new baby sister. Her name (which she later changed) was Cynthia. Just like that.

I felt distinctly odd. I screwed up my face in strong disapproval and whined in disappointment. While glad it was a girl, I'd hoped for a more normal name, like Judy. With my sister only a few hours old, already I felt left out. Nobody had asked me what name I liked.

Shirley now had two young children to contend with and no extended family to draw on for support. One incident stands out while the four of us still lived in the High Park flat. I was wearing my little blue coat with the black velvet collar, which I quite liked. My mother and I had just returned from a walk with my new sister, sound asleep in her carriage. We were at the top of the stairs. I must have said or done something to really annoy my mother – perhaps I disobeyed one of her constant commands – because she suddenly got very angry, grabbed me by the shoulders, and shook me quite hard. As I struggled to break free, I went tumbling backwards all the way down the stairs.

"Are you all right?" whispered Shirley from the top of the stairs. I don't know what I replied. She continued, "Serves you right! That'll teach you! See what happens when you don't listen to your mother!" I began to sob. Shirley told me to be quiet so I didn't wake the baby. There was nothing to cry about.

When was I ever going to learn! She didn't come down the stairs to see how I was or to hold or comfort me after the fall. That wasn't how Shirley operated.

My mother probably didn't know how to soothe a crying child, never having received that type of compassion herself. Instead, she seemed more concerned about her new daughter and acted as if the whole thing was my fault. This soon became par for the course. Surprisingly, my new sister slept soundly through the whole exchange. This memory has always been so very clear that I've wondered why I've hung on to it. I believe my fall was accidental. While Shirley had a vicious and mean temper, she usually expressed it verbally, if hysterically. When I was small, she could spank me. Most parents spanked their children back then, and Shirley reacted a lot out of frustration. But I don't believe my mother would ever deliberately harm anyone physically. Even an irritating, disobedient child like myself.

Unlike me, who had been difficult to manage, my sister was a delight. She went to sleep without a fuss, ate whatever was given to her, and rarely cried. My sister turned out to be the child my parents had always wanted. Easy to manage, docile, pleasant-natured, and bright. From as early on as I can remember, my mother compared her two daughters out loud and in front of others. I was dark-haired, my sister was fair. I had a pale complexion, hers was golden. I was fussy, she was easily satisfied. I was most often a naughty girl, while Cynthia had neither the character nor the inclination to be naughty.

Despite the comparisons, I liked my baby sister (apart from her name) and was curious about her.

The only problem for me was that she took my place as Daddy's little darling. I was now "the big girl" and expected to behave as such. That's when things started to slide downhill fast. I really didn't want to be a bad girl. And I wanted so very much to be a good girl, especially for Daddy. But no matter how hard I tried to be good, somehow I always ended up doing the wrong thing. My sister, on the other hand, from an early age, did everything right. At least on the surface.

The relationship between my sister and me was essentially beige: neutral, calm, and pleasant. Given the frequent high drama in our household, neutral was a good thing. The comparisons between us that began after her birth steadily increased as we grew older. As infants, I was the difficult crybaby who never wanted to go to sleep. She was easy to manage and slept all night. As toddlers, I was a chatterbox, always getting into trouble. She caused no trouble at all. She quickly became the "good girl," unlike her bad older sister.

"Don't be like your sister!" she was frequently told. I imagine that from her perspective, this would be the last thing she'd want. According to Shirley, my sister was generous (she shared her candy), and I was greedy (I gobbled mine up quickly). She was obedient and did what she was told. I was obstinate and never listened. She was cooperative, I was impossible. She was often out playing with her friends, while I was unsociable, usually staying inside by myself. She was thoughtful and considerate, and I was a selfish cow. She studied and worked hard at her schoolwork, and I was a lazy cow. She was athletic, and I was a fat cow.

Now that I think about it, my sister was never called a cow; that honour was reserved exclusively for me. While I wished I could be more like her, I was glad my parents had at least one bright spot to enjoy (since it took some of the heat off me). I also felt quite guilty when Shirley accused her of taking food I'd stolen from our kitchen (cake, cookies, desserts), which in turn triggered my craving to consume even more.

By the time she was ten, my sister got back at me in subtle ways. For example, while sitting beside me in the den, where we watched TV, or walking past as she entered or left the room, she'd suddenly wave her hand up and down in front of my face, imitating a Three Stooges[18] gesture. Palm up as her fingers fluttered from chin to forehead less than an inch in front of my nose, and palm down as the fluttering moved in the other direction. She usually made a squeaky noise to accompany this motion, which she'd do twice. Perhaps it took five or six seconds. Long enough for Robert to laugh heartily at my reaction. At the time, very annoying. Now I see it for the hostility it conveyed.

My sister's given name, Cynthia, was one we both disliked for its pretentiousness. But mainly because it didn't suit her down-to-earth nature. She wanted me to call her Cindy, and I was happy to oblige, although it took a while. As an adult in her twenties, Cindy changed her name once again, but legally, to Tsiporah (which means "bird" in Hebrew). It's quite a pattern in our family, this name- changing. I'm the only hold-out. So far.

I now know how awful it was for my sister to have to hear and watch the abuse I received. Her response had been to become as unproblematic as she could. This only strengthened Shirley's comparisons. I, on the other hand, went the other way. Dr. B describes it like this:

> There is one 17-year-old sister who is the antithesis of our patient. She, however, worships her older sister ... [Natalie] feels that this sister tries to compensate for what Natalie has not given the family. The sister is editor of the yearbook, a member of a sorority, a class representative and on the Student Council, and gets along well with the family.

My sister didn't worship me, but was impressed when I, at age seventeen, went off to university, while she had to stay home in dull old Niagara Falls. She survived in constructive ways, however, by getting out of the house as much as possible and participating in her life.

It took me until the 1980s to realize how envious I was of my sister. At the Clarke, I was oblivious. The hospital records show that I recalled "no sibling rivalry at the time of Cindy's birth." Such obliviousness could be because my sister and I got along most of the time, rarely fighting or even arguing. I suppose, in part, because we were already exposed to enough crises. Our favourite memories to this day involve doing the dishes together. I'd wash, she'd dry, and we'd take forever. We'd have the radio on and dance around to Elvis or Motown tunes. We'd develop poke-fun-at-Mom routines, based on something ridiculous she'd said.

Shirley hated the idea that we took so long in the kitchen to do a few simple dishes. Her way was one-two-three and it's done. *Pfft!* It also probably bothered her that my sister and I were having such a good time on our own. Without her.

From left to right: Me, Shirley, Cynthia (her given name) in Midland, Ontario. Sometime in 1954.

**My sister Cindy (as she wanted to be called)
as a drum majorette, mid-1960s.**

The Shadow

In the 1950s and '60s, the term "eating disorder" hadn't yet been invented. It didn't appear as such in the medical literature until 1980.[19] If you suffered from an eating disorder, you had no reassuring label or diagnosis to let you know you were not alone.[20] To let you know you weren't a freak. Being unable to stop eating was unheard of. A young girl stealing food and lying about it, also unheard of. Starting around the age of eleven, I began to do this. No single event sparked its entrance in my life. Just a gradual but growing sense of alienation and confusion, coupled with prepubescent physical changes. And of course, the gibble-gabble.

I couldn't help it. I'd sneak into the kitchen, lift the lid off the cake tray on the counter in the corner, and slice off a skinny little piece of that chocolate cake. The one my mother had bought for my sister. After all, to quote my mother, she wasn't going to "deprive" my sister just because of me.

Shirley thought I was too fat and needed to watch what I ate. Shirley watched what I ate all the time. So I had to sneak the cake. Eventually, the slices got larger, until whole sections of the cake went missing. "Who ate the cake?" Shirley would ask. "Not me," said my father. "Not me," said my sister. I said the same thing. But of course, it was me.

Within our family constellation, my binge eating disorder (BED) was the shadow, a term coined by noted psychiatrist Carl Jung to describe the darker, often hidden side of human nature – the unconscious, negative aspects of our characters. In my family, the Shadow was the disruptive evidence that all was not as it seemed.

It's important to note that not everyone with BED comes from a home like mine, but many do. Some have loving, caring, and nurturing homes and families, yet something in their lives, within the culture, within their relationships, helps create the fertile ground for this potentially chronic, and for some, fatal, disorder.

In the 1950s, girls in public school often played a little call-and-response game. We called it "Zing, zing, zoom, zoom." You could do it with three people, but it worked best with five or six. We'd all stand in a circle holding hands, and number off. Then we'd all swing our arms in and out of the circle in unison, reciting this refrain.

Zing, zing, zoom, zoom! My little heartie goes boom!
Who stole the coo-kies from the cook-kie jar?

Arms in on the first zing, out on the second. Arms in again on the first zoom, and out on the next. And so on. Without missing a beat or swing, number one would start.

(Number one) Was it you, number three?
(Number three)- Who me?
(All) Yes you. (Number three)- Couldn't be.
(All) Then who? (Number three) Number five.

That girl would reply and deny, also without missing a beat or swing, then supply another number. The object was not to miss a beat or swing. If you did, you were out. The refrain, questions, and responses would continue alternating until only one girl remained. The winner.

At home there was no refrain. No winners. Just plenty of questions with unsatisfactory responses. But my little heartie always went *boom!* Imploding inwards, it split into tiny fragments as I perfected the pattern of theft and deceit. I learned to lie as easily as I learned the schoolyard singsong routine. "Who me? Couldn't be." *Zing, zing.* I never missed a beat.

Eventually, it got so I was wolfing down entire cakes bit by bit at first, and later all at one sitting. When Shirley asked who ate the cake, I'd reply, "What cake?" *Zoom, zoom.* Sometimes I'd sneak to the store, and buy a new cake to replace the one I'd polished off.

Soon, I graduated from the forbidden chocolate cake to other goodies, which were stashed around the house as Shirley tried to thwart the thief. She hid the treats everywhere. In cookie boxes tucked away at the back of cupboards where pots, pans, and cooking utensils were stored. In drawers holding special dish towels. Inside serving dishes brought out only when company came. Behind canned goods stacked in the pantry. And downstairs in the basement, inside other storage containers, or in the extra fridge or freezer. After the war and its scarcity, Shirley and Bob were never going to be without something to eat. "Preppers," ahead of their time.

Over the years, the game grew more complex. My mother often made treats for a bake sale or bazaar, or just to have around for company. She carefully recorded the exact quantity on bits of scrap paper and then tucked the papers inside each container. After demolishing what I guessed was an unnoticeable amount, I'd carefully rewrite the number. The smarter Shirley got, the more devious I became. *Was it you, number two? Who me?*

My sister got blamed, my father got blamed, and I got blamed. And Shirley got ever more hysterical about the missing goodies. Like the paranoid Captain Queeg in the movie *The Caine Mutiny*[21] feverishly cross-examining his subordinates about missing strawberries. But no one ever directly accused me. I've often wondered why not. Because there was one major clue staring us all in the face. One elephant, so to speak, in the room. As the refrain from a Mamas and Papas song goes, "And no one's getting fat except Mama Cass."[22] No one was getting fat except me.

My fatness became my mother's albatross, her deepest shame. Shirley's mission in life: get Natalie to lose weight. She'd goad me into it, shock me, shame me, push me, beg me, cajole me, tease me, bribe me, rant and rave at me. She'd do anything, pay anything, say anything and try anything to get me to lose weight. And she wondered why I didn't feel the same.

It wasn't as if I wanted to be fat. I didn't. At least not consciously. I wanted to lose weight and be thin. Then I'd have the wonderful life and future sure to follow, as Shirley promised. "You can have anything you want," she'd say, "the world at your feet! But you have to be thin!"

Being fat in a thin world is a special hell of its own. Back in the 1950s and '60s, fatness and obesity were not the almost norm they are today. If you were fat, you really stood out from the crowd. I didn't understand why I kept doing this hurtful thing to myself when I tried so hard not to. No one knew how hard I tried *not* to steal the food, *not* to eat the food. I just couldn't help it.

The general theory today is that compulsive eaters or binge eaters simply "perceive" a loss of control, when in fact, they actually have control, but fail to understand this – an idea I strongly dispute (see "The Power to Choose" in chapter 16).

I actually *was* out of control. I was obsessed with food and eating it. I had my favourites, but if they weren't available, anything edible would do. Eating stopped the gibble-gabble's push into action, stopped the food thoughts and images from tormenting me. As soon I heard my parents' car pull out of the driveway, I'd rush to the fridge or the cupboards. Often I wasn't even aware of how I got there. Suddenly, I'd just be in the kitchen, standing in front of the open fridge, cupboard, or drawer. Eating. Gobbling up what I found in a frenzied manner. Until I was overly full. Or until the food was gone. It was so scary. I didn't understand. Why was I doing this when I wanted to lose weight? Was I crazy? Maybe I needed a psychiatrist.

Crazy in those years was absolutely not chic or cool. It was a daunting and intimidating subject, surrounded by far more myth, fear, and social stigma than today. Take, for example, the classic 1948 movie *The Snake Pit*, whose main female character, confined for months, survived electroshock therapy, hydrotherapy, and "truth serum" injections. The film was based on Mary Jane Ward's brave autobiography about the dehumanizing horrors of American psychiatric treatment in state-run mental institutions.[23] The title refers to the primitive custom of throwing mentally ill people into a pit of snakes, on the theory that what would make normal people insane would make insane people normal. I saw this film on TV as a teenager, and it freaked me out.

I felt enormously ashamed of my increasingly fat body. But I couldn't admit it, especially to Shirley. The gibble-gabble kept busily trying to figure out why I stole food in the first place. My great sorrow and humiliation. My dark secret. My nightmare. I had no words to describe it. No context for it. I could tell no one what I was doing. It was too disgusting and appalling to believe. Shirley would shriek, "What's wrong with you!" after discovering some carefully hidden food item was missing. Nobody knew the answer.

It was probably something horrible. If I could just have some peace long enough to figure it out, I assumed I'd then be able to *do* something about it. Which was, of course, completely and utterly wrong. But nobody knew it then.

Shirley was very big on *doing* something about it. In frustration, she'd plead with me. She'd tell me she could understand if I was a "cripple," because a "cripple" couldn't *do* anything about their condition. But I was fat, and fat was something within my control. Fat was something I could *do* something about. Except that I couldn't. No matter how hard I tried.

Peace was a rare commodity in our house. Shirley went on frequent raging rampages, outbursts that were always my fault. No one could deny that. Not my sister, whose cake I stole and who got blamed for whatever else I ate. Not my father, so ashamed of his big daughter and so annoyed when I opened my "big mouth" and set Shirley off. Once riled, like a tornado, Shirley would flatten whoever was in her path, sometimes my dad or sister. This was my fault, too. If I hadn't made her angry in the first place, she wouldn't be yelling at them.

She'd screech at me, often out of the blue. "For God's sake, Natalie! How can you let yourself get like that?" Or, "How can you stand to *look* at yourself!" She'd place her hand on her face, aghast, as if in shock. "I can't stand the *sight* of you – you're so fat!" Or, "You should be ashamed of yourself!" Or, "Look at you! How can a girl with such a pretty face let herself get so fat?" And my favourite, as she grabbed my midriff (what we euphemistically now refer to as love-handles), "Ugh! Ugh! You're disgusting!" Followed by, "How can you stand to let anyone *touch* you?" (Unspoken answer: I couldn't.) She'd often end with, "You make me sick!"

That's a lot of guilt, blame, and shame to be lugging around with you, weighing you down wherever you go. *Zing, zing.*

There was more. At the time, understandably, I hated Shirley. And I felt guilty about that. After all, she was my mother and was only trying to do what was right for me. Nobody else was ever going to care about me the way Shirley cared. Shirley cared with such passion and devotion, she could barely contain herself.

Zing, zing, zoom, zoom. My little heartie went *boom*! Because it was me who stole the cook-ies from the cook-ie jar.

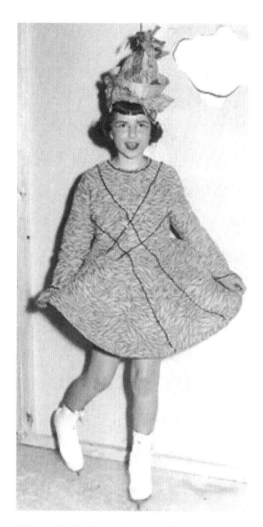

Me as a skating pineapple at age 10 or 11 in Niagara Falls. Shirley was already calling me fat. So was I.

CHAPTER 4: OPENING NIGHT

Noelle

Unlike the movie *Girl Interrupted,* my stay at the Clarke was no mere interruption in my life. It fundamentally changed my life. The Clarke was a marker, a huge neon marker, dividing my life into two portions. Before the Clarke, with my miserable, confused and tormented existence. And after the Clarke, with the rest of my life. Every year, I note March 31 and April 1 as an anniversary.

Being at the Clarke enabled me to break with my past and, more importantly, helped me understand that I *needed* to break with my past. It was the first real help I got. I came out of the cold, albeit into confusion and chaos. But I wasn't so alone, and I wasn't ever as confused or distraught, and I certainly wasn't interrupted. I *began.*

And while I can write all these positive things, I still have some shame, which is another reason to continue writing, so I can let it go. I've come to believe I must finally deal with it, settle myself with it, and come to terms that it happened and what it meant.

It took me a while to muster up the courage to write my story. It's such an emotional issue.

Memories of that first eventful night at the Clarke so many years ago were with me frequently. Not every day, but often enough to occupy a substantial space in my memory bank, at least until I finished this book.

I can picture myself in Gilda's office, sitting in the chair on the left side of her desk, lined up against the west wall. She had to swivel around to see who came through the door, but I had only to look up.

Gilda must have called for the two nurses who knocked on her office door. I met them in the hall, where Gilda introduced me to Miss Fish and Miss Lord. No kidding. Those were their names. When I heard Miss Fish's name, I thought "Fish? Fishy.

Hmmm, there's something fishy here all right." Then I met Miss Lord and made an instant association with the old gospel song "It's Me, oh Lord." I thought, *Oh lord, oh lord. I'm standing in the need of prayer.*

Later on I was to meet a black male nurse named Moses, which also spawned some eyeball rolling, I can tell you.

The Misses Fish and Lord (dressed in street clothes and not in uniforms, as was the custom at the Clarke) had come down to Gilda's office to escort me to the ninth floor. At this point, I wasn't too clear on what was happening. They were taking me somewhere. I felt very tired and scared. Where were we going? They seemed pleasant enough, so I went with them. Up in the elevator. The numbers flashed into view: 7, 8, 9. And then we stopped. The elevator doors opened, and directly across I spotted a bunch of people behind a Plexiglas wall, doing paperwork.

My escorts guided me left, and then left again, past some sort of lounge area, to a room at the end of a hallway, where I was promised I could rest since I felt so tired. I lay on the single bed against the wall and looked out the window at the greying sky. Still daylight.

As far as I can remember, my room was a busy place, with various people coming and going throughout the evening. An Austrian woman named Shotsie, built like a wrestler, was on hand mainly for emergency situations. I'm not sure if someone was with me all the time or not, but if so, it would have been the Misses Fish or Lord.

I don't recall what was happening too clearly, because there was so much going on inside my head and inside my body. I felt super-sensitive, as if I'd broken through some multisensory barrier and could perceive more and more clearly than ever before. I felt as if I knew, for example, exactly what the nurses were thinking as they stood beside me, and what they were feeling, what they thought of me, and how happy they were with their lives. Don't ask me how or why. I just knew. Months later I learned I'd been correct about many things.

Each of the next few events stands out clearly from an otherwise muddy background, although the order may not be accurate.

At one point, I felt extremely cold lying there on the bed, despite the camel-hair suit, so some people helped me cover up. Then I was brought some pills, which I didn't want to take. No thank you. No. Definitely not. I didn't need pills. I just needed some sleep. Why wouldn't anyone let me sleep? Why all this to-ing and fro-ing? Just leave me alone and let me sleep. The Clarke people, however, insisted the pills were going to help. I don't recall taking pills. But I do remember feeling very thirsty and restless. In an incoherent and agitated state, I must have mumbled that I was thirsty. Someone asked if I wanted something to drink. Would I like some orange juice? Yes. Orange juice. So they brought me what looked like orange juice. But it tasted foul. Like mustard. Instantly I spat it out. Is it possible that pills were mixed in with the orange juice? I thought so.

They tricked me, I said to myself. They lied about the drink. This had happened to me before, but I couldn't remember when or where. What the Clarke people had brought me tasted like mustard. From then on, I believed and trusted no one.

I remember lying on the bed, eyes closed, as I experienced going through the birth canal. In my mind, I was being reborn. My sensory hallucination, or if you prefer a less diagnostic term, my fantasy, felt very real. I struggled and squirmed for a long time in the dark, feeling scared and alone. Anticipating my rebirth, I knew I needed a name. I didn't want to be Natalie anymore. That was no fun. That didn't work for me. I knew Natalie meant "child of Christmas," so I figured Noelle would be a good substitute. I liked the sound of it and felt relieved to have discovered it in the nick of time.

The moment was fast approaching when I was to enter the world. Push! Push through the darkness! I could feel myself moving slowly down the birth canal, twisting and turning, struggling to be free. And yet, strangely resistant. I wanted to be reborn. And I didn't want to be reborn.

I could feel myself enter the universe. I began to call out, but couldn't make a sound. I tried to scream, to cry out, but no sound came. Very scary. In that infinitesimal instant, I wanted my dad. Where was my dad? I tried to call out for him, but all that came out was "Dddduh, duh, duh ..." In a nanosecond, I realized not only that my dad couldn't be there, but also that he wasn't the right person to call, wasn't the right name. And as facial images of my dad and several men named David flashed through my mind, the one I ultimately settled on belonged to the young man I'd been infatuated with about a year earlier, David

X. And the name I shrieked out instead of Dad was David. "Duh, duh, duh ... David! David!" At the top of my lungs. People came running. Including a tall, very thin male nurse apparently named David.

"Shush, shush! ... Stop making so much noise ... What's wrong? ... David is here!" Whatever they said at this point only irritated me more. Who were they trying to kid? This wasn't David X! I became increasingly restless, and began tossing and turning. They took hold of my arms and tried to restrain me, but the more they did this the more I resisted. I didn't want to be there now. This was a huge mistake. These people were not on my side.

Everything felt so hostile, so unfriendly. I'd just been reborn, and here they were treating me with lies and contempt. But the more I squirmed and screamed, the more they tried to quiet me and hold me down. And the more they tried to hold me down, the more vigorously I thrashed about and the louder I shrieked.

The battle ended with me lying on the floor. People on either side had me pinned down by my arms, shoulders, and legs. I remember seeing them beside me, feeling the comforting, cold, hard floor beneath me. Solid. Dependable. I could also feel hands on my body. They felt both calming and disturbing at the same time. People were touching me – and I was alert to Shirley's warnings that people would get sick with disgust if they touched me. Yet at the same time I longed for them to hold me, like the kids at Brown Camps were held. After all, I'd just been reborn. I needed to be held. But I could no more have said this than I could fly to the moon.

Soon nurse Shotsie gave me an injection. I could feel myself drift off to sleep right there on the floor.

Brown Camps

Brown Camps was a private residential facility for emotionally disturbed children, founded in 1966 by John L. Brown after he left Warrendale,[24] a conflict-ridden government-sponsored children's mental- health treatment centre. An old camp counsellor friend, Jerry, had suggested I apply to work at Brown's and that I'd be great with these kids. But my memories and the hospital records both confirm that I was already over the edge when I applied for a job there in the first or second week of March 1967, only a few weeks before I entered the Clarke.

At that time, Brown's offered a revolutionary and controversial treatment program. Staff members were trained to restrain wild and unruly kids with their own bodies, "holding" and enclosing them on the floor in a safe way. The kids could then yell and scream without hurting themselves and without artificial constraints, such as drugs or straitjackets. I'd heard that the holding technique built trust.[25]

In the mid- to late1960s, therapeutic intervention involving human touch was in the early experimental stages and considered highly questionable. But I sometimes wonder what would have happened to me if I'd simply been held my first night at the Clarke, whether drugs would have been needed.

My initial interview for the Brown Camps job was conducted by Dr. F at his office in the northern outskirts of Toronto – in an area called Oak Ridges, now part of Richmond Hill – but accessible by public transit. The Clarke records show his real name, but I prefer the letter "F" for his capital-F Failure to detect my slipping grip on reality. A rather heavy-set older man in a tweed jacket, Dr. F said very little, in typical psychiatrist fashion. At the far end of his large office, I couldn't help but notice that a luncheon buffet had been set up, with plates of food arranged attractively on the table. I wondered if it was some sort of test just for me as I pondered whether to choose the celery or carrot sticks, the fruit, the sandwiches, or the pastry. I thought it strange they'd know this weakness of mine ahead of time, but didn't pursue this line of thinking to its obvious rational conclusion that indeed, they did not.

Instead, I just sat there, resisting the temptation to sample some of the food, which was becoming quite a distraction. What was really going on here? Of course, I mentioned none of my suspicions to the doctor. I wasn't going to risk talking about food unless he mentioned it first. Since he ignored it, I pretended to do the same. I don't recall much of the interview, but I must have passed muster, because Dr. F arranged for me to meet a man named David V at the camp residence, a few blocks away. Since it was a beautiful sunny day, I didn't mind walking, although I felt quite nervous and apprehensive. I was meeting another David.

If you're feeling a bit confused about the Davids, imagine how it must have been for me, in my less-than-together state of mind.

As it turned out, David V was a very tall, attractive man, who essentially ran the place. After an informal chat in his ground-floor corner office, he took me on a tour of the facilities.

Since it was midday, our first stop was the lunchroom, which was far from what I expected. Chaos reigned. Several rows of picnic-style tables and benches were filled with happy, noisy, energetic kids, jumping up and down, waving their arms about, shrieking at one another, and laughing as they grabbed food off each other's plates. Boisterous adults at each table made little effort to calm them down. Shirley definitely would not have approved.

Was I hungry? David V asked. Would I like some lunch? No thanks. I wondered if this was yet another food-related test. Temptation loomed its ugly head, despite the chaotic atmosphere. But I would never eat in front of a potential employer, or anyone, for that matter.

He then escorted me outside to see the grounds and the home from a different perspective. The snow had melted all around, leaving enormous puddles and oodles of mud in the driveway and parking area behind the building.

Enviously, I watched some of the kids play in the puddles. Splashing, jumping, sinking into the mud, oblivious to the mess they were making or how dirty they were getting. Their freedom, their joyful abandon, struck me profoundly. How much I wanted to splash in the puddles with them and sink into that mud. I longed to know how it felt to slide deep into the ooze. I even mentioned this to David V, who shrugged and said I could join them if I wanted.

No. I couldn't. I wasn't dressed for it. My best black wool coat with the fur-trimmed collar, and my dark royal-blue, double-knit, three-piece suit (a tight skirt, shell top, and three-quarter-length, double- breasted jacket with gold buttons down the front) was not how you'd dress to jump anywhere, let alone into mud. With such an outfit, I also had to wear several girdles, to keep the fat from squeezing out. With midriff, tummy, hips, and thighs so restrained, plus suspenders and nylon stockings, submerging myself into the mud with abandon was not something I was physically capable of doing. Of course, my clothes were really just an excuse. Even if I'd been wearing loose clothes and rubber boots, psychologically I was nowhere near free enough to play. My unmet desire to do so made me feel uncomfortable, so I pushed it away.

David V and I returned inside to attend the daily staff meeting. There, my attention focused on everyone's peculiar idiosyncrasies. As we all sat in a circle in the staff lounge area, what I observed were all the gestures, mannerisms, and movements the staff made – the nose-scratching, eye-rubbing, earlobe- tugging, lip-licking, leg-stretching, leg-crossing, arm-crossing, finger-tapping, and so on.

From my current perspective, these seem to be normal movements people make while sitting together casually and comfortably. But at the time, my perception had somehow shifted into slow motion, as if a camera had zoomed in to show close-ups of moving body parts in a choreographed dance. Viewed this way, these people seemed weird. I wondered what was wrong with them and if they were okay enough to look after emotionally disturbed children.

When the staff meeting finished, I expressed my concerns back in David V's office. He seemed surprised by my comments and not too impressed with my keen powers of observation. After a while, he told me I wasn't really suitable to work at Brown Camps and escorted me to the spacious front hall to bid me goodbye. But I didn't want to leave. I wanted to stay and persuade him that I was an excellent candidate.

I'm not clear exactly how it happened, but let's just say he noticed my reluctance to go. As he took my arm at the elbow to lead me closer to the door, I resisted and pulled away. But the more I physically resisted, the more insistent he became that I leave.

Other staff members soon arrived on the scene, some taking hold of my arms to move me out of the hallway. I recall sinking to the floor, at first saying I didn't want to go, then yelling "No!" And then at the top of my lungs, "Don't make me go!" The staff and David V grabbed me by the arms and lifted me up, as I kicked and struggled to get free. In the end, four of them had to physically carry me out of the building, like a sack of potatoes.

On the front verandah, David V waited with me as I gathered myself together. He told me I couldn't stay at the home and said if I wanted help, he'd give me the number of someone to call. Yes. Help would be good, yes. So while I waited outside, shocked at my own behaviour, he went back to his office and returned in a few moments with the phone number of someone he vouched for. This is how I got Gilda's number at the Clarke.

After my humiliating eviction, I remember walking along the gravel-coated roadside, clutching the phone number, this lifeline, in my pocket, mulling over the phrase "want help." I'm now incredibly grateful for that help. Without that number and the assurance that I'd like Mrs. Gilda Katz, who knows what would have happened to me. I can tell you this much. I would never in a million years have thought of calling the Clarke Institute on my own. I didn't even know a place like the Clarke existed.

Everyone knew about the mental health centre at 999 Queen Street West, Toronto's official "loony bin." We all joked about it. That's where I might have ended up, with who knows what results. Several well-known Canadian authors and mental health advocates have written of their experiences[26] in the Canadian mental health system – which makes me realize how fortunate I was back in the 1960s. Sadly, the type of support I received is no longer available.

So a huge thank-you goes to my messenger, David V, whom I never saw again. Until you said the words "if you want help," I wasn't aware I needed any. It took several weeks before I actually got it.

When I was younger, so much younger than today, I never needed anybody's help in any way.[27]

Here's what astounds me about my Brown Camps experience. Despite my sad and sorry mental state, I managed to fool the psychiatrist who screened me. And I also fooled David V, enough for him to show me around the place. His suspicions weren't raised till I told him mine.

Then again, I'd been fooling people my whole life. My adult act, practiced since I could talk at the age of two, was polished to near perfection. I'd learned early on that the smart way to get along was to give people what they wanted. Tell them what they wanted to hear. You'd have less trouble, and they might even like you. Problem was, I'd started to believe my own BS.

CHAPTER 5: CONNECTS AND DISCONNECTS

The Source

Shortly after Shirley's death (in 1993), as my sister and I sorted through a box of old black-and-white photographs, we found many taken during the wartime years. Several showed our mother posed in a one- piece bathing suit. All featured messages scrawled across the back to her beloved husband stationed overseas. On one, the question, "Do I look fat, or don't I??"

Shirley in 1943 and a note on the reverse side of photo to my father, who was away in the war. It shows Shirley's preoccupation with weight a few years before I was born, and probably was sent after her miscarriage.

Shirley worried about her own fatness before I was born. A stunning revelation! This was England in the early 1940s. Movie stars were slim. Slim therefore became fashionable. But Britain's cultural landscape lacked today's constant barrage of "be thin" multimedia messages. Shirley must have developed her thin fixation all on her own. Perhaps the photo was taken after Rosemarie's sad, brief appearance, when my mother was trying to lose pregnancy weight.

Physical appearance meant a great deal to Shirley. Correction: physical appearance was almost everything to my mother. It was how the world judged you. It showed how proud you were of yourself. And it was the decisive factor in a woman's ability to find a husband, her ultimate raison d'être.

According to Shirley, if a girl wasn't decent-looking (that is, thin), she didn't stand a chance.

The System

There always has to be someone in a dysfunctional family to be the bad guy. The black sheep. To take the blame for what does and doesn't happen. In Family Systems therapy, this person is called the "scapegoat."[28] In my family, that role was mine. No one officially decided. And we certainly didn't vote on it. But given our family dynamics and the personalities caught up in the dance, the negative focus on me evolved over time, especially after my younger sister was born.

My mother and father were both control freaks. Otherwise they were total opposites. Shirley was irrational, emotional, and often hysterical. With an attention span of about five seconds, she could go off at a moment's notice. You never knew when the volcano would erupt. And you certainly never had to guess what she thought. Because Shirley told you straight out, whether you wanted to hear it or not. If she thought it, you got it. To Shirley, there was a right way to do everything. Hers. And a wrong way. Ours.

Nobody could ever do anything fast enough, or good enough, or right enough for my dear mother. As a result, most of the time she lived in a perpetual state of dissatisfaction, which we all paid for. But I bore the main brunt.

On the other hand, Robert was a study in contradictions. His outer manner was calm and measured. He liked to portray himself as someone thoughtful, who reasoned things out and enjoyed thinking along rational and philosophical lines. When he spoke, it was usually in a straightforward but intimidating, authoritarian manner, befitting a Mafia boss. Seemingly in charge and in control.

In public, my father could be absolutely charming, but at home he was tuned out much of the time. I sensed, however, but couldn't articulate, a turmoil within. A silent, ever-present threat of stored-up anger and pain. Waiting, hovering, and simmering below the surface. Ready to explode in a flash. One stern glance from Bob, and my sister and I morphed into obedient servants. Whatever you want, boss!

My father also tried to be kind to me. He didn't scream at me or call me names like my mother did. At least not about how I looked. He aimed more at my intelligence. "El Stupido" was his favourite joke-insult for me. I don't think he had one for my sister. Of course, El-Stupido hurt, but so much less than the fat attacks. My dad explained he knew I was intelligent, which made it okay for him to call me stupid. It was a joke. No big deal.

While I hated my mother and felt guilty about it, I adored my father, who tried to help by explaining my mother's rampages. He'd tell me she didn't mean it. She loved me, wanted what was best for me. She meant well. But she just couldn't help it. He'd also tell me not to answer back, to try to understand her. He'd glare at me during my mother's hysterical rants, warning me with his eyes to keep quiet. When I didn't, he'd sigh and shake his head from side to side, while tsk-tsking. He expected me to know better next time. Maybe I was nine or ten when I first started hearing this advice, perhaps even younger. But I didn't know better next time, or the hundreds of next times after that.

I did try to understand my mother, though. Because my dad asked. But I failed miserably, despite my father's promptings. It was almost impossible not to answer back. After all, I had to defend myself.

Over time, I learned to let most of the fat comments go, hurtful though they were. I got used to them. Besides, Shirley's rhetorical questions had no answers. I didn't know how I could let myself get so fat. But all other criticisms were fair game. I usually opened what my father called my big mouth. Except when she'd ask the heavens what she had done to deserve a daughter like me. Or when she'd accuse me of hating her. "You *hate* your mother, don't you?" That was always too close to the painful truth. Silence was the only answer.

Even more painful was the fact that I didn't completely trust my father. At the time, I couldn't afford to admit it. So I denied and disowned my sense that all was not as it seemed. I pushed it aside because I needed him to be on a pedestal.

At that time, trust was a foreign concept. This simple, one-syllable word wasn't part of my vocabulary, spoken or unspoken. It wasn't a category I considered when figuring out the world. Or the people in it. Who I did or didn't trust was a non-issue. I had no word to describe the sense of safety or security trust implies. Nor did I have any experience of it. I certainly didn't trust myself. How could I trust myself when I swore I'd stop stealing and sneaking food, but then repeatedly return to that behaviour? I couldn't. The shame of this permeated my being. I also don't recall feeling safe or secure while growing up, even though my material needs were always met.

When figuring out the world and its people, I relied on other important categories. Did I like or dislike you? Were you a user or a usee? Were you sincere or phony? Did you have a good personality or not? Were you fair-minded or prejudiced? And were you honest or dishonest? No mention of trustworthiness.

In my later years I was quite shocked to discover how I really felt about my father. Now it makes perfect sense. But as a teenager, I needed someone to think of in positive terms. Obviously, I couldn't face the prospect of being against both parents. Then I'd have nobody.

The Great Pretender[29]

Looking back, I wasn't *that* fat during high school. So said my school friends and acquaintances when I brought the subject up. This was my way of testing people. If I liked you and wanted to check that you were on my side, I'd follow the "I'm-so-fat" script. I'd tell you I was fat and that I wished I wasn't. I'd describe how I couldn't lose any weight. Or I'd say I really wanted to lose weight. And inevitably, my potential pal of the moment would say, "You're not *that* fat!" Very reassuring, especially compared to the constant drubbing at home.

Sometimes in disputes with Shirley, I'd tell her "I'm not *that* fat." And she'd tell me not to be silly and that of course I was a big, fat lump! I'd say my friends didn't think so. That really got her going.

According to my mother, people who told me I wasn't *that* fat were not my friends. Friends told you the truth, even if it wasn't pleasant. Even if it hurt. Like her friend Sally. Anyone who told me I wasn't that fat didn't really care about me. Not the way my mother did. According to Shirley, my so-called friends actually *wanted* me fat, so I'd be less competition. I found this ridiculous and refused to think so poorly of people who tried to be kind.

Like other addicts, I used food and eating to keep pushing my feelings away. Food, as I consumed it, was a drug. The sugars and starches I ravenously and compulsively scarfed down stimulated my brain, like liquor or cocaine.[30] I was zoned out much of the time, which I probably needed to be just to survive. All I had to work with was my mind, which was busy-busy all the time with the gibble-gabble.

I also blamed my mother. If only she'd lay off for a while, give me a breather. Then maybe I could psyche myself up enough to go on a diet and stay on it. But Shirley couldn't lay off. And every time she'd insult my appearance, I'd lie to myself. I'd pretend not to care. I'd also pretend I didn't mind what I weighed, whatever the number. I rarely knew the number.

To get Shirley off my back, I'd go on pretend diets. And I'd pretend to get on the scale in the mornings. When my mother could see no weight loss, I got sneakily creative. I'd tell her I only lost a pound, perhaps two. Sometimes I'd even say I gained a few pounds, and act all upset and confused. How could this could happen when I'd been so careful? Or I'd tell her I wasn't getting on the scale till such- and-such a date. She always remembered my previous fake weight number.

Lying to my mother did little for my self-esteem and was not the best way to start the day.

Eventually, Shirley began to suspect I was making it all up. The fake weights I invented made no sense. Sometimes, amidst my howls of protest, she insisted on watching me get on the scale. "You don't *trust* me!" I'd wail. No, she didn't. "You don't *believe* me," I'd complain. No, she didn't. It was a mean game, played out on my body and on both of our spirits. A game nobody won.

So we'd both trundle upstairs to the tiny, second-floor bathroom where the scale was kept. As my mother crouched down close enough to get a clear view of the number, I'd rest my arm on the sink.

Leaning carefully and applying just the right amount of pressure, I'd watch for a reasonable weight number to wobble into focus. Then all would be calm for a while.

My mother was not a patient person. Back then, no one in our family had much of that quality. Nor was Shirley intellectually inclined. But she knew things and she sensed things. Her gut instinct and strong intuition informed her much of the time. I find it amazing that she played the scale game for so long. Especially when she knew I was lying.

We were both slaves to different masters. Mine, an addiction to food, especially sugar, even before the commercial popularity of high-fructose corn syrup,[31] and eating. Hers, an abiding belief that no woman was going to get anywhere in this life if she was fat or ugly, no matter how smart she was. Or how much talent she had. If a woman was fat or ugly, forget it. She didn't have a chance! Eventually the two words became synonymous with one another and bonded tightly together in my mind. Fatandugly Uglyandfat.

This woman was so committed to my well-being she'd move heaven and earth to make sure I wouldn't grow up to be fatandugly. This, I now painfully know, is how my mother loved me. Enough to engage in senseless daily battles. Enough to spend many of her waking hours scheming to prevent me from ending up with the fatandugly curse on my life.

Once, she dragged me downtown in Niagara Falls to a little place with fat-reducing machines. Most gyms in the early 1960s were mainly for boxers, wrestlers, and body builders, not for the general public, and especially not for women. I must have been sixteen, because I drove us to this converted storefront.

The owner, a woman clearly ahead of her time, explained how the two main machines could take off fat without exercise, by breaking down fat cells. One machine looked like a stationary treadmill, with a wide belt to place around your hips and butt. At high speed, the belt apparently jiggled your fat away. The other was like a roller-drum, which was about two feet high. You sat on the floor and leaned various fat parts of your body against round, curvy wooden rollers. When turned on, the rollers spun, theoretically pummelling your body part into shape. I have no idea how much Shirley spent on these sessions. But I do know they didn't work.

Convinced no one would want to marry me if I was fat, Shirley insisted I come with her to the doctor. Our family doctor. He regurgitated this nonsense to me in a pseudo-authoritative, matter-of-fact way. Probably as a favour to my mother, who suffered from high blood pressure. According to Dr. A, no one would want me or want to marry me at this weight. That's what he said as I stepped on the scale in his office. How humiliating. How shameful to hear this from such an unsmiling nasal-sounding little man.

This scene may be the origin of my lifetime interest in informing the medical profession about eating disorders and how to help, not humiliate, their patients.

Dr. A's warning failed to inspire me. In fact, it had the opposite effect. Marriage was the wrong carrot to dangle in front of this horse. I was dead set against it, in theory and in fact.

I studiously watched my parents and drew my sad conclusions. I saw my mother screech and yell and harass my father too many times. And felt sorry for him. No one deserved that. I swore I'd never treat a man like that. Robert rarely wanted to be around her. I never saw them together in a romantic way. And I never saw my dad kiss my mother on the lips. Sometimes she'd get a peck on the cheek when he arrived home. More often than not, it was Shirley who planted a smacker on his face as he waited for dinner to be served. Shirley adored Robert. Her whole life essentially revolved around him, and from what I could tell, the feeling wasn't mutual. That was my picture of marriage. Bob and Shirley's fate was not anything I wanted for myself.

To me, marriage was the antithesis of freedom. And freedom was what I craved. Freedom from and freedom to. Easy now to understand why a slave to addiction would long for freedom. Freedom from all the confusion, from the gibble-gabble, from the habitual, unthinking reactions. From the compulsion to eat, whether hungry or not. Easy now to see the special allure of freedom from parental control, from being bossed around, from being forced to sit in boring classrooms day after day. Easy, too, to understand why freedom would be such a powerful concept to me. Freedom to do what you want, say what you want, go where you want, whenever you want.

Most of all, freedom meant that nobody owned you. Freedom! I dreamed about it, listened to songs about it, sang songs about it. The old spiritual gospel songs. Soul songs, songs about your spirit being free. These I loved. These sustained me. I wouldn't be here today without these songs to feed me, hold me, and contain my deepest hopes. The hopes I didn't know existed, the ones I couldn't even imagine. "Oh Freedom!" I'd sing that old civil rights gospel song as if my life depended on it. And to a certain extent, it did.

And before I'll be a slave, I'll be buried in my grave
And go home, to the Lord, and be free!

It still moves me.

Mealtime at Our House

The deal in our household was that my father controlled his work domain, and my mother ran the household. This division of labour was not so unusual for that era. My mother ran a tight ship. All meals were served at specified times. You ate whatever was put on your plate, with very few exceptions, and you ate all of it, without complaint. No choices here. Choices did not exist in our household.

We could voice approval of particular foods – oh, good, rice pudding! Or hurray, baked beans on toast! (Many of my mother's menu selections were British, not a country known for its haute cuisine.)

While appreciation was acceptable, you didn't want to risk Shirley's reaction if you disliked what she served. This I learned at the age of seven or eight, when our house in Midland was close enough to the school for me to come home for lunch.

Shirley had spent one morning making a new dish, what she called chicken fricassee. It smelled foul and looked like someone had vomited into a plate. So I turned my nose up and refused to eat it. Shirley was in no mood for this. I remember her yelling and me whining, and then a sudden strange noise, as the plate of hot, steaming chicken fricassee crashed over my head. I don't recall what happened afterwards. Except that I never again turned my nose up at any food on Shirley's table. At least not so she could see.

When my sister and I first learned to speak, we learned "manners." For example, "Thank you for my lovely breakfast, please may I leave the table." This applied to every meal. We had to finish what was on our plates, or we didn't get to leave. We should eat what was put in front of us because there were starving children somewhere in the world (who would somehow benefit when we finished what was on our plates).

Our family ate dinner together every night except Thursdays, when my father worked until 9:00
p.m. Actually, we were in the same room and sat at the same table. But we didn't all eat at the same time. My mother busied herself the whole time, serving the various courses, cleaning up as the meal progressed. While we ate the soup, she washed the salad dishes. Shirley was notorious in her family for her constant clearing up, and her siblings joked that if you lifted your cup to sip your tea, when you put it down, the saucer was already washed, wiped, and back in the cupboard.

Shirley didn't actually sit at the table until we'd all been served the main course. By then, my father would have almost finished eating. Between the two of them, mealtimes always felt hectic, not peaceful or calm by any means. Robert could consume food in record time. He prided himself on how fast he could eat, actually bragged about how much he could demolish in a short time. He'd stand at the fridge, *voorsht* (kosher salami) in hand, and boast how he could eat the whole thing in one sitting with an entire loaf of bread. That's what he did in the old days. Before he got married, before he met my mother. Such were my father's few reminiscences from the past.

Dinnertime conversation was usually sparse. According to my father, mealtime was for eating, not talking. However, in brief bite-size statements, in between mouthfuls, Bob told Shirley what happened at the store. Who tried something on, who bought or might buy a particular item, and who popped in to say hello. Then he'd deliver any gossip he'd learned about the community, Jewish and gentile. Who died, who had an operation, a baby, and so on. None of this dialogue was directed at me or my sister. We were expected to sit there, eat, listen, and not interrupt. Unnoticed diners, except when under fire.

Shirley's conversational sphere included our school accomplishments. "Tell your father how you did on your exam," she'd demand. My sister and I would report our grades, usually quite high. Perhaps 97. The interrogations would then begin. "Humph! Why didn't you get 98 or 99?" Our class ranking was never good enough. If we came third, who came first and why didn't we? I recall no praise, no congratulations, and absolutely no celebration of accomplishment. Even a perfect grade got a lukewarm response. "Humph! That's more like it. Why don't you do this more often!"

Sometimes Robert would wink at us, while still chewing, to let us know he understood. Or that he knew Shirley was off the wall. Or to show how much he was enjoying the chicken. It didn't matter what that wink meant. It wasn't negative or hostile, to us, anyway.

But at other times he'd glare at me in disapproval because of a smart-aleck response to Shirley. For example, I'd explain I didn't come first because it was someone else's turn, or I didn't get 99 or 100 because that's the way the numbers added up.

Shirley saw her comments as positive reinforcement, and not as the demoralizing perfectionism they really were.

Being ignored at the table was vastly preferred to the other main conversational topic. By the time I'd reached eighth grade, the question of who stole the cookies from the cookie jar placed a heavy negative focus on the whole family. It often made supper a living hell of accusations, nasty looks from my father, and growing hysterics from Shirley.

To counteract our father's high-speed eating, our mother's busy-ness, and my deceit, my sister developed the habit of eating slowly and deliberately. She'd purposefully (and annoyingly) savour every morsel, pause between bites, lick her lips, and thoroughly clean the fork or spoon with her tongue before taking more. Surprisingly, Shirley found this amusing and simply cleaned up around her.

Gabby Girdle Gold

During my early days at the Clarke, I made one decision that I've honoured ever since. Never to wear a girdle again. Ever. And I never have, not even control-top pantyhose. This may not seem like a big deal, but I assure you, it was and still is.

You'd have to be an overweight woman to really understand how it feels to severely encase and restrict major parts of your body with tight, heavily reinforced, thick elastic undergarments. In those days, these were made with metal and whalebone, which dug into your skin after you'd worn them for a while, leaving deep red gouges, as if you'd been run over by a horde of tiny cyclists.

By the time I entered the Clarke at the age of twenty-one, I usually wore a three- or four-girdle ensemble as a matter of course. One knee-length panty girdle held in my thighs. Another provided excellent tummy control. A third girdle zipped up tightly to cinch me in at the waist, with suspenders for my nylon stockings. Pantyhose had become popular in the mid-60s, thanks to skinny miniskirt model Twiggy.[32] But even if available in my size, I wouldn't have worn them. I counted on the triple girdle effect, because it worked. I also wore a long-line bra to lessen midriff bulge and to contain the tops of the other three girdles.

As you can imagine, unlike today's lightweight Lycra and spandex undergarments, my heavy elastic armour took considerable time and effort to put on and take off. Going to the bathroom was a daunting proposition, so I'd ignore my bodily signals as long as I could and go as infrequently as possible during the day. This wasn't too difficult. I was so out of touch with my body's needs that I was usually unaware of the physical signs that signal you have to go. Like many people with chronic binge eating disorder, most of my bodily sensations and signals were filtered to mean one thing – eat!

Instead of a garter belt to hold up my nylon stockings, I began wearing a girdle when I started high school in 1959. Thanks to Shirley, I realized that a girdle really did hold in my stomach. And I thought it helped me look less fat. Pure fantasy on my part, and the great myth of overweight people everywhere. (Girdles may help smooth out a few minor bulges, but they won't make you look thin if you're not.) Aided and abetted by women like my mother, the myth flourished with only a modicum of advertising by the undergarment industry. At least compared to today. In that conservative era, bras and girdles were not a topic on radio or TV programs. Nor were they featured in public fashion shows. It was really a fuddy-duddy time.

Despite countless changes in fashion, textiles, and women's underwear, one thing hasn't changed. The shame and discomfort in the girls' locker room before and after gym class. Actually, the situation may be even worse today. There's still shame about bodies. What they look like, how they're maturing. Shame over every imperfection, no matter how slight. At how they don't measure up to the unrealistic standards set by today's pop and fashion icons. Nowadays, with surveillance cameras and smartphones everywhere, someone's embarrassment can be quickly broadcast to the world on any number of social media outlets.

At my current gym, to avoid such dangers, many young teen and pre-teen girls change in and out of their exercise gear in the toilet cubicles.

When I attended Stamford Collegiate Institute in Niagara Falls, changing for gym class became even more unpalatable, thanks to the gym teacher, Miss P. As I look back, I can see that this woman had some psychological problems, which she apparently took out on her students. She had her favourites, the girls who were physically fit, capable, and cute. And she had her unfavourites, who were just the opposite. She was wonderful to the girls with athletic ability. She supported them, encouraged them, joked and laughed with them, and had them demonstrate new exercises to the class. Nothing wrong with that, you might say, and quite understandable.

However, what's harder to accept is Miss P's meanness to girls who weren't physically fit, a category I not only belonged to, but exemplified. She'd ridicule us in front of the class when we did something the wrong way. She seemed to want to punish us for being unfit. She'd even time us in the locker room, and penalize us with extra ridicule or additional exercises if we took too long to change.

Those were the days of the hideous, bright, royal-blue gymsuit. A ghastly one-piece outfit with a short-sleeved top, tailored collar, white buttons down the front, and elasticized waist with ties usually fashioned into in a bow at the back. The best part: the puffy bloomer pantaloons with elastic around the thighs. Delightful!

To avoid drawing attention to my fatness, and to avoid any teasing or torment from my peers, I tried to hide the fact that I wore more than one girdle. Because it took too long to remove all three, I kept one on during gym class, with the garters tucked underneath my panties. If you thought this restricted my freedom to move you'd be correct. But it hardly mattered, since I was already at the bottom of the physical prowess barrel. It hadn't always been this way, but by the time I reached high school I saw myself as unfit, uncoordinated, and not in the least athletic. Shirley said this was because I was lazy and much too sedentary.

One day in gym class the unthinkable happened. One of the garters became untucked and hung out of my bloomer pantaloon. Miss P spotted it. She stopped midsentence, pointed, asked if that was a garter, and was I wearing a girdle in gym class. I hung my head in shame and dread. Yes. Well, that set her off. She announced to everyone that a girdle was not to be worn in gym class because it wasn't healthy and because it restricted movement. She then suggested this might be why "Gabby Girdle Gold" wasn't too great at gym. Everyone laughed. A lot. And the name stuck. From then on, Miss P derisively referred to me as Gabby Girdle Gold.

But that wasn't the worst. As punishment, I was to learn how to change in and out of a gym-suit quickly, without a girdle. Miss P wanted to know just how fast I could move, if I put effort into it. So every morning for two weeks I came in early and changed in and out of my gym-suit at least a dozen times. I'd head straight down to the locker room and get into my gym-suit. Then I'd run up to Miss P's office in the corner of the gym for inspection, to show her I was in my gym-suit sans girdle. Sometimes she checked the pantaloons to make sure I was garter-less. Then I'd rush back down to the locker room, change into my clothes, and hurry back to Miss P's office to show her I was in my clothes. And then I'd repeat the routine eleven more times, before Miss P let me attend my first morning class. If I was late, Miss P promised to tell the teacher why. They probably knew. Word of this ritual spread around the school pretty quickly.

The "Gabby" part of the name came from my talking too much in class. When you repeatedly can't do something, even though you've been shown how and have tried many times, when you watch others easily master what you cannot do, and when shame, humiliation, and low self-esteem are your constant companions – well, you have to tune out and deaden yourself just to survive. Just to keep breathing. But the deadening takes on its own aura, which feels like a hideous boredom. An overwhelming, endless, numbing boredom. It's actually a sign of depression.

To relieve the boredom, I talked. Sometimes the energy from talking made it seem like I was alive. Not dead or numb inside.

Nowadays young people sometimes cut themselves to feel their way through the numbness. But that didn't occur to me. Talking came naturally. Was the one thing my parents encouraged me to do as a child. They'd say, "Listen to that little *pisk!*" (Yiddish for mouth, describing someone who talks a lot).

I actually got the strap for talking in first grade at Toronto's Humewood Public School, when we lived at the Pinewood Avenue duplex. The teacher, Mrs. Richmond, was probably approaching retirement. A heavy-set woman with close-cropped, white hair and thick, horn-rimmed glasses, she strapped me in front of the class for talking too much. And for talking when I wasn't supposed to. As usual, I hadn't intended to talk or disobey. But I'd finished my work ahead of time and was bored. So I tried to get a girlfriend's attention. "Psst!" I whispered three times. The third try came out too loud. And that was the final straw for Mrs. Richmond.

I was so glad we moved from Toronto to Midland in the middle of first grade. At six years old, I could hardly believe my luck. Instead of mean Mrs. Richmond, there was a lovely, gentle lady named Miss True (honest, that was her name). She, too, wore thick, horn-rimmed glasses, but that was their only similarity. Miss True spoke to everyone, including me, in a kind manner. Her soft, lilting, singsong voice is how you'd talk to a kitten or puppy. I loved her. I caused no trouble in Miss True's class.

But the talking persisted, all the way up to high school. Especially in gym class, where the athletes got to practice and the non-athletes were just as happy to watch. This situation was rife for talking. So I talked, to Miss P's consternation. Her perfect solution? "Gabby Girdle Gold." That extra little bit of humiliation got me to shut up fast. She only had to look in my direction. I'd make sure not to utter a word and to stay away from anyone who might speak to me.

Since talking was out, I took to chewing gum to relieve the boredom and misery of being such a loser in gym class. Not surprisingly, Miss P caught me chewing during a basketball practice. My penalty: wash basketballs every evening after school for two weeks. Very inventive.

The worst and meanest thing Miss P did was to reveal my weight to the whole class. It's hard now to imagine a teacher being so insensitive. But Miss P truly was. For some reason, she decided to weigh everyone at the beginning of the tenth-grade fall season. I'd acquired a serious chunk of weight that summer and felt even more ashamed and appalled than I had the previous year. I didn't know exactly how much I'd gained, since I was playing scale games with Shirley. But none of my ninth-grade shirtwaist dresses fit. So I knew it was serious. (Incidentally, back in those yesteryear days, the dress code demanded that girls wear only skirts or dresses to class. The idea of young women wearing slacks or jeans was unthinkable.)

The big scale, like the ones in doctors' offices, was moved next to Miss P's office in the gym. We each took turns getting weighed, gym-suit and all. Miss P called out the weight to someone standing by with a clipboard. That was the procedure. Miss P had the choice to speak loudly or softly. Clipboard person called my name, and Miss P seemed delighted to welcome me to the scale. "Ah, it's Gabby Girdle Gold!" I know I asked her to please just whisper the weight. Begged her with my eyes to keep this obviously huge number between us. Not surprisingly, and in keeping within her known character, or lack thereof, Miss P didn't just ignore my plea. She took extra pleasure in bellowing out the number. "Gabby Girdle Gold – 183!" That's how I know what I weighed at the beginning of tenth grade. (Back then, I couldn't know that in years to come, I'd yearn to return to this much lower weight.)

I feel sad to write this now. Sad to think about the cruelty of some people. Over my lifetime, I've often wondered what makes people mean to others. Especially those in a teaching or power position.

There is no single answer, other than because they can. I don't know if Miss P is still alive. I suspect she had many unresolved issues. And to be honest, at times that notion brings me a little satisfaction. At other times, I am actually able to feel compassion for those who treat others in a heartless and insensitive manner. Including Miss P. People who enjoy tormenting children can't be truly happy inside.

Splits

You don't have to be fat to disown your body and live in your head. But it helps. Lots of non-fat people do it, too, for different reasons. But the effect is the same.

The fatter I got, the more I grew to hate my body. Moving around became increasingly uncomfortable. And buying clothes that fit became an ordeal. I felt betrayed by this starving mass of flesh that demanded to eat. And I definitely felt ashamed.

So, I distanced myself from my body. When I looked in mirrors, I focused upwards, from the shoulders or neck. And ignored the rest. I lived in my head, preoccupied with the gibble-gabble. Always busy thinking. But I wasn't in contact with any other part of myself. My body was an entity quite separate from who I was. It was just something I was forced to inhabit. And to cart around with me wherever I went. It brought me no pleasure or joy. There was me, who lived in my body. That was the main connection. Shutting off helped me survive. Helped me avoid feeling my emotions.

We're given reason and emotions to help guide us through life. Both are important. Both have roles to play and work best when integrated. But I didn't know how to feel my emotions. They were too dangerous. If I started feeling emotions, I might explode. I couldn't cope. So I had to keep shutting off, pushing the feelings away. That's basically what depression is. Emotional shutdown. Emotions pushed deep into your body. So you miss the important signals from your heart and your guts. The signals telling you what you feel, what you want, what you need. You don't get that information.

How can you make good decisions or choices without all the right information? You can't, of course. I didn't consciously choose to see things this way. None of this splitting was on a conscious level. It probably started when I was around seven or eight. Maybe even before. I wrote a little play once, when I was seven. It was about "The Why" and featured my deceased maternal grandfather, who was asked a lot of questions by another character (probably me). I think that may have been the begin-ning of the gibble-gabble. That's where some of the unexpressed emotional energy went. Into my head. Fuelling the questions. Spinning the thoughts and ideas.

When you shut your emotions off for any length of time, you have to learn how to handle them when they start to surface. How to recognize and tolerate them. How to integrate them into your being. Scary stuff. Without learning it, recovery from an eating disorder is less likely to take root.

CHAPTER 6: EARLY IN THE NINTH

A Teensy Bit about the Clarke Institute of Psychiatry

I didn't know until this writing that the Clarke Institute opened its doors at 250 College Street West in June 1966,[33] less than a year before my rather peculiar arrival. As the University of Toronto's psychiatric teaching hospital, the $9-million Clarke (which lacked the usual barred windows and straitjackets)[34] was to focus mainly on research and training.

The Clarke was unique and "set apart" from the general hospital system. Designed and built by a committee who apparently had "peculiar ideas about what psychiatry was about," the Clarke "had a bit of everybody, and it never came off quite right for anybody."[35]

The hospital was named after Professor Charles Kirk Clarke,[36] the then-distinguished but later controversial public policy advocate for "mental hygiene" (likely where the term "mental health" comes from). Clarke had worked at various "lunatic asylums," as they were called in the bad old days of the early twentieth century,[37] which is the origin, I suppose, of the derogatory term "loony bin," one of Shirley's favourites. Clarke was also reputed to be a eugenicist,[38] (a subtle form of racism relating to genetic makeup) along with a host of other notable psychologists and scientists of that time.

In 1998 the Clarke and several other institutions serving people with various types of mental illness were merged into the renowned Centre for Addiction and Mental Health (CAMH).[39] While this merger was intended to improve the public's outlook on mental health (a worthy but still ongoing uphill struggle), I suspect the loss of the Clarke name and its unpleasant negative association was welcomed within the psychiatric and psychological communities.

The ninth floor of the Clarke was designed like an H with a hat on top. The elevators and nursing station faced each other across the middle bar, while various rooms lined the legs and hat. If you stepped off the elevator and turned right, you'd just see a bunch of doors leading to different rooms. But if you turned left, you'd see a spacious lounge area with large picture windows along the outside wall.

For an institution, the lounge looked relatively comfortable, with upholstered, royal blue sofas and chairs, assorted small wooden side tables, and a large wall unit with a built-in TV along the south wall. The top part of the lounge extended into the dining area, with tables and padded chairs available for meals, coffee breaks, card-playing, drawing, or the big favourite, simply sitting and staring into space. The cafeteria counter formed the inner wall of the dining area. At mealtimes, you'd line up with your tray and choose from that day's menu options.

The Original April Fool

During that first long, dark night at the Clarke, images of several Davids I'd met paraded through my mind as I called out. But the David I settled on was David X from the youth centre, who quickly became my obsessive focus, the glue that seemed to prevent me from shattering into a million pieces. My love object.

Obsessive people are by nature reductionists, or simplifiers, who cope by shrinking the world into an easily understandable formula. We simplify our universe into one major stream of thought, one catch- all, multipurpose filter. Every stimulus, idea, thought, or image to enter the mind's eye is processed through the lens of this single entity. In my case, it was David X. If I looked nice, it was for David X. If I needed to brush my teeth, David X would appreciate it if he knew. If I said something, I debated whether or not this would interest David X. And so on.

During my first eighteen hours at the Clarke, people must have gone to my little basement apartment near Lawrence Plaza to collect some of my things. Among them, all three of my knee-length housecoats or robes. For a long time, these were what I usually wore around the hospital. One bright pink cotton garment featured white polka-dots, capped sleeves, and white buttons down the front. The cream- coloured, rayon muumuu with short puffy sleeves had a wide neckline so you could pull it over your head, and large, hand-drawn pink and blue flowers that looked like children's art. If these don't sound too fetching, it's because loungewear for fat people was not in high demand back in the day. No fashionable plus sizes for women larger than a fourteen. No comfy track suits, either. Only cheesy-looking outfits or appalling dark-coloured gear suitable mainly for elderly widows.

My favourite robe buttoned down the front, had three-quarter sleeves, and was made from some type of shiny, satin-looking fabric. Woven into the black background were thin, vertical strips of multicoloured ribbon – pink, pale orange, yellow, aqua, green, and violet. A belt from the same fabric tied under the bust empire-style, leaving the back loose and full. I wore this ribbon robe a lot. And enjoyed the biblical reference to Jacob's coat of many colours.

How long I slept that first night at the Clarke, what time I awoke, and whether it was morning or afternoon I don't know. However, I do remember it was the first of April, April Fools' Day, which I found extremely amusing. "I'm the original April fool," I kept saying out loud to myself, since no one else was around.

Somehow, during the night, the staff must have undressed me and put me into a hospital gown. Definitely not something I appreciated. I scanned the familiar friendly robes brought from home and changed into the cream and flowered muumuu. No other memories of that day remain, but I could have slept through most of it.

The next day, I was delighted when the nurse woke me to say I had company. I opened my eyes to see my mother and my friend Karen in the room. I felt happy to see them. "Hey, Ma!" I shouted. "Look at me! I'm in the loony bin." I began bouncing on the bed, laughing at the irony. During her frequent fits of pique, Shirley would often say I was going to send her to the loony bin. But look, it was *me* who ended up here! I found this hilarious. Delightful. The more I bounced up and down on the bed chanting "I'm in the loony bin" in a childlike, singsong voice, the less happy Shirley looked. (Big payoff, indeed.)

When Shirley got upset, a combination of distress, frustration, worry, shame, anger, and perhaps even sadness flashed across her face. Picture anyone's expression when a horrible, foul-smelling stench suddenly permeates the atmosphere. That's how Shirley looked when she was upset. "Oh, Natalie," she said. Then I told her my name wasn't Natalie, but Noelle. Yes. Noelle. I explained that Natalie actually meant child of Christmas, but Shirley remained unimpressed. So I continued to bounce happily on the bed. My visitors were a drag. They couldn't see the humour in the situation. They'd heard I was the original April fool, but were not amused. Apparently, it was too much, and they soon left.

My father was absent that day. Perhaps the situation was considered too stressful for someone who'd recently had a heart attack. I have no idea how my mother got to Toronto.

Thirsty Girl

After my visitors left, I was told I could have a bath if I wanted. I wanted. The bathroom doors didn't lock, but nurse Bev was just outside, and I was to call her if I needed anything. Every so often she'd peek in to check that I was okay. Lying in the bath, looking up at the ceiling, I tried to count the little holes in each ceiling tile, which I found somewhat comforting.

Less comforting, however, was the thought that a hidden camera might be stashed somewhere, perhaps in one of the ceiling tile holes. But no matter how carefully I scrutinized the ceiling, showerhead and faucets, I found nothing. Everything looked okay, but then again, what did I know about photographic equipment? As it turns out, however, my concerns were not so farfetched. The Clarke apparently had peepholes in the patients' doors.[40]

My attention soon turned to playing with the neat bath bubbles and watching the soap float. Talk about regression. I was probably two or three years old emotionally, perhaps even younger. At one point, I felt thirsty. With no glass at hand, I improvised and sucked on the wet washcloth. I thought this was quite inventive and felt proud I could get a drink without bothering anyone. At that particular moment, Bev popped her head in the door and saw me, washcloth in mouth. She shook her head in disapproval and frowned. "Oh, Natalie. Don't do that." I felt embarrassed. It had seemed like such a good idea at the time.

Strange how I functioned at different emotional and psychological levels, and shifted in and out of different states of awareness and consciousness. Even though I was emotionally a toddler, I still had some concept of shame, of being wrong, and of feeling hurt, embarrassed, or disgraced when spoken to in a critical way.

I certainly disliked being told what to do or not do, and always had. My being at the Clarke didn't change that aspect of my personality, drugs or no drugs, neuroses hidden or in full display. Besides, it was usually counterproductive to give me instructions, since I'd end up doing the opposite. Even if I agreed with what I'd been told, my psychic reflex was to disobey.

When I emerged from my bath, clean and dressed again in my cream and flowered muumuu, it was time to get something to eat. I remember feeling excited to learn there were other people out there, outside my room. And I wanted to meet them. It would be fun, like a party. Clearly, while I knew I was in a mental hospital, it took a while before the full impact of being in such a place actually sunk in. Perhaps because of the drugs I was on, or because of some natural protective mechanism. But everything seemed new and fun, an adventure. Like a very young child's state of mind.

It was lunchtime, and I could hear the muted sounds of dishes clattering, people talking, and chairs being moved about. The nurse told me to get ready, that she would accompany me. During those early days, I was to go nowhere unattended, not even on the ward. So, I changed into my pink, polka-dot robe and eagerly ventured forth to meet the people. I have no idea who I actually met, or what I did for the rest of the day.

Chrysanthemum

Certain images and scenes from my days at the Clarke have stayed with me all these years, while others have long since disappeared. These bits of mental flotsam and jetsam pop into my awareness at odd times, like remnants from a sunken ship that suddenly float up to the water's surface. Strange curiosities.

One of my earliest memories from the ninth floor took place around the supper hour. I was getting ready to leave my room, performing some last-minute grooming rituals to make myself more presentable. My short dark hair, however, would simply not lie flat. Various clumps insisted on sticking out like little spikes, not fashionable in 1967. So I tried to slick them back with Noxema, a non-greasy, strongly mentholated cream, (which I used to wash my face, instead of soap). But instead of making my hair lie flat, the spikes stood out even more. In the mirror, all those stand-up spiked bits of hair made me look like a flower. Sort of like a chrysanthemum. To complete the picture, I smeared a thick coat of the mentholated Noxema on my face. Delighted with my creativity, I felt ready to dine with the people.

The cafeteria folks said nothing and just smiled. But people at every table I approached didn't want me to sit with them and turned away in disgust. I must have looked and smelled quite unappealing. At the time, I didn't realize what all the fuss was about. Didn't anyone have a sense of humour? A nurse escorted me back to my room to make myself less flower-like and more humanly presentable. Shirley often used to try to get me to look more presentable. But by that, she meant thinner.

Pandora Talks

Most of the thirty-four patients on the ninth floor[41] suffered from depression. Not me. While I'd unknowingly experienced depression at various times before my arrival, by the time I got to the Clarke, depression was the least likely word to describe my condition. You could say I had a nervous breakdown, but I've always thought of it more as a crack-up. A manic explosion outward, as if a hundred squelched cats finally escaped the proverbial bag. Or the lid blew off Pandora's Box. The result: an outpouring of pure, unprocessed verbal gibble-gabble. More like blither-blather, because the sounds and images remained.

Drugs or no drugs, I talked incessantly. As if I was on speed, which I wasn't. Just the natural high of expressing almost twenty years of pent-up energy and emotion. Non-stop talking. To myself or to whomever was around.

During the early days, there was always someone around. I pretty much had twenty-four-hour company. Various nurses took turns sitting in my room, listening, usually without interruption. Silent hostages. They probably weren't really listening, but lost in their own thoughts. I wouldn't have noticed and didn't care. As long as they were quiet and didn't disturb my flow. Questions, interruptions, changes of topic, they all generated enormous frustration. They interfered with the steady torrent of my words and thoughts. And often cut me off, just as I was about to reach some incredibly important conclusion or insight.

Jagged Little Pills

Other than my relentless chatter, many of those early days on the ward are somewhat blurry, thanks to the passage of time and all the drugs I'd been fed. Drugs seem to be automatically given to people in mental hospitals. The quick and easy answer. I suspect it's more to help hospital staff manage potentially unruly patients than to bring comfort or relief to those in their care. Don't get me wrong – I'm not assigning malicious or harmful intent to people who work within the health care system, far from it. But I suppose the humane alternatives to drugs take too much time, effort, and trained personnel, and are not cost- effective.

I'm going to elaborate a bit on the specific drugs given to me, because their side effects had an impact on important decisions made about my treatment.

Other patients on the ward said I was probably on Largactil, apparently one of the drugs given to new arrivals. They were right. The medical records show I was on 100 mg (a rather large dose) several times a day, along with 2 mg of Cogentin and some chloral hydrate, if needed.

Largactil[42] was one of the first antipsychotic drugs used in the 1950s and 1960s to treat schizophrenia and manic depression. It essentially blocks dopamine receptors in the brain. While dopamine is a feel-good neurotransmitter (chemical messenger in the brain), too much can overstimulate its receptors (landing pads) and create psychotic types of behaviour, like mania.[43] So, my felt sense of a crack-up or inner explosion was close to the mark. My little dopamine receptors were overstimulated.

How *about* that. Largactil is often referred to in Britain as "liquid cosh" for its knockout potential. Nowadays it's rarely used to subdue patients. Many side effects include weight gain, Parkinson's symptoms (for example, twitching or uncontrollable movements) or drowsiness.

Cogentin[44] was probably prescribed to counteract any Parkinson's symptoms created by the Largactil. But the side effects of Cogentin include blurred vision, impaired thinking or reactions, confusion, hallucinations, depressed mood, memory problems, and unusual thoughts or behaviour. Ill- advised if you do anything that requires alertness! Finally, chloral hydrate[45] was included as a sedative in case I couldn't sleep. It slows central nervous system activity and has side effects that can impair thinking and reactions.

These were the meds I was on when given the first set of evaluative tests. The dosages weren't reduced until I'd been at the Clarke two weeks, and then, only temporarily.

Food, Glorious Food

Sometime during my first week, Dr. B and I had a little chat. That is, she chatted, I listened. But I only remember one thing she said. She looked me straight in the eye and in a very clear, firm tone told me to "eat everything, including the fat of the meat." What a bizarre thing to say. And quite an assumption. I never ate the fat of the meat. Never wanted it, never thought about it, didn't care about it. Shirley would've been horrified at such a command.

In fact, I wasn't a big meat-eater to begin with. And weight-fanatic Shirley made sure, even in the 1950s, not to serve fatty meat to her family. Yuck. So why anyone wanted me to eat the fat seemed suspicious. What were they playing at? Did they want me to gain more weight?

While Dr. B's idea hints at some awareness of my struggle with food, no way was I going to take advice about food from another fat person. Surprised and repulsed by her instruction, uncharacteristically I said nothing in response. Now I see it as either an attempt at reverse psychology, or Dr. B was trying to alleviate the pressure of resisting a forbidden food. I decided never to eat the fat of the meat. Double yuck. And I never did.

Incidentally, Dr. B's approach is currently used in many eating disorder treatment centres, where clients are encouraged to eat everything, despite the fact that we now know some things we eat are addictive. Sugar, for example, has been proven addictive by many reputable scientific studies over the past few years,[46] and yet most eating disorder treatment centres require all patients to eat sugary treats. I understand that not everyone is addicted to sugar and that refusing to eat sugary products, along with many other foods considered fattening or "bad," is part of the unhelpful restrictive thinking of many who suffer from eating disorders. Here's an idea -- one size does not fit all. But I digress.

All the people who worked at the Clarke's ninth-floor cafeteria during my ten months as an inpatient deserve a medal for doing their jobs far above and beyond the call of duty. For me, every meal felt like an adventure, where I got to pick and choose the food I wanted. Not only that, I also got to choose the dishes it was served on. What fun! The cafeteria workers patiently went along with my time-consuming and erratic requests. For example, sometimes I'd insist that the peas be on a separate little plate so they didn't get mixed in with anything else. At other times, I'd want them in a dessert dish beside the yellow corn, since the colours looked pretty together. Or I might want all food items on their own separate little plates. I went through phases of favourite dish types, like the saucer phase or the cup phase, where everything had to be served in saucers or cups, maybe with one exception, which I'd decide on the spur of the moment. Now I can see the strong indications of obsessive-compulsive disorder (OCD), which was never mentioned on any hospital note. Ever.

The gracious, always accommodating cafeteria people usually greeted me with smiles on their faces, no matter how annoying I was. And as you can imagine, "annoying" would be the operative word. When I think of their generosity of spirit, I feel grateful to these people who obliged my whims and fancies without complaint or judgment.

At the Clarke, as mentioned earlier, I regressed emotionally to a very young age, and wafted in and out of various emotional states. The daily choices of food and dishes had a profound impact. I'd never been treated this way at Shirley's table, or at university, or even when I lived on my own in my little basement apartment. While I'd shopped and bought food, I rarely cooked. A steady stream of three personally selected meals a day, day after day, was revolutionary, compared to my norms of strict diets or wild binges.

Gilda's First Take

By April 21, 1967, Gilda had met with me individually six times and with my parents twice. In her report of that date, she stated that the symptoms of my apparent schizophrenic break had cleared up after a night's rest. To Gilda, my problems stemmed from my obesity and my birth into a middle-class upwardly mobile Jewish family with high expectations. Gilda noted:

She appears of average intelligence, but seems to have to strive for an intellectual position above her level ... Her current difficulty with abstract thoughts, her tendency to ramble and her difficulty focussing might be a product of her illness, rather than an indication of her potential. It never occurred to anyone at that time that my intellectual difficulties might be due to the various drug combinations I'd been given.

However ... she is functioning on an average or slightly below average level. Much of her energy seems to be used ... in defending herself and playing games with her parents. At times she deliberately disappoints them and at times she deliberately does things to please them. She seems to fear honest confrontation with her parents...

At this point, Gilda was unaware that you couldn't really confront Shirley and come away unscathed.

Natalie expresses generalized resentment to both parents, sometimes taking one side, sometimes another. She is, however, very concerned about her actions and their effects on her father. She has been told by her mother that her name was a "forbidden word around the house" and that Mr. Gold's heart attack and Natalie's irresponsible behaviour and obesity were associated with her father's illness.

That's one way of putting it. Shirley actually blamed me for my father's heart attack. She may have had a point, though not in the way she thought. My absence from the family home could have been a factor. Since I absorbed so much of the household's negative energy, my being away at university and then in Toronto probably created a negative vacuum. First, my mother lost her anger outlet, her dumpee, so to speak (me), and some of this energy may have spilled over onto my father. Second, my father didn't have me there to control and manipulate, or to carry the emotional load.

... She defends herself with observations about their marriage ... stating that she herself would have been a better wife to her father than her mother was. However, at times she supports her mother against her father's domination.

Part of my fantasy about my father, encouraged by him, was that I differed from Shirley because I could listen to him. I could understand him. And I obeyed him. For many years I believed I would make him a better wife than Shirley. While sexuality did not overtly come into the picture, it was an undercurrent, nevertheless. One of the many I undoubtedly ate over. At the same time, I had some inkling of my father's true domineering nature. I didn't learn about "emotional incest" for decades. When I did, I struggled with the term. I still do. Even now, as I write, I am reluctant to admit the true nature of our relationship. Unlike physical and sexual incest, the shadow cast by emotional incest is subtle and corrosive, like rust.

She presents as an immature, unrealistic young lady with some insight, a tendency to avoid problems by skirting around them and is developing a dependency around the hospital, hiding behind its regulations.

Yes. I skirted issues, having learned from some top-notch skirters. And yes, I did become dependent on the hospital. But I couldn't completely acknowledge that to myself. I feared leaving, but since fear had never been an option, I couldn't accept it.

The patient is cooperative in interviews and seems to be seeking help, at least superficially. On the other hand ... Natalie has no realistic plans for release. She toys with the idea of returning to school, rejecting schools where she might be eligible. She would like to become either an actress or a social worker. She does not seem to want to commit herself to a five year course at university.

True. I didn't want to commit myself to university. Because I knew I lacked the necessary self- discipline, as would anyone with the gibble-gabble and a compulsion to eat running their life. But Gilda et al wanted to help me and came up with a five-point treatment plan:

> *(1) Setting the discharge date for two weeks and limits on her freedom in the hospital. This will probably motivate her to move towards discharge.*

> *(2) Encourage the patient to make appointments for interviews with prospective employers.*

> *(3) Permit ventilation and offer the patient observations about the game she plays with herself, her parents, etc.*

> *(4) Make clear to Natalie when her plans are unrealistic, while acknowledging her right to try them.*

> *(5) Psychological testing to help the patient decide about a job.*

They didn't really understand my state of mind, my emotional state, or the games I played with myself. They didn't understand addiction, especially a food addiction, and what a chronic eating disorder does to self-esteem and the ability to function. And they didn't yet see the whole picture. Neither did I, despite how hard I tried.

Decades would pass before mental health communities would even begin to understand the impact of binge eating, a situation that's ongoing as I write, almost fifty years later.

CHAPTER 7: O-BLAH-DEE-O-BLAH-DAH

Location, Location, Location

Until I wrote about them, I couldn't figure out why memories of certain places stayed with me. As the song says, "Some forever, not for better, some have gone, and some remain."[47]

Who Wants to Be a Millionaire?

I didn't want to move from Midland to Niagara Falls, away from fun girlfriends and the boys I'd kissed. But we did, right after I finished fourth grade in 1955. I was nine and a half. My dad had gone ahead six months earlier to set up the store and find a place to live.

The move came about thanks to a business deal gone sour – something I learned about only years later. A few doors down from our Midland home, in the house on the corner, lived a family of Polish immigrants. Sam, his wife, and two young sons occasionally invited our family for dinner. I liked Sam's wife, who often wore see-through nylon blouses with fancy coloured slips underneath. But I disliked Sam, a lot. Something about him bothered me. He was too nice, gushy, and tried too hard to please. He gave me the creeps, an opinion I kept to myself.

Sam and my dad became partners in a fur-dyeing venture, with a unique process my dad invented. But Sam double-crossed him. My father had expected the process to make him a millionaire, but instead it led to betrayal and financial ruin. He never trusted anyone again, not that he was the trusting sort to begin with. The bankruptcy was one of his greatest disappointments. But as the song "That's Life" goes, he just picked himself up and got back in the race.[48] Started all over again, in his mid-forties, with a wife and two kids.

He never said why he picked Niagara Falls. Neither of my parents explained the move from Midland, or anything they did, for that matter. So I filled in my own blanks. I blamed myself. After all, I knew Sam was creepy but hadn't warned my father.

My mother was glad for the move. Niagara Falls was bigger than Midland, with a synagogue and an actual Jewish community. And besides being one of the Seven Wonders of the World, it was right next door to the United States, which made it seem glamorous. It wasn't.

We lived at three locations in Niagara Falls. Geographical links that help bring the past more clearly into focus.

Safety First

The Strathmore Crescent house ushered in a lot of firsts during the year we spent there. We got a piano, a mixed blessing. Lessons were great, but I didn't want to practice, giving Shirley another reason to yell at me. We got our very first TV, black and white of course. One Saturday night the babysitter let me stay up late to watch a concert of Gershwin's extraordinary "Rhapsody in Blue."[49] My first introduction to a jazz and blues sound.

I also became aware of my slightly changing body. I wanted to go on a diet, like a few of the older girls on our street. But Shirley said no, don't be silly, I didn't need to diet. And that was that. I doubt if I even knew what a diet was, exactly. I just wanted to look tall and pretty, like the other girls. To compensate for the ugly, corrective eyeglasses I had to wear.

One mid-winter evening, after an event at the synagogue, someone's dad was kind enough to drive me and several others home. Deep snow everywhere, roads icy and slippery. Our driver chatted endlessly to someone in the back seat (I was in the front), waving his arms, paying little attention to the road, especially as it curved left at the bottom of the hill. Suddenly, he lost control as the car slammed into a snowbank. As we all lurched forward, an arm swiftly moved across my body so I wouldn't fall head-on into the dashboard. (Seat belts weren't mandatory back then.)

For some reason this memory has remained. Perhaps because this man saved my life. Or perhaps because my developing breasts were the body parts that interacted with his arm. I know I felt very strange afterwards.

Now I look back with a different understanding. This man protected me from harm, and no one had done that since I was an infant. Being protected wasn't part of my perceived entitlement. Certainly no one protected me from my mother's wrath. After this minor accident, I became more attuned to imminent danger, albeit not on a conscious level. Not just in cars, but in general. Things could happen beyond your control, things that had nothing to do with you. Or maybe they did. It was hard to know.

Figuring out the world, especially the part I lived in, took on a greater importance, thus elevating the urgency of the gibble-gabble. Deciphering all the clues and understanding how things worked, how people worked, would give me a chance, maybe just a little chance, to have some effect. Or at least a chance to protect myself from harm.

Mea Culpa

Just before I started sixth grade in 1956, we moved to the three-bedroom apartment on Dorchester Road. Finally, a room of my own. Blissful privacy. My period arrived a year later, just in time to celebrate my first day in seventh grade at Princess Margaret Junior High.

That morning, before putting on my favourite pale pink cotton floral dress, I noticed some bleeding. Kind of weird. Quietly, I tiptoed into my parents' bedroom and gently tried to wake my mother. "Mom," I whispered a few times before she opened her eyes. When I told her about the blood, she mumbled, "You know what that is, don't you?" Yes, I did, although no one ever told me about menstruation. (Like many other girls, I'd managed to piece together some vague information from various sources.)

Shirley whispered directions, then quickly returned to sleep. Sure enough, I found the Kotex box, read the instructions, but couldn't find the stupid-looking belt to hold the pad in place. Back to the bedroom, more whispers, then Shirley's final comment, "Don't let your father know, don't let him see anything."

Apparently he wasn't aware of menstruation, and we were to keep it that way. This is how I officially became a woman, although I didn't feel like one.

I'd started wearing a bra the year before at Shirley's insistence, and wondered if people could tell what was underneath my twin set as I self-consciously rode my bike along Dorchester Road. Together with my full, black felt skirt, it was one of the few outfits I liked, even though I didn't choose it myself.

My father actually chose most of my clothes during his regular forays to the Toronto wholesalers on Spadina Avenue. One day, he brought home a three-piece brown tweed suit, with a tight skirt, matching vest, and a hideous, mustard-coloured, V-neck pullover sweater. Wow. I was old enough for a tight skirt. When I modelled it for Bob and Shirley, to their delight, and my dread, it fit perfectly. Creepy how my father was familiar enough with my body to guess my correct size. It took away some of the pleasure of the tight skirt.

Puberty was one thing. Violence another. I was wearing my favourite pale pink cotton floral dress when I got beaten up for being Jewish. Right in front of the synagogue, around suppertime, as parents dropped kids off or picked them up from Hebrew school. From the front verandah of the house next door, a group of tough girls had watched as I made my way to the synagogue's side entrance. My hunched-over posture and self-conscious manner clearly signalled *victim*. They began to call me names. "Hey, kike! ... Look at the dirty Jew! ... Hey, Christ-killer!" The usual crap. I walked faster and tried to ignore them. But I was scared.

Fighting back? Not an option. Not that I was a total pushover. But my spunk, nerve, and scrappiness only surfaced to rebel against authority. Not in response to bullying. Not against abuse from outside my family.

When Hebrew class was over, the name-callers still occupied the verandah. Quickly I shuffled towards the front of the building, headed for the bus stop across the street. But I wasn't fast enough, and the girls smelled fear. Four of them approached. I steeled myself for trouble, but didn't believe they'd do anything in front of all the adults chatting on the synagogue steps as they waited to chauffeur their children home. It all went so fast. More name-calling, right to my face. Little finger-jabs, pokes, and shoves escalated quickly into hits and punches. I tried in vain to get away, but I was outnumbered. Even under attack it didn't occur to me to fight back. The girls pulled my hair, scratched, shouted, spit. Suddenly, I was down on the ground. But no adults made a move to help. The question flashed across my mind: why didn't they do something? Say something?

Then, out of the blue, a sudden screeching sound announced the arrival of Mrs. Lilly Greenspan[50] as she crashed her car into the curb, jumped out, waved her arms, and shouted at the bullies to stop. She then bravely stepped into the fracas, physically inserting her body as a shield between me and my attackers. She pulled me away. The bullies let go and abruptly took off, laughing and joking a little less, as Lilly threatened to call the police if she ever saw them around there again.

After checking me over to make sure I was at least in one piece, my rescuer, dear Mrs. Lilly Greenspan, drove me home. This was the second time someone from outside my family had protected me.

When I arrived home at the Dorchester apartment, my parents had already been alerted by phone.

Shirley was serving dinner to my father as I walked in. She asked if I was okay, and I told her yes. She said "Bastards!" And that was the end of it. No hugs, no kisses, no holding, no talking. Nothing. My parents had no idea what to say. I understand now that this incident was possibly terrifying to anyone, especially any Jewish person, who had lived through the war.

Well, there was a *little* talking. During supper, my father asked me if I did anything to provoke the attack. I said I didn't think so, but I never knew for certain.

The problem: it was tricky to know exactly what you did to make people mad at you. Sometimes it was obvious and other times less so. That's how it had been for me my whole life. But it was important to find out, so I could learn. Shirley and Bob both told me, "You never learn." So I tried desperately to make it otherwise. I wanted to learn. I wanted to avoid causing trouble. I wanted to bring my parents *nachas* (pride and joy, pronounced like the "ach" as in "Bach" and the "as" as in "us") and not *tsuris* (trouble and sorrow, pronounced soo-ris). So I spent even more time trying to figure it all out.

Me and National Geographic

Halfway through seventh grade, just before Christmas 1957, we moved to Barker Street, the house where my life took a noticeable turn for the worse and where the bad times sorely outnumbered the good. Once again, my sister and I had to share a bedroom. She was almost eight, and I'd just turned twelve.

In that house, the milkman began to deliver the fateful chocolate cake, and the weight war was declared. One night during dinner at the oval kitchen table, Shirley proclaimed I was too fat, needed to diet, and that it was time for me to lose weight.

Shirley devised no formal diet plan for me, except doing without dessert. She also bought various diet items marketed in the late 1950s. Metrical,[51] a rather foul-tasting drink in a can, which also came in a powder version to mix with milk or water, or cookies, which tasted like dog biscuits. The Ayds candies[52] were for her. Little cellophane-wrapped butterscotch or chocolate caramels. Supposedly, one or two before meals would decrease your appetite. I'd sneak handfuls at a time, which only increased my desire to eat more. Of everything.

At twelve I was somewhat round and pudgy, with fully developed breasts, to my supreme discomfort and shame. Peter, a classmate, laughingly pointed at a photo in *National Geographic* magazine, saying I looked like the half-naked African woman with very large, droopy breasts. Did I? Did I look like that? I didn't think so, but how could I be sure? If Peter thought I did, then maybe I did. How very upsetting.

What others thought and believed about me took precedence over what I thought and what I sensed or knew about me. Being so shut off from my feelings, I had little information to work with. Just what I figured out in my head, which was becoming an increasingly busy, crowded place. The gibble-gabble shifted from constant companion to commander-in-chief, and now began to run my life.

Bob and Shirley, at the Barker Street house, late 1950s.

Bob and Shirley, in their typical spots in the den,
with their granddaughter, probably mid-1980s.

May I Help You Out?

Some years after both my parents died, my father's only sister,
Hannah, told me my father had wanted to leave my mother. Apparently, this was during the tumultuous early years in Niagara
Falls. He had asked Hannah, a concentration camp survivor, for
advice. She would never suggest anyone abandon their family, let
alone her brother, another Holocaust survivor. Besides, in those
days, divorce and marital separation were much less common
than today. "Till death do us part" meant just that.[53]

If my father had asked me, I'd have told him to leave immediately. And to take me with him. One of my major fantasies: my
father and I would live together after he left my mother. Or after
she died. Two guilt-making scenarios, but the only way out I
could see. Besides, what was a little more guilt to the ever- growing stockpile?

Auntie Hannah's advice probably wasn't what kept Robert from leaving. Unlike me, he couldn't have handled any more guilt. Nor could he have broken his deathbed promise to my grandfather to always look after my mom. No minor matter, to be sure. According to Hannah, my mother threatened to tell Robert's secrets if he left. (More about my father's secrets later.) Ridiculous. Shirley might say something like that in a fit of temper. But she'd never follow through. Who would she tell? And what would she say? More important, what would people think? Also, my mother was too dependent on my father. She couldn't drive. She hadn't worked in decades and had no marketable skills. She was unwise in the ways of the world. But she was smart enough not to risk her security. The idea was preposterous. I doubt my father believed it, but Hannah did.

My dear aunt, whose story is memorialized in the Shoah Foundation's tape library,[54] was and is a very strong-willed woman. A survivor, in every sense of the word, despite diabetes and numerous other illnesses and ailments. During our regular phone conversations, she still reveals bits and pieces from the distant past. Like many people in their mid-eighties, her long-term memory is sharp, and I listen with a pen and paper nearby. But Hannah will *not* divulge certain parts of my father's story. Absolutely refuses. Because she, too, can keep secrets. Because my father made her promise to keep his, on his deathbed. Too many people in my family seem to control things from their graves. Very annoying.

Hannah and her husband did not come to visit our family in the Falls very often. She told me it was because my uncle couldn't bear to watch how my mother treated me. Thank you, Uncle. I'd like to think your being there would have helped. But that's unlikely. Any attempt to interfere would have added fuel to Shirley's fire. The fact: she was out of control a lot of the time. And while I hate to admit it, my father's diagnosis was correct. She couldn't help it. Much of the time she probably didn't real-

95

ize the full horror of what she was saying. Or the deep wounds she was carving into my psyche.

During the early years of Shirley's abuse, my father had tried to intervene on my behalf. "Shirley," he'd say, interrupting her diatribe in his calmest voice. But she'd immediately yell back, "Don't you Shirley me! Don't tell me you're going to take her side! That's the thanks I get! I'm trying to knock some sense into her, and you're telling me 'Shirley'? Go on! Take her side! Let her grow up to be a fat ugly lump! How do you like having a fat ugly lump of a daughter!"

My mother would then work herself up into an emotional fervour. She'd bellow at my father, my sister, and me. Whoever was around. All my father's attempts to help clearly backfired. In fact, his feeble efforts made things worse. I actually got down on my knees and begged him *not* to help. Pleaded with him to say nothing. "Please don't help me. Please don't!" High drama. And absurd, if it wasn't so sad. Lesson learned: people can't help. Corollary: don't even bother to ask.

And so my father and I conspired. He'd stay out of it when Shirley fell into one of her rages. I'd know his good intentions, but he had my permission not to try to help. Doing so would make my mother, despite her good intentions, angrier. Our convoluted little agreement made sense at the time, still does.

And the best part of it was that I was my father's confidante.

While I didn't want my father's help, I desperately wanted him to stand up to Shirley for his *own* sake. I wanted him to threaten to leave. I never told him that, of course. But I believed if he could convince my mother he was serious about leaving, she might settle down. A ridiculous notion, perhaps. She was out of control, so nothing would have worked.

Several years later, however, after I'd escaped to Toronto, Robert did threaten to leave. Sort of. And it did work. Sort of. He had a heart attack. That scared Shirley, all right. But I'm getting ahead of myself here.

My father used to tell his customers a joke if he spotted them looking through the clothing racks. He'd say, "May I help you out?" And just before they responded, he'd add, "Which way did you come in?" And they'd laugh together heartily. And usually, the bonding and chit-chat would continue. Little of that friendly bonding and casual chit-chat reached our house. Especially during my teen years, when Shirley was in her forties and heading into menopause. I remember most exchanges as overwhelmingly intense and fraught with negative overtones.

Now you may wonder how three people with such good intentions (I include myself here) could make such a mess of things. There is no answer, but there is a lesson: some questions have no answers. I didn't know this back then. So I felt compelled to keep searching, questioning. Relentlessly trying to figure it all out. Without success. Fuel for the gibble-gabble.

Ms. Personality

My father's inability to defend me and his ineffectiveness against his wife were too awful to contemplate. I couldn't accept the idea of my idol off his pedestal. So I ignored my disgust with him. I swallowed it, in fact. I swallowed my disgust, my hopelessness, my grief, and my shame. And of course, my guilt. And I ate.

My life got too confusing, so I began to buy into my mother's fantasy. If only I could lose weight, then I could go anywhere, do anything. Thinness became *the* goal, the route to a full, successful, satisfying life. I began to simplify, to think of myself as having only one problem – I was fat. And if I could just solve that problem, then my life would be perfect. My mother would love me and not nag me anymore. My father would be proud of me. People would want to be around me. Because I already had a pretty face. I had talent and smarts, according to Shirley. Plus the real biggie, I had personality! Just like the name of that 1959 hit song. [55]

Ever since I spent a month at a rich kids' summer camp, I knew that popularity demanded more than looks. The whole camp adored Gretchen, even though she wasn't a pretty girl. As Shirley might say, she was a "plain Jane." Gretchen, however, was not fat. She had a winning personality. She was fun and had a great sense of humour, and she played the ukulele. So personality counted at least as much as looks. This was a Big Deal for me. A very Big Deal.

Gretchen's existence fed right into my idealistic theories about the true importance of appearance. The plan: develop one incredibly terrific, capital-P Personality. So when I finally did lose weight, with my face, slender figure, and capital-P Personality, I'd have no problems. Ever. Quite a scheme. First, I got myself a ukulele. Okay, it was the late 1950s and guitars weren't "in" yet. Neither were ukuleles, but nobody told me. I practiced a lot, learned several songs, and was all set in case anyone wanted to sing around a campfire.

I also honed my humour skills on my sister and even on my mother, who in her good moments could laugh with the best of them. I discovered if Shirley wasn't too deeply into her anger, I could jolly her out of it, before it escalated into an unstoppable force. Here's where Shirley's short attention span paid off. If she started to laugh, she'd forget why she was angry. By the time she remembered, the harshness and cruelty would be gone from her voice. For example, she might begin, disgustedly, "Ugh, Natalie, how many times do I have to tell you –" I'd interrupt and answer in a silly, high-pitched voice, "Duh, let me see now – seven?" Or I'd do a cheerleader version of what she'd said. "How many times, rah! How many times, yay! Does anybody know, rah! How many times, yayyy!!" Or maybe say in a sing-song tone, "Over and over again until I get it, that's what mothers are for!" Okay, not too funny now. You might even find some sympathy for Shirley and the bratty behaviour she had to put up with. But the divert- and- distract tactics worked, which was all that mattered.

My terrific new capital-P Personality not only involved music and humour. It included being sincere (never phony), kind (never mean), generous (never stingy), caring (never selfish), thoughtful (giving only praise and compliments, as long as they were sincere), considerate of others (always putting them first, ahead of myself), being a good listener (letting people talk first), never burdening others with my problems, and always being there for a friend. If you needed me, I'd be there. No matter what. In other words, I taught myself how to become a doormat. Or, in more modern addiction-related lingo, codependent.

The Within

Two other qualities took precedence in my self-reinvention and boosted my pseudo-ego. Being deep and being entertaining. Most people I knew were overly concerned with looks, clothes, money, status, cars, and things money could buy. Shallow, very shallow. I would be the opposite. Deep. And therefore wisely detached from material things. What a person was on the inside, *that* was important. Not how they looked or what they wore.

Various philosophical ideologies bolstered this belief. As did my father's disapproving description of my mother as vain. "Your mother is very vain," he'd say, after her sermons about my appearance. In his eyes, being too concerned about how you looked was not a good thing. And I did want to be good for my dad. I'd read somewhere (probably in one of Shirley's *Reader's Digest* magazines) that the most important change comes from within. Since I incurred only failure trying to lose weight and change my physical appearance, I felt encouraged to work on my "within."

I set about trying to become a Better Person. This is how I distinguished myself from others my age. Whenever the conversation turned to clothes, makeup, hair – the usual topics for teenage girls – I'd immediately categorize the speaker as shallow. And possibly unworthy of my friendship. That's one way I protected myself from the pain of social exclusion. No cute clothes were available for someone my size. And makeup or hair products couldn't compensate for the main repellent feature, my fatness. Who'd notice anything else, once people realized I was fatandugly? So I told myself I was deep, on the inside, where it really counted.

The other element of my self-created persona came about more naturally. I was a born entertainer, apparently, who loved being centre stage. This meant I was not boring, unlike so many others. Were you feeling a bit down? Did you need a little cheering up? You wouldn't have to say anything. I'd sense it, and immediately become funny, or animated, or dramatic. To distract you from your troubles.

Complementing the perception of myself as deep and unique was my growing disdain for money, rumoured to be the root of all evil. The actual biblical quote says that the *love* of money is the root of all evil. But the inaccurate version supported my developing pseudo-belief system. In a major push to be good and not evil, I decided not to want money. No thanks. Everyone else wanted money, including Shirley and Bob. But not me.

My thinking along these lines fit with the 1960s rebellion by young people against their parents' middle-class suburban values. But in the late 1950s, I was simply going against the trend, the usual way I made my stands. If everyone else wanted something, automatically I didn't. If everyone else believed something, I took the opposite stance.

How long has it taken to unravel what I created in my early teen years? Decades, and I may not be finished even yet.

My main motive for trying so hard to become a better person with a great personality was to make people like me. Everything else was secondary, except for losing weight. Because once I was thin, nothing else would matter.

Great Expectations

When you build your whole life on a lie, you're headed for big trouble somewhere along the line. My own foundation was a rat's nest of lies and half-truths, based on what I wanted and needed to believe.

I can picture myself now, snuggled up all comfy-cozy in the study, tucked inside the big old, rust- brown canvas chair in the corner of the back room. We called it the study. The room was square, with no desk, no writing table – actually, no writing surface at all – and no books. But it was the study because I was expected to do my homework there. A lamp stood sentry beside the chair. Opposite, an old upright piano camouflaged the wall, before its banishment to the basement. A portable record player balanced on top of a rickety, plastic TV table. My study equipment.

Rarely did I do homework, except to cram the night before exams. Parked in the chair, schoolbooks scattered on the floor, I'd dream. Or try to figure out the world, what it was like. More importantly, what it *should* be like. I'd reflect on how the world would be a much better place if only, for example, people weren't so shallow, so inconsiderate, and so focused on material things. Everyone fell under my critical scrutiny. Family, friends, teachers, neighbours, kids at school. Religious leaders, people who attended synagogue, politicians. Characters in movies or on TV. And ordinary members of society. I developed enormously high expectations of us all, which were rarely met. So I lived in a constant state of disappointment.

I can see how I copied Shirley and Bob in this critical evaluation, because no one could live up to their expectations, either. Especially me, but not only me. The world and its people also fell far short of what my parents wanted and needed. But they couldn't control the world and its people. They could, however, control me. Or try to. And therein lay the battle.

Not only was I their embarrassingly fat daughter, I didn't "apply myself" enough at school. This was one thing they agreed on. Shirley usually did the talking. Bob did the sideways head shakes and the tsk-tsking, often accompanied by the disapproving glare. Teamwork.

Shirley believed she was encouraging and motivating me. But this insatiable lust for perfection had the opposite effect. Good enough didn't cut it. So by the time I reached high school, I stopped trying. Why bother? The notion that education mattered was one I rejected. Because everyone believed it. And because school was such an intolerable bore. High school seemed like a colossal waste of time. Worse, it felt like being in prison. I hated being treated like a four-year-old. Hated having to sit in class and listen to teachers drone on.

Funny how fat people, people who are larger than others, can be both highly visible and invisible at the same time. Invisible in the sense of being overlooked. Unheard, even if they have great personalities. Even if they wave their hands in class when they know the answers. But teachers don't want to hear only from the hand wavers. They didn't want to hear from me all the time. So I stopped putting my hand up. Why bother? So much for education.

To compensate for the non-stimulating atmosphere, and to cope with what was going on at home, I often got into trouble. Mainly from talking, but also from acting out or daydreaming in class, a pattern well-established since first grade. I remember one particular incident from tenth-grade geometry, taught by "Mither Marthy," a name students gave him because of his slight but noticeable lisp. Irritated at my daydreaming demeanour, he demanded that the geometry proposition of the moment be written out ten times and handed in first thing next day. Of course, I reacted to this unfair penalty in an overly dramatic way. So he doubled it, I reacted again, and the same punishment continued until I had racked up an impossibly high number of propositions to do, under threat of a failing mark. He specified these were all to be handwritten in full, with diagrams.

At first I felt overwhelmed. But then I realized he hadn't actually said they had to be written by me. Many classmates sympathized with this injustice, and offered to help. We began writing out propositions right there in class and continued till the final bell rang.

By the end of the day, word had spread around the school. "Mither Marthy's Proposition Party" was on at my place, starting around four-thirty. Even the teachers seemed to know about it. I'd phoned Shirley to see if it was okay to invite some classmates over to do "homework" together and to see if we had enough snacks on hand. Of course we did. I knew she'd be pleased that her daughter was bringing people home. I'd invite people over as often as I could, because they could act as a sort of buffer between Shirley and me. And my mother was always good about it, hungry as she was for social interaction.

Many kids from my high school dropped by that evening and each wrote out a handful of propositions. Even some of the very cool kids. I was thrilled. But Robert wasn't. He insisted I apologize to the teacher the next day and say I was willing to write them all myself. My father's party-pooping move took some of the joy out of the event. I dutifully told Mither Marthy I'd do them all myself, but I did not apologize. He could barely contain the smile on his face when he said he'd let it go. This time.

I suppose I did learn some things in high school. I learned to speak French rather well. Or at least to pronounce it, thanks to Mme De Montpier and her phonetics approach. She'd get the class to stand up. Then she'd strut around the room feeling our diaphragms to make sure we breathed correctly as we repeated *"pûpitre"* (desk) to her satisfaction. Madame would say *"très bon"* (very good) when we succeeded. We were all *très bons.* Ninth-grade French class was probably the only place in the universe where I was considered très bonne![56]

Basement Magic

After Shirley relocated the piano in the basement rec room, she inadvertently created my second escape route. My single year of music lessons meant I could read music, albeit slowly. So I bought a songbook and spent countless hours practicing songs like "Sentimental Journey," "Cry Me a River," and "Dear Hearts and Gentle People."[57] I often lost track of time. Soon I learned that most songs had certain chord structures, and I figured out how to play simple pop tunes on the piano, like "26 Miles."[58] But most importantly, I'd sing, without inhibition or self-judgment. I didn't really like how my voice sounded, but I loved how good I felt during the song and afterwards. Always.

Feeling good singing was a surprise, especially since no audience was with me in the basement, not even an imaginary one. Music let me get lost in it. A respite from being me, requiring no one else. No analysis, no figuring out anything but chords. No one to impress, or worry about impressing. No sad folks to cheer up. Don't get me wrong – I hadn't given up on entertaining. But it was simply not a factor when I sang in the Barker Street basement.

I was six or seven years old when I first learned how amazing it was to be in front of a live audience. We lived in Midland at the time, and my family vacationed at some kind of summer camp for a week or so. One evening was set aside for a talent show, on a little stage, in front of what seemed to be a fairly large crowd – perhaps eighty to a hundred people.

Despite feeling nervous, I experienced a strange sense of comfort and safety up on the stage in front of people. Dressed as a gypsy, with tambourine in hand, I sang a cutesy little 1914 tune called "Aba Daba Honeymoon" about a monkey, a chimp, and the big baboon who married them.[59] At the end of every line, I banged on that tambourine. And people laughed! Wow. What a thrill. People were laughing and happy. So I banged on the tambourine again and again. More laughter. And applause when I finished. The noise was kind of scary, but from then on, I was hooked on audiences. And applause. But mostly on the feeling of being okay and at home on the stage.

But the magic of doing music in the Barker Street basement was that the music itself was enough. I didn't need a stage, an audience, or applause.

Dotter

Absorption. That's what happens to children in malfunctioning families. The kids absorb the tensions and conflicts and take the energies into their little bodies, into their little emotional, psychological, and spiritual systems. It's automatic. Unaware, they have no way of defending themselves from the negativity. They soak it in, like thirsty sponges. This isn't my own made-up theory. Many professionals providing emotional therapy subscribe to it. But John Bradshaw's name[60] comes to mind, especially his books and PBS specials on shame and on the damage caused by family secrets.

Absorption is my word, not Bradshaw's, and describes what happened to me. I soaked up the angst and negative energies of my parents into all my systems, and carried them around with me wherever I went. I didn't know how to protect myself from them.

Eventually, the energies became fused or enmeshed with my own, so I couldn't tell the difference. Guilt, grief, and rage from my father, unresolved anguish from my mother. I carried some of it. And it became mine and part of me. That's the tricky aspect of repression. The energy doesn't disappear, it just goes underground. In fact, as it simmers on the unconscious level, it takes on more power. I believe some of my mother's hysteria and rage were also ways to express what my father could not.

Many times my dad bragged how he could control his temper, unlike my mother and me. Because my father's temper was a dangerous thing. If he ever let himself go and got really angry, he didn't know what he'd do. Once he got started, he might not be able to stop. He implied that he'd killed someone because of his anger. I assumed during the war. This wasn't stated specifically, for my father was never that unambiguous. But the intended warning was clear. Do not make your father angry, you don't know what might happen. That's how a great dollop of fear was added to my already turbulent emotional mix.

Somehow I got the idea that I was my father's favourite. Possibly from my dad's stories about when I was an infant, which he occasionally told with pride and fond remembrance. He and Shirley would wheel me in the huge pram though the park in London, England. If my mother took the pram handle, I'd scream until my father took over. That was his version, which Shirley never contradicted. I can now imagine Shirley interpreting such behaviour as proof that even at an early age, I hated her.

Another story my father liked to tell was this one: whenever he sang me to sleep in my crib, "Ave Maria" was the only song that got me to stop crying and go to sleep, which I never wanted to do. Shirley's theory was that I didn't want to miss anything. But perhaps my dad's singing helped foster the belief that I was special to someone, or at least somebody's favourite. That need became pretty important.

If I wasn't someone's favourite, then I'd be nothing. Just like the song says, "You're nobody till somebody loves you."[61] So, I'd sign birthday cards to my dad or letters from camp "Your favourite eldest dotter." I only included the word "eldest" so as not to offend my sister, in case she saw it.

Robert probably knew that. After all, he could often tell what I was thinking, or so he said. And I believed him. I believed my father could read my mind. Not all the time, but a lot of the time. So I had to be careful not to think certain things when he was around or when he paid attention to me. Then, to be on the safe side, I had to make my mind blank.

The energies in our home were so strong I had to expand to contain them all. Another reason I ate. Fat wasn't just a tension and shock absorber, but a protective shield, as well. Maybe in some ways, eating – or rather, overeating – saved my life.

Over the years, I've often felt grateful that my compulsivity expressed itself with food and not with other more deadly substances or addictive behaviours. Like drugs or gambling or serial killing.

Note to people who think compulsion can be cured: it cannot. You get remission. You learn how to cope with repressed material so it doesn't fester inside your system. And how to bring unconscious material to the surface. How to feel, how to identify feelings. You learn healthy ways to respond to the stresses and strains in your life. How to make healthy choices. To stay balanced, emotionally and psychologically. But the compulsive tendency never totally goes away. It's always there, lurking in the background. Waiting for the right moment, when you're not paying attention. When you get the urge to act in that old familiar way. In my case, to eat. To binge. To stuff so much crap into my body that I fall asleep from sheer digestive exhaustion. Or from a sugar high-low reaction.[62]

As a teenager I knew none of this. I kept thinking there had to be a reason I ate. One single reason, one answer to my problem. To set me free and unlock the mystery.

My belief that I was my father's favourite was shattered one evening after I overheard a conversation he had with my mother.

Where's Oprah?

As I mentioned earlier, Dr. B's intake report stated, "Previous depressive illness with suicide attempt two years ago." The timing was off by several years, due to my muddled cognitive condition when I first arrived at the Clarke. But it was no mere attempt.

In autumn 1962, after an extended summer holiday on my own in England, I began grade twelve two weeks late. I'd hoped to turn over a new leaf, and not act out in class as I'd done for years. But all the teachers had saved seats for me at the front, where it was surprisingly easy to tune out. Teachers usually focused on kids at the back of the room.

The twelfth grade is mostly a blur. My head hung down in shame about how I looked. How much fatter I'd grown over the summer. Uncharacteristically, I wanted to avoid drawing attention to myself.

Everyone should just leave me alone and let me be. For the most part, they did.

My life was a drag. In the evenings, I'd curl up in the old armchair in the study and try to figure out what was going on. Early in the semester, I knew I wouldn't be getting my usual good marks. No more proficiency awards. No more easy A's or B's. I wasn't retaining information like before, barely paid attention in class, and lost the ability to cram the night before a test. My courses all seemed useless, irrelevant. Latin, a dead language. And chemistry. Bor-ing. In a strange way, I hoped to hit bottom and fail. Finally. Maybe *then* I'd learn. Exactly what I'd learn was anyone's guess. But something was missing. Some big piece of the puzzle that would make sense of things. Nothing made sense anymore. Or seemed to matter.

Clearly I was depressed. But in the early 1960s, depression and feelings weren't part of any equation in the world I inhabited. Feelings and emotions weren't encouraged or discussed. Talk-radio topics were mainly impersonal, and TV talk shows[63] were news or entertainment-oriented, lacking any in- depth psychological content. No Oprah, no Dr. Phil. You had to be pretty far out there to seek psychiatric help. Ordinary people rarely did.

Despite this, before the summer holiday, I'd made a luke-warm attempt to get help of some kind. But it led nowhere. Robert kept trying to persuade me that Shirley didn't mean the horrid things she said, that she couldn't stop herself. My response – maybe she needed a psychiatrist. My father believed my mother would never talk to a stranger under any circumstances, let alone a psychiatrist.

Then Bob came up with a plan. He'd arrange for a psychiatrist to come to the house, ostensibly to see me. That's what he'd tell my mother. But the psychiatrist would actually be there to see *her*. Clever, eh? Once they'd met and talked, she'd feel better, more open to ongoing psychiatric help. She'd get what she needed, and everyone would live happily ever after. A fantasy doomed for failure. It wasn't even tried. My father never made the appointment. Whenever I'd ask, he'd scowl, close his eyes, and shake his head. That meant drop it.

I wondered if his little plan had me as the ultimate target of a psychiatric home visit. But how unnecessary that would've been! I'd have jumped at the chance had it been offered directly. But that wasn't how Robert operated. You never knew where he was coming from.

When I suggested professional help for myself, my father initially nixed the idea. An informal home visit was one thing. A daughter of his seeing a mental health specialist was another. People talked in the small community of Niagara Falls. But I finally managed to persuade him to set me up with someone. It didn't even occur to me to make my own appointment. Even though I was sixteen and quite able to dial a phone number, I still needed Daddy's approval. So Robert arranged for me to see a psychiatrist in Welland, a town less than a half-hour drive from Niagara Falls, but far enough away to prevent wagging tongues.

An older man with greying hair slicked back off his forehead, Dr. McSomething wore a dark suit and tie, and then-unfashionable wire-rimmed glasses. He sat behind a desk, and every so often would light and relight his pipe. I wore a sophisticated white linen sheath dress (from my father's store, of course) that zipped up the back. I have no idea what we talked about. He asked questions. I answered. The appointment ended. I drove back to the Falls. And that was the end of that.

He reported back to my father that I was fine but I wasn't told. Astounding. Because I was definitely not fine. I was depressed and couldn't stop binge eating. But I'd fooled him. I'd put on my very polished adult act, practiced since the age of three, and it worked. This isn't unusual in the therapeutic process. Patients avoid change, even when they want it. It's a push-pull kind of thing, called resistance. So while I was desperate to get help, I was also terrified of it, and relieved. When I returned from England that fall, since seeking psychiatric help hadn't worked, I set my sights on extreme failure as my salvation. As that song I mentioned earlier says, once you've hit bottom, "the only way is up."[64] That was my plan for the rest of 1962.

One evening, while getting into bed, my sister fast asleep across the room, I overheard Shirley shouting at my father from the TV room downstairs. She began with a slight scream that built up into a loud shriek. "Oh Bob ... You can't tell me you *like* the way she looks! Now can you? Can you? *Can you!*" Silence. "Can you?" Still no answer. Obviously they were discussing fatanduglyme.

Then, from out of the silence, I heard my father's voice. Quiet. Calm. Resigned. "No," he said.

I heard nothing else after that. The world crashed in around my ears. *No.* He'd said no, he didn't like the way I looked. At first, shock. I couldn't believe it. But I'd heard it all right. He'd said no. I began to cry. At first just a few tears. Then a fast and furious torrent. I couldn't stop sobbing. I was utterly broken. Shattered shards of glass where my heart used to be.

If he didn't like how I looked, that meant he didn't like *me.* Despite my mental efforts to believe the person "within" counted most, my true emotional beliefs were the same as Shirley's. How I looked was *who* I was. How I looked was *me.* The one person I could count on just said he didn't like me! That was the night my spirit died. That was when I lost all hope. When I didn't want to live anymore. No more worry about hitting bottom. This was it. I was nothing. I was no one. And I wanted to die.

The Pharmacological Challenge

Over the years, teen suicide has been increasing and is one of the top three leading causes of death for young people in both the United States and Canada.[65] Many more try it than succeed. The subject gets a lot of media coverage. Newspaper and magazine articles. Blogs. Documentary specials. They all ask why it happens so often. Here's why. Despair. Hopelessness. And no foreseeable way out of the pain.

The night my father finally told the truth, I cried myself to sleep. Silently, of course, still considerate of my sleeping sister. The morning came, I went to school. I didn't care. The days passed. I didn't care. I failed most exams, and didn't care. Then one evening, when my parents were out, I noticed pills in the medicine cabinet in the downstairs bathroom. The label warned not to exceed more than four per day. I decided to take the dozen or so left in the bottle.

Fortunately, I was pharmacologically impaired. It was Excedrin, a fairly benign headache remedy. I took all the pills, slowly, one or two at a time. Believing with each swallow that this was my final night on earth. I wouldn't wake up tomorrow. There was no tomorrow for me, a comforting thought. I wouldn't have to be here anymore. This was goodbye. My life would soon be over. If heaven or hell existed, I'd find out soon. Maybe I'd even get a chance to talk to God.

As I lay in bed that night, I didn't feel weird. I felt almost happy. Peaceful. I wouldn't have to endure one more day. I figured my parents would be angry, but that was just too damn bad. I didn't consider how my sister would feel to wake up and find my dead body. I left no note. I thanked God for all I'd been given, told myself this was the end, and promptly fell asleep.

The next morning, I awoke, furious to discover I was still here. And very angry at the stupid pills. Evidently they weren't strong enough. I felt disgusted that I couldn't even kill myself properly! Just one more thing I couldn't do right!

Shirley was yelling from downstairs to "get a move on" or I'd be late. And with that, I washed my face, brushed my teeth, threw on my clothes, and stomped off to school. I wore a black A-line skirt and a purple angora sweater with three-quarter sleeves and three white angora stripes across the boat-neck top, just under the neckline. I've always associated that dreadful morning with that purple sweater.

111

I'd failed to kill myself quickly. But a slower, more circuitous route was already available through my binge eating disorder. One soul-destroying binge at a time.

CHAPTER 8: MEASURING THE MARIGOLDS[66]

Family Therapy

Within my first week at the Clarke Institute, the hospital set up a family meeting with Shirley and Bob, Gilda, Dr. B, Dr. Shugar, and myself. This must have been traumatic for my parents, to see their daughter in a mental hospital. How confused and scared they must have been. Ashamed, too, having total strangers know their business.

I walked into that ninth-floor meeting on April 5, 1967, barefoot and dressed in my favourite ribbon-robe, my usual hospital attire during the first few months at the Clarke. Most hospital staff gave up trying to get me to wear shoes. In these early days of the hippie movement, bare feet weren't totally unheard of. However, the head nurse, an attractive woman whose short dark hair framed her usually flushed face, was always after me. One day, she caught me heading into the lounge, barefoot as usual. "You can't go in there like that!" she said in exasperated tones. How absurd. Of course I could. "Yes, I can. Just watch!" And I stepped into the lounge area. Easy-peasy. She didn't look very happy, so I revved it up a notch. I stepped back into the hall and said, "See, I *can*!" And then repeated this stepping back and forth routine muttering, "Wanna see it again?" till she just walked away. I could see other nurses giggling behind their Plexiglas cage. Telling me "You can't" was like waving a red flag in front of a bull.

As soon as I entered the ninth-floor meeting room, I spotted my mother perched on the edge of a wingback chair, looking extremely upset, as if she'd just witnessed an accident. Or spotted some rotting road kill. Shirley squirmed and frowned the moment she saw me. Dismayed at my apparel, she put her hands to her face and shrieked, "Oh, Natalie!" This didn't get us off to a good start. After several similar outbursts, I slammed out of there. The hospital records validate my recollection:

Because Natalie referred to the parental relationship as a source of conflict, it was decided to see the family jointly, and to explore the extent and nature of this conflict. The first session ... was a very difficult one for the family.

Mother felt that the therapists were on Natalie's side against her, contradicted all of Natalie's statements by saying "Natalie, you know that isn't true," and contradicted all statements from both doctors and social workers. She stated her points of view and then asked for doctor support. If she didn't get it she stated that that was her position. Mr. Gold was visibly hurt by Natalie's statements and very anxious to prove "No one is guilty," "Let's forgive and forget."

How typical of my mother to deny reality. And how typical of my father to want to sweep it all under the carpet and pretend nothing happened. The second attempt at togetherness on April 17 (which must have taken place in my room) didn't fare much better.

Natalie refused to talk when her parents and the doctor were present, curling up in bed, using baby talk, and interrupting with irrelevant questions when Dr. Shugar or I spoke of her relationship with her parents, her current behaviour, or tried to bring any structure into the interview.

It seemed that Natalie had learned not to try to contradict her mother, and the aftermath was too painful for her ... A decision was made that the family stop seeing Natalie and see the social worker alone until Natalie was better able to cope with her parents.

Great plan for me. Not so much for Bob and Shirley. Another joint session with them wasn't tried until early June.

Drugged Tests, Part 1

About a week after I arrived at the Clarke, the staff psychiatrist in charge of my case, Dr. Gerry Shugar, had a little chat with me. Tall and lanky, with short brown hair, blue eyes, a soft voice, and gentle manner, he told me I'd be taking what turned out to be the first in a series of evaluation tests.

The plan was to get me out of the hospital and back into the workforce as quickly as possible. That meant office work. The occupational therapist (OT) was to assess my readiness, but I didn't understand the true purpose of the tests she gave. Her report detailed my education, training, work experience, interests, hobbies, and participation in social groups.

Included were some highly unflattering observations. I was "obese, and not concerned with grooming." Apparently, proper job interview attire didn't include bare feet, a robe, and unshaven legs (I probably wasn't allowed a razor). However, it's unclear whether the OT took into account the high doses of meds I was on, with those side effects of impaired thinking, slow memory, and slow reactions, among others.

Meds weren't mentioned in the OT report, but it did say I was "stuporous [sic] and apprehensive," worked at a "very slow pace," and "dawdled much of the time."

Reading this made me smile. After living with Shirley for so long, if I didn't have to rush, I was going to take my sweet old time. Shirley always wanted things done immediately. And *her* way, the only right way. She'd often repeat, "Get a move on, we don't have all day." So when left to my own devices, I let myself be slow.

The report also cited my average intelligence, poor organization, and indecisiveness. And that while "anxious to talk" about myself, I never referred to my problem. Hard to believe, since I often referred to my problem. The listener either wasn't trained to pick up on my cues and clues, or the test materials gave little or no leeway to do so, or both.

The OT also assumed I lacked awareness of others. Like anyone with a background of emotional (or physical) abuse, I was keenly aware, perhaps even vigilant, when other people were around. In the context of the OT room, however, I just tuned other patients out. If I hadn't, my attention would have been focused on them and not on the task at hand, whatever it was (probably making a basket, or a potholder, or some other item that was unlikely to come in handy at the hospital). The others used their intuitive antennae, as well, and kept their distance.

Alarming

All ninth-floor patients were subject to various restrictions on their movements. All comings and goings on and off the ward were monitored by staff from the nursing station opposite the elevators. If you were a danger to yourself or others, or out of it (as I was when I first arrived), you had to be accompanied everywhere by a nurse or student intern. When mentally fit enough, the ninth floor was yours to explore: the lounge, cafeteria, music and crafts rooms, and other patients' rooms.

"Hospital privileges" were given only when you were competent enough to move freely about the hospital. Eventually, you could leave the building on your own.

Visits to the locked forensic ward on the fourth floor were always accompanied by nurses. Some of us went there regularly to play cribbage or cards, usually euchre. No one asked why anyone was at the Clarke, an unspoken courtesy. I hated being locked inside, but that was the deal. Occasionally, the fourth hosted well-supervised alcohol-free parties. I'm not sure if we celebrated Halloween on the ninth or fourth floors, but I know I went as super-skinny model "Twiggy,"[67] in a costume decorated with twigs. The closest I could come to being stick-like.

On or about April 11, 1967, according to hospital records, I had permission to go anywhere in the building by myself, including the coffee shop on the ground floor and Gilda's office in the basement. The doctors had even started lowering my Largactil dosage.

I was usually happy to see Gilda, one of the few people who seemed to hear what I said. Most of the time, she tried to understand me, and even if she wasn't successful, I appreciated her effort. One day during that particular mid-April week, I got off the elevators, not too far from Gilda's office. Barefoot and feeling pretty chipper in my cranberry-red woollen coat-dress (with engraved gold buttons down the front and on the long-sleeved cuffs), I sauntered along the hall. My attention was suddenly drawn to the shiny, bright red fire alarm on the wall, exactly at my eye-level.

I'd never noticed it before. It wasn't behind glass, so I moved closer to get a better look. From just an inch or two away, I could easily read the directions, "Pull in case of fire," printed clearly above the silver lever. Dramatic white letters against a black background, my favourite colours. Curious indeed. What could this mean?

Slowly, I edged closer to the lever, till I could almost touch it with my nose. I wondered what would happen if there was a fire. You were supposed to pull the lever, but did you pull it up or down? I read the instructions again. "Pull in case of fire." It didn't say which direction, up or down. "Pull" probably meant out, so you'd move the lever towards you, in a downward motion. Or it could mean up. How very confusing. This was the trouble with lots of written directions. They were often vague and left you to figure things out for yourself. Which could be very time-consuming, especially in an emergency, like a fire, for goodness' sake!

What if there actually was a fire? You'd have to figure out what to do with that lever. I was pretty sure you'd pull it down, but not a hundred percent sure. Also, the sign said, "in case of fire." Did that mean if there *might* be a fire, or only if there actually *was* a fire? What did "in case of" really mean?

As I pondered this riddle, I moved my index finger very slowly and very carefully towards the lever, curious to know what it felt like. Not as smooth as it looked. Fascinated, I then began gently, so very gently, to brush my finger across the lever, as if stroking it would somehow magically impart what to do in case of fire. Suddenly, an unbelievably startling noise erupted. It sounded like a fire alarm! Omigod! What a coincidence! Here I was, ready and waiting, in case of fire – and now there was a fire, apparently! I froze, right there.

Ear-splitting sirens whined throughout the ten-story building. Bells rang, people's heads popped out from office doorways along the hall. Like a superbly choreographed dance, they looked right, then left, then right again. Was this a real fire or a test? Then I saw people moving quickly along the halls. This was serious! People wanted to know where the fire was. There was no smoke, at least not in that basement hall.

As the sirens and hubbub continued, I remained glued to my position beside the fire alarm. It had all happened so suddenly. So quickly. Maybe there really wasn't a fire. Maybe, just maybe, I'd accidentally moved the lever and set off the alarm when I only wanted to explore it. Uh-oh! That would be quite a mistake. This thought struck me as so funny, I began to laugh. At first slowly, then I could hardly stop. The more I laughed, the more I felt like laughing.

No doubt I made a strange sight, standing there beside the alarm, doubled over at the waist from laughing so hard. I looked up and saw Gilda, who instantly understood what had happened. "Did you do that?" she asked. Yes, I told her, amidst my laughter. "Yes, but I didn't mean to, it was an accident." More laughter. She ordered me to wait in her office until she returned. She probably went to inform the authorities that it was a false alarm, there was no fire, and that the culprit had been caught. The rest of that day is a total blank.

This event, apparently, contributed to the decision to post-pone my scheduled April 19 release with outpatient follow-up and keep me at the Clarke a while longer.

Was setting off that alarm an unconscious cry for help? Probably. I was in no way ready to live on my own. "Discharge to be postponed," stated the April 18 doctor's orders. Dr. B thought it was due to

... *patient's lack of concrete plans and inability to work through her problems, especially relationship to her parents. Demonstrates mixed feelings about the latter. Patient is however appropriate in thought and affect, though at times somewhat facetious.*

Yes. I was unable to work through my problems with Shirley and Bob in the first two weeks at the Clarke. With this expectation, is it any wonder I was facetious? Here's Gilda's take:

Approximately two weeks following admission, at a time when discharge was being considered, her behaviour again became inappropriate with an air of frivolity. She showed unwillingness to formulate definite plans and her parents' constant interference appeared to warrant a further stay. By this time, however, her behaviour appeared to be of an acting-out nature and a diagnosis of character disorder was entertained.

Gilda was correct about the acting out, but not so much about this second diagnosis, which was based on the very limited options available in the *DSM-I*.

By April 21, I was back on 100 mg of Largactil for "acting-out behaviour." I got more drugs instead of therapy. Drugs to control my behaviour. Drugs, instead of helping me see my acting-out as a substitute for honest expression of feelings, which I needed to learn. Maybe they didn't understand that themselves. I certainly didn't.

Drugged Tests, Part 2

After the decision to keep me a while longer, I was put through another series of tests[68] on April 21 and May 17 to better gauge my IQ and job suitability. Updated versions of many of these tests are still used as assessment tools, except for the Rorschach, seen as too subjective. While assessments and other diagnostic tools are considered objective, they still require some sort of subjective interpretation, as do statistical results, survey questions, and other measurement instruments. In my view, there's no such thing as a truly objective test.

The Psychological Report described my initial reluctance to provide biographical information. I found it tiresome to be repeatedly asked the same questions. But I'd apparently discovered a more acceptable reason for coming to the Clarke, a "problem with self-control." This wasn't explored, or else the report would have mentioned that the "problem" referred to my out-of-whack food binges and eating habits. As my interview progressed, my responses apparently became "more free and eventually rambling." No surprise here. The gibble-gabble was getting another chance to be expressed. Held back for years, torrents of words and images poured out. Unstoppable. I'd get lost in them. them.

At one point, I was brought to a little room to complete several tasks. I clearly remember two of them.

First, I was to assemble bits and pieces of little jigsaw puzzles to look like familiar shapes or objects. I don't know if I was given oral or written directions. But I do remember how annoying these puzzles were. One piece, unmistakably an elephant's trunk, led to the blatantly obvious conclusion that the finished puzzle would be an elephant. I figured it couldn't be that simple, and that an idiot could create an elephant, or a giraffe, or a kangaroo out of these shapes and colours. So I got more creative. I invented different animals. It was fun to play with the different pieces and create brand-new species. Much more interesting than making the same old boring ones.

The second task relied on several sets of black-and-white cartoon drawings,[69] which when placed in the correct order, would tell a story. The set I remember involved fishing. One cartoon showed a little boy seated at the end of a wooden dock, his fishing rod suspended over the water and an empty pail beside him. Another showed the boy walking to the dock with the rod and empty pail in hand. In a third, the boy was walking back along the dock, with the fishing rod and a pail full of fish. The set included several more such drawings. I was to put them in proper sequence, so they made sense and told a story.

Here again, the intended story was too obvious for words. I could barely contain my contempt at the simplicity of some of these tasks. So, like the puzzle test, I created new stories to fit whatever sequence I fancied. For example, I chose to begin with the drawing of the boy leaving the dock with his fishing rod and pail full of fish. As he walks home, he remembers the details of his catch, and recalls sitting at the end of the dock with his empty pail, which became the second picture. For the third, I chose the one showing him heading towards the dock with his rod and empty pail, hoping for another great catch. This was a much more interesting tale to me than the obvious one, and I felt quite proud of myself for not doing what was expected.

Both examples show that my perspective was a tad off, to put it mildly. While I knew I'd been given tests, I think I assumed they were all related to IQ and creativity. The thing is, I don't recall being told what the tests were for, but for sure, no one ever asked me to explain what I'd done. If the testers had questioned me, they might have discovered that I could have finished in a normal fashion, if not in normal time. I remember being uncharacteristically careful and relaxed while working on the tests and not in my usual revved-up, mile-a-minute thinking mode. Again, this was possibly due to my drugged condition.

The report adds that I destroyed the tests I'd been given to complete on my own, since I wanted no more testing. But I co-operated next time, except for the vocational interest test.

A short time later, I overheard Dr. Shugar tell several people I'd not done very well on the tests. This came as quite a shock. I'd always seen myself as bright and above average. I'd done rather well on previous IQ tests.

Lots of teachers had told me I was smart and expressed displeasure or disappointment when I hadn't lived up to my potential. But maybe I really had. Maybe my potential wasn't as high as everyone believed. A bitter pill to swallow. No wonder Dr. Shugar didn't give me the bad news in person. Now, I was not only fatandugly and a mental patient, but also not too bright. What chance did I have for the future? Yes, it was better to find out and be prepared than to go through life thinking you were smarter than you were. So I'd better get used to being average. What a bummer!

The actual news, in the Psychological Report, was even worse. I tested at a low average, with an IQ of 92, which included a verbal performance IQ of only 83. Me. The talker. The one who got in trouble throughout school for talking, who won oratory contests. The one with the "gift of the gab," according to Robert, a girl who could talk her way out of a paper bag. That's what he'd told me when I phoned him in a panic a few years back, near the end of my second year at university in Buffalo, New York.

At the time, I was having a complete identity crisis. I couldn't stop crying and was struggling, unsuccessfully, to keep myself together. Robert drove to Buffalo. As we sat in his car in the university parking lot, I told him, amidst sobs, that I didn't know who I was. "Is that all?" he replied with relief. He'd just learned the high school valedictorian was pregnant and was terrified his daughter was in a similar predicament.

What irony, I remember thinking. How could I get pregnant when I couldn't let any man touch my body in case he threw up in disgust at my fatness? This reminder of my super-virginal status made me cry even harder. This is when my father tried to comfort me, by telling me I could talk my way out of a paper bag. When I think about it now, I realize how difficult this must have been for my dad. Given his own false identity –more on that later – my little crisis must have seemed insignificant by comparison.

The writer of the Psychological Report attributed my low IQ score in part to "difficulty with concentration and attention," adding that I was probably functioning below my "intellectual potential." But I wasn't told that. Nor was there any mention (again) of the drugs I was on.

Ironically, the projective tests somewhat more accurately diagnosed my personality. Note that Freudian theory still dominated psychiatric thinking at the time, as shown by the language used.

On the Rorschach, she ... is in severe conflict of many varieties. Whenever any feelings are activated, there is a general arousal of strong anxiety and a struggle to avoid feeling or awareness of drives; at the same time, she ruminates considerably about acts or behaviour which express these drives. Therefore, feeling arousal is stressful ... under stress, her behaviour could appear psychotic-like. The main stressors ... appear to be closeness needs and expression of aggression; failure ... appears to be very painful ...

On the DDT [Differential Diagnostic Test] ... she reacts to stress by becoming over- controlled and using a system of defences which are rigid and not adjusted to meet the particular situation. The effectiveness of these habituated defences is diminished under stress.

On the MMPI and 16PF [Minnesota Multiphasic Personality Inventory and 16 Personality Factors] tests ... she shows herself to be somewhat rebellious and non-conformist. It seems that she would tend to be an isolate, to avoid close personal ties, and be reluctant to reveal her feelings and attitudes. She appears to be impulsive and distractible and would find it difficult to apply herself to any single task for an extended length of time; oc-

cupational inefficiency would be probable.

I wasn't reluctant to reveal feelings, but simply unaware of them, having avoided feelings my whole life. I had no idea how to recognize and/or identify feelings, let alone tolerate them. Often, I felt overwhelmed by them. My parents modelled the extreme ends of the emotional expression spectrum. Shirley was hysterical, Robert repressed. And me, I went both ways, but mostly ate in order to shut out my feelings. But the tests weren't designed to show that.

Also, I'm pretty sure I revealed my attitudes. You could say, in fact, that attitude was something I definitely had.

Bob and Shirley at the Clarke, Take 1

Between April and August 1967, my parents visited the Clarke ten times. They met mainly with Gilda, but sometimes also with various psychiatrists (Dr. Shugar, Dr. B, or Dr. Abbott). The sessions were quite an ordeal for them, and totally unknown to me until my later scrutiny of the hospital records.

Her family, particularly her mother, are deeply entrenched in Natalie's difficulties. Mother is extremely resentful of the father's leniency and interest in the daughter. Mother, once extremely attractive and vivacious, appears to want to live vicariously through her daughter but is frustrated by Natalie's weight problem, 200 lbs., 5'4½" and lack of desire to socialize with the Jewish community in the hometown of Niagara Falls.

Father: tall, good looking 52 years old, appears well.

Mother: a carefully dressed matron with dyed hair, who devotes a great deal of attention to her appearance.

Here's a better description of my mother. Picture comedian Ray Romano's mother, played by actress Doris Roberts in the TV sitcom *Everybody Loves Raymond*. Add a slightly worn British accent, and you've got Shirley.

My father is harder to pin down. Imagine Dr. Phil. Tall, broad-shouldered, balding, and with a moustache. Now add a bit more weight, change the southern drawl to a British accent with a slight eastern-European tinge, and you've got a fairly decent image of Bob.

The parents seem to control each other and their children through illness. Mother has high blood pressure, father had a heart attack and Natalie's recent hospitalization may be a part of this family pattern.

Parents both do a great deal of nagging, especially mother, and one feels both are very conscious of their position in the community. Mother expressed the fact that she is ashamed to walk with Natalie and Natalie also is aware of her mother's feelings. Guilt feelings dominate. Father didn't visit until the Wednesday after admission.

Gilda's notes show the extent of my parents' denial, brought about by their embarrassment and guilt.

The parents feel Natalie's problem is her weight ... and none of their threats or rewards, such as a trip to England or Israel, helped. They feel her relationship with both parents is good and close ... This [hospitalization] is the first time the family had any indication of a mental problem.

Mr. Gold feels Natalie likes him better, "quite naturally, the Oedipus complex," but that things always went well at home.

Even now, I shake my head in amazement when I read the above. Things were going well at home? But here's my favourite part. Welcome to my world.

In interviews with the parents, they tried to control the therapist, contradict each other and frequently talk at the same time. Mr. Gold feels his position on the White Cross Guild [an advocacy group for mental patients and mental health] in Niagara Falls has given him a great understanding of his daughter's behaviour.

This reminds me of a brilliant plan I concocted after I'd been at the Clarke only a few weeks. I was going to alert the local Niagara newspapers to a wonderful heart-warming story of transformation – how the daughter of the president of the local Mental Health Association was hospitalized for mental illness, and got the help she needed at Toronto's Clarke Institute. Various headlines would sensationalize this event. I told myself this inspirational account would help reduce the stigma of mental illness. But the truth was, fueled by disowned resentment, the public revelation I sought was payback to Bob and Shirley. Like most of my fantasies, this one (fortunately) didn't materialize.

What set Bob and Shirley apart from most of the North American public who misunderstood mental illness due to lack of knowledge, is what Gilda observed:

Both parents claim to want instruction about how to deal with Natalie, but find difficulty in accepting such instructions, constantly pointing out loopholes ... Mother especially is concerned that the hospitalization interferes with their normal social lives.

Both used much of the interview time in (1) speaking of their daughter's brilliance and beauty and her school accomplishments. (2) Finding out what the Clarke is doing for Natalie, how many times I see her each week, what we should do, etc. (3) Expounding on theories of mental illness, for example red is bad for mental patients, Natalie should not pick up things dropped on the floor, we should put Natalie on a diet, etc.

They have also suggested I should be more than a case-

worker to Natalie and take good care of her. In short, the parents have a tendency to turn their anxiety outward.

They really didn't get the hospital concept.

CHAPTER 9: THE UNWINDING

During the months preceding my entrance into the Clarke, the threads weaving my life together, loose as they were, had begun to unravel. My got-it-all-together act was unsustainable.

Within a mere eight-month period, many difficult things and major stressors happened. I lost weight, then regained almost twice as much. I became severely depressed and lost my job. I found a new job, was sexually assaulted, and moved. Then I lost my car, lost my second job, and literally got thrown out of a children's mental health residence. Oh yes, and I almost killed my father.

Who Are You?

My first Toronto job was as a junior clerk-typist in the creative department of the ad agency Vickers & Benson (V&B). In other words, a lackey for creative people. Eventually I worked my way up to secretary, work I still saw as demeaning. It was hard to keep a lid on my self-pity, envy, and resentment. After all, I was just as creative as some of the people there. But I was fatandugly in an environment where only beautiful people were admired and celebrated. Shirley was right.

Soon after receiving a pair of tiny, see-through bikini panties as a Secret Santa Christmas gift, I decided to lose weight. Over a seven-week period, a doctor injected me daily in the hip to boost my metabolism (probably injections of HCG),[70] and also put me on an extremely low 500-calorie-a-day diet. Not surprisingly, I lost a lot of weight quickly.

One weekend, very pleased with myself, I tried on a peach-coloured linen suit (size sixteen, equivalent to an American size fourteen) I hadn't worn for several years. The straight skirt and tailored jacket fit perfectly! I felt so celebratory I got a new hair-do to match. That Monday morning in April 1966, I arrived at work feeling pretty spiffy. But no one recognized me. Not at first. Every time I entered my boss's office she'd throw up her hands and say, "Who *are* you? Who is this strange person in my office?"

She meant to be supportive and complimentary. But her remarks and others' reactions freaked me out. Being fatandugly had been my identity. And with it came some pretty negative expectations. Heavily reliant on external cues to tell me who I was and what role to play, I felt completely lost when others failed to give me clear signals. Compliments only created confusion and discomfort, unaccustomed as I was to receiving them. Or accepting them.

In typical fashion, within a few months, I'd regained the lost pounds, plus. And could only fit into a size 22 or 24. In the mid-1960s, finding any plus-size clothing with colour and style was almost impossible, since no special stores existed for plus-size women. (Years later, I relied on pretty-looking maternity clothes.) But back then, I actually found something: a lime-green, straight-skirted, cotton shirtwaist dress with white polka-dots. I wore it often as I sat outside the V&B producers' offices. And I mean sat. Day after day. Gazing off into space, doing nothing with the stacks of files piled high on my desk.

Depression had set in, along with a side order of numbness, hopelessness, and incredible disappointment with myself and my going-nowhere life. My producer boss, Kenny, didn't want to hear about my period, or any other embarrassingly inappropriate excuse I offered. Eventually, the poor guy had to fire me because I wasn't doing my job. I felt bad for him, but hadn't wanted to be a secretary in the first place. After ten months, he'd done me a favour.

The Ontario Red Cross hired me within a month as a youth worker. More accurately, as a youth talker. Something I excelled at. I'd be travelling to high schools in central Ontario to give talks about the Red Cross and their volunteer youth program. Good thing I had Boris,[71] my little white British Anglia, which I'd lent to a young married couple shortly after arriving in Toronto. The deal: they'd drive Boris, look after all related expenses (parking, garage rental), Boris wouldn't sit idle, and I could use the car when needed. This mutual favour was really a way for me to ingratiate myself with them. Now, having Boris meant I could take turns driving to various speaking gigs with Helen, the other youth worker. Helen was a tall, blonde, truly beautiful young woman. Gorgeous on the outside and also a lovely person inside. Try as I might, I couldn't dislike her. One rainy winter day, Boris broke down en route to a speaking engagement in Hamilton. Helen and I were late and missed the student assembly. (No cell phones back then, to let anyone know what had happened.)

My little Boris, it turned out, was ready for the scrap heap. Apparently, the married couple had driven it into the ground. Losing Boris meant losing the Red Cross job, and losing my main connection to this couple.

Not a Rape

The minimization and denial of trauma is nothing new, and people working with individuals who have been sexually abused or assaulted know this from sad experience. I was sexually assaulted in the fall of 1966, about five months before I entered the Clarke.

But it took me almost forty years to confront what had happened. In the interim, if it came to mind at all, I'd simply brush it off as too embarrassing and inconsequential. From a Gestalt therapy perspective, we usually become ready to deal with a particular experience when other, perhaps seemingly unrelated experiences have been more fully processed.[72]

Here's what happened in November 1966. I know the weather was cold because I was wearing my long, black winter coat with the black fur collar. As I got off the Bathurst bus and began the two-block walk home, I felt some foreboding. It was a dark and stormy night. (And yes, I've wanted to write that corny line for a long time.) But it really was. No moon, no stars. Only a glimpse of thick, shadowy cloud shapes hovering across a darkened sky. The wind howled as it tossed odd bits of litter and loose leaves into the air. And blew drops of rain mixed with snow into my face.

As I turned the corner onto my street, I spotted a man following slightly behind on the other side. Medium height and build. Shoulder-length dark hair. Dark pants and a black leather bomber jacket. I decided to ignore him.

Here's the crazy part. Instead of speeding up and walking more quickly to my house at the end of the block, as they teach in any decent self-defence class, I actually slowed down. I began to balance on the cement curb lining the road, carefully placing one foot directly in front of the other, as if I was measuring the curb by foot-lengths. I sigh now even as I write this. I didn't want to hurt the man's feelings, you see. I didn't want him to think I was afraid of him or worried about him (which I was). And I didn't want him to think I saw him as a creep (which I did, and he was).

And here's the kicker. I didn't want him to think I was concerned he might attack or rape me, because I was too fatandugly to be raped. Yes, that's what I believed. I saw rape as a sexual offence, a view held by much of 1960s society. And given that I was fatandugly, especially after regaining so much weight, I believed no one would want to touch me or have anything to do with me sexually, including rape. To manage my fear, I hummed the melody of a song learned in childhood – "I Whistle a Happy Tune" – which is really about not letting on you're afraid.[73]

The punchline comes at the end of the second verse. "For when I fool the people I see, I fool myself as well." Message: don't show your fear; pretend. I was pretty good at pretending. This also fit right in with Shirley's approach, whenever feeling scared came up. She'd say, "Don't be silly, there's nothing to be afraid of!" Lesson: don't trust your feelings. Don't trust your God-given intuition and evolution's instinctive gift.

So I dawdled, hummed, and balanced my way along the curb. The guy suddenly ducked into a driveway across the street, headed towards the back of one of the residences. Phew! He was gone. Again, instead of picking up the pace and hurrying home past the few remaining houses, I continued my unafraid act.

Suddenly out of nowhere, I felt a hand from behind reach across the right side of my face and cover my mouth. For an instant, I thought it was my old friend Jerry playing a "guess who" joke. But in a flash, I knew it wasn't Jerry as the hand yanked my head backward and the rest of me with it. As I was pulled back, I felt another hand grasping under my coat, roughly moving up my legs, fingers stretched out and reaching to get inside me. By this time, I heard strange, high-pitched noises come out of my mouth.

Shrieking, I fell all the way back until I hit my head on the curb. The guy's hand was still grappling under my coat, poking and prodding. But he was having a lot of trouble because I wore the ultimate anti-rape protection: several heavily elasticized panty-girdles. He'd gone as far as he could, and given all the noise I was making, he took off quickly into the night.

I managed to stand up, quite shaky and still screaming. In shock, I screeched my way to the side entrance and the relative safety of my little basement apartment.

That night, two young male officers sat in my wood-panelled basement room asking questions. I felt as if I was making a big production out of nothing. After all, the guy didn't rape me, so what was the big deal? I imagined the police might wonder why anyone would want to rape someone like me in the first place. Maybe the pervert realized how fatandugly I was and changed his mind.

The officers asked me to describe exactly what happened. And I did. Except I left out the part about the panty-girdles. I'd rather have died than tell them that. And I didn't mention how I'd dawdled, an aspect that bothered me. Because in my mind, my slowness made me partly responsible for the attack. I should have hurried.

After the police left, I also called a woman who'd befriended me at the ad agency. Sort of. She was one of the people I worked for, who actually talked to me, albeit with a somewhat benevolent condescension. I told her what happened, only this time I included the girdles. She laughed, which I took as encouragement to further develop the funny side of the story. So I said all the guy did was goose me. And this is how I managed to minimize and take the blame for a traumatic experience. Turning it into a self-demeaning, humiliating episode best forgotten as quickly as possible. The Clarke records make no mention of it, and I'm sure I blocked it from my mind.

One more thing. During the assault and my loud screeching, no one on that street opened a door to see what the noise was about. I soon found another little basement apartment.

Basement Daze

Most of that month before my arrival at the Clarke on March 31, 1967, was spent in and out of a fog. Yet several very clear remnants highlight my gradual disintegration.

Going Numb

My seventeen-year-old sister phoned one night, wanting me to call "Mommy" at a friend's place, but wouldn't say why. Shirley got on the phone and told me my father had suffered a heart attack. He was resting now in the hospital, and it was all my fault. "This is all your doing," she said. "I've told you time and again, but you never listen! You upset your father."

Just to clear the fog, I said, "You blame me?" And Shirley, never one to mince words, replied in a frenzied but relatively loud whisper, lest her friend overhear, "Yes, I blame you for this. Of course I do.

Who else brings him so much *tsuris?*" (Trouble and sorrow, remember?) I had no answer. I could only listen in silent shock as Shirley added how I was both a worry and a disappointment to my father. I can't say which caused me the greater grief – the shock of my father's encounter with mortality or my mother's accusations. Because I went straight into numb mode, where I stayed, more or less, until I entered the Clarke. Helped, of course, by enormous amounts of food to suppress any and all feelings.

Culture Shock

I imagine most of my repressed emotional energy became so abundant that it moved into my brain. From there, it accelerated the speed with which thoughts and images roller-bladed through my mind. Since I'd lost my Red Cross job at the end of February, I'd spent most of March in a haze. Or a daze. Or a hazy daze. I used some of my savings to live on.

During that time, I recall reading two books in particular. J.D. Salinger's *Catcher in the Rye*, whose main character, Holden Caulfield, writes from a mental hospital. I knew exactly what Holden meant and why he felt so enraged. [74]And James Joyce's *Ulysses*,[75] which I acquired during university days but never read or understood. Now it made sense. Perched on my bed at one end of that little basement room, I recited certain passages out loud. Could actually smell the snot-green sea he described. Impressive, my deep and profound connection with literature. Who needed university? Not me.

Music also moved me, literally. Inspired by one of my favourite record albums by Herb Alpert and the Tijuana Brass,[76] I performed a Mexican hat dance in the centre of the room. A sombrero, inherited from one of my sister's dance recital costumes, formed the centrepiece. I'd draped it with chains from a hardware store. Who needed dance lessons? Not me. Who was in chains? Not me. And this is what I desperately wanted to believe.

Calling, Calling

I only remember a few of the many telephone calls I apparently made in the last two weeks of March before heading downtown to meet Gilda.

The pizza guy asked me how many people were going to eat the extra-large pizza I'd decided on. We'd been chatting for a while before I placed my order. Without thinking I answered "me." For the first time, I'd admitted to another human being that I was eating way beyond a normal amount of food. The man's response came in a soft-spoken Irish lilt, with no hint of judgment or derision. "Ahhh," he said. "You don't want to do that, do you?" Yes, I did.

His mellow tone stayed with me and made me sad, even as I wolfed the pizza down. When you're starved for kindness or compassion, when you finally get just a little taste of it, sadness isn't unusual. It stems from the grief of recognizing what you haven't experienced before. That's why I've never forgotten the pizza guy. But sadness was exactly what I didn't want to feel, was afraid to feel. There was just too much of it. Once I started to feel sad, I might never stop.

Unfortunately, my friend Karen was another recipient of my phone outreach. We'd met in 1960 at Union Station while waiting on the platform for the train to northern Ontario. Noticing a girl my age with similar duffle bags, my father asked her if she was headed to the same camp as me. Yes, she was. What a coincidence. Robert proceeded to tell her about my three ocean voyages (when I was two and a half and three and a half), assuming she'd be as impressed as he with this historical feat. Karen wasn't impressed, but her sense of humour and keen perception helped her see the situation for what it was. A father embarrassing his daughter.

We became good friends after that. Often, we'd reminisce. "Hey, remember the time we met at the train station?" It became one of our many in-jokes.

Karen lived in Toronto, and over the years I'd visit from Niagara Falls. We'd joke around a lot, and she'd listen patiently to stories about Shirley and Bob. Her mother was the opposite of Shirley. Kind and comforting to be around. After grade thirteen, Karen decided to do her second university year overseas, which I experienced as a tremendous loss. When she returned, she was different. She'd fallen deeply in love and married her sweetheart. To my dismay and shame, I was still a virgin at twenty-one.

Karen and I grew apart. I'd dropped out of university after my second year, while she'd attended grad school. But she was still important to me. And so, in my confused and sorry state I phoned her a number of times, according to the Clarke records. My disjointed conversations must have been incredibly disturbing to her, because I remember her telling me she had to get off the phone. I felt as if I'd said something wrong or crossed some sort of line. Or perhaps confirmed my worst suspicions: we weren't going to be close friends anymore. One more loss. A rejection, which I couldn't fully digest at the time.

But I had a sense that she'd moved on. It happens all the time. People come together for a time and then go their separate ways. So I can only thank the universe for sending me Karen to help me keep it together during those traumatic and difficult teen years.

I also phoned David X, from the downtown youth centre where I'd volunteered. Tall, dark, and handsome, with a slow, dreamy, soft-spoken voice, I found him highly appealing and non-threatening. His mellowness probably came from smoking pot, but that wouldn't have occurred to me back then.

When he answered the phone, I played "guess who," until he got tired of the game and asked what I wanted. Taken aback by such directness, I blurted out, "To marry you." I was probably as surprised to hear myself say those words as he was to hear them. Looking back, I suspect what I really wanted was sex, something I was quite confused about. Those were the days when the "free love" movement was moving into full swing and practiced by many of my generation. But an equally strong pull towards old-fashioned morality, a leftover from the straitlaced 1950s, also flourished. I belonged in the latter category, not so much by conscious choice, but by weight. I was simply too fatandugly to be desirable.

David X didn't laugh. And he didn't hang up. I have no idea what he said, except it wasn't yes.

And it wasn't no, which I would have remembered. Nor was I asked to clarify or explain. He simply drew the conversation to a close. Told me to take care, have a good night. If I hadn't already fallen in love with the guy, what I saw as considerate treatment clinched the deal.

It's clear now that my usual social restraints had long since dissolved, before I even got to the Clarke.

CHAPTER 10: CHEZ CLARKE

On the Move

A few days after I arrived on the ninth floor, I was shifted to a shared room at the opposite end of the hall, along the inner corridor. A room without windows.

My roommate, Olivia, a married woman in her early thirties, suffered from major depression. She looked like a typical farm girl, with her freckled face, blue eyes, and shoulder-length, strawberry-blond hair held back off her forehead with a headband. Her usual outfit was a pale blue skirt and jacket, with a printed brown silk blouse. A gentle soul, she was always kind to me. On the ward, we all knew Olivia was getting electro-shock treatments. Several times a week, she'd disappear into a room down the hall.

Strapped to a padded table, with electrodes attached to various parts of her body, a series of strong electric jolts would apparently eradicate much of her memory.

Despite the relative harmony between Olivia and me, I wasn't keen on sharing a room. When I heard a patient had died and that a vacant single room was available, I took this as a sign from the universe. If you want something, go get it. Long before the "occupy" movement, I decided to occupy the room before the nurses assigned it to someone else. I confided my secret to Olivia, assuring her this wasn't personal, and she wished me luck. I quickly packed my belongings into a suitcase.

The next morning, I awoke before daybreak, donned my ribbon-robe, and began the move. The suitcase couldn't have been very heavy, but that morning, it seemed to weigh a ton. Maybe waking up so early meant I was still under sedation. This could explain the extraordinary amount of effort it took just to move my body, let alone to push a suitcase along the floor. Fortunately, my destination was just down the hall and around the corner, close to the nursing station and in view of the elevators. Such a seemingly simple undertaking stands out in my mind as one of the most physically and mentally arduous tasks I've ever tackled. Like Sisyphus pushing a huge boulder up the great mountain, I struggled, stopping periodically to catch my breath and to motivate myself with encouraging words. My whole life seemed to depend on accomplishing this particular task. Finally I reached my new room, quietly closed the wooden door, and began to unpack my things.

Later that morning when the nurses discovered what I'd done, they were not amused. "You can't do that," they each said as they walked into my new room to witness my self-declared occupancy. To me, this was the stupidest, most irritating thing the nurses ever said. And unfortunately, they said it all too often. They seemed to love telling me I couldn't do things that I clearly and obviously could do. And did. They didn't get it.

Once I realized I was going to be at the Clarke for a while, I wanted my things with me. The end of April was fast approaching, and I had to vacate my basement apartment by then. So I phoned my pal Jerry, who kindly agreed to pack my stuff into a few boxes and bring them to me at the Clarke. Guess what the nurses said a few days later after the boxes arrived.

True to form, each nurse said something like, "You can't do that! You can't bring all that stuff in here!" Idiotic, really, because right there in plain sight, sprawled across the floor in my room, was a lot of stuff. Boxes containing most of my worldly possessions: books, records, odd bits of jewellery, clothing. And assorted knick-knacks, such as a bright-yellow, pear-shaped ceramic ashtray, the Mother's Day gift I'd given to Shirley when I was a kid. Shirley didn't smoke and never had. But the ashtray was really pretty and ultimately became mine. Shirley never liked most gifts she received. So no big deal.

Other items Jerry brought included my knitting, a small transistor radio, my Mexican sombrero, a portable record player, portable typewriter, my old teddy bear named Timothy (which I still have), and some plastic-coated chain-link strips from a hardware store. I'd draped these on the wall and around the ugly light fixture in the centre of that basement room. Last but not least, Jerry brought my guitar.

"You can't have all that stuff in here," said the nurses again. Obviously I could, since the stuff was there. I managed to restrain myself and simply smile, shrug my shoulders, and gesture with my palms up to show this was now beyond my control, a *fait accompli.*

Finally, the head nurse arrived. "You can't have all that stuff here," she repeated. "It belongs at home. You need to send it home." That was the final straw. My restraint disappeared in a flash. "This *is* home!" I shouted at the top of my lungs, which I must tell you, is extremely loud. "I *am* home! Home is wherever I am, and I'm *here*! I have *no other* home. I live *here* now, and I need my stuff *with* me, at *home. This* home, where I *am*!!" I must give the woman credit. She listened to my diatribe, thought for a few seconds, turned, and walked out of my room back to the nursing station. That was the last time anyone ever said anything to me about my stuff.

The people in charge decided to let me stay in my new room for the time being. Olivia and I became former roommates who rarely associated with one another, with one exception. She loved to sit in the lounge and listen to me sing as I accompanied myself on guitar. In fact, one of the greatest gifts I ever received came from Olivia's father, a distinguished gentleman in his sixties who visited her quite often.

After witnessing his depressed daughter come to life during those musical interludes, Olivia's father brought me a songbook. It makes me cry just to think of it. I was so touched, so appreciative. I still have this gift in support of my musical abilities from someone else's father. But a father nonetheless. To Olivia's dad, wherever you are, I thank you. Your gift has warmed me more than I could ever say.

Guitar

In June 1963, after freshman year at university in Buffalo,[77] I got my first guitar. Before that, while my grades weren't great, I'd managed to rack up a fairly impressive list of non-academic accomplishments, such as being elected to the Freshman Class Council, to the Goodyear Hall (the female student dorm) Council as Vice-President, and to the Student Senate. I couldn't wait to tell Shirley all the good news. Her immediate response was to ask if I'd lost any weight. In fact, she told me not to come home for the summer if I hadn't. I hadn't, so I didn't.

Instead, I got a live-in job as a mother's helper in Buffalo for Mrs. S, a recent divorcee with a little boy of two and a little girl of five. The job involved plenty of responsibility, including car keys and lots of money for grocery shopping. My weight soared that summer. I don't know the exact number because I avoided the scale. But I had to get new muumuus and dusters (short cotton housedresses), since I quickly outgrew my wardrobe.

Mrs. S told me to buy whatever food I wanted. Still, I felt compelled to sneak, steal, and hide what I ate, typical binge-eater behaviour, lest anyone think I got fat from eating. One afternoon, I heard Mrs. S arrive home and enter the kitchen, right next to the family room, where I was sprawled on the sofa chomping on an enormous baloney sandwich. My immediate impulse was to get rid of that sandwich. I shoved it deep down into the sofa, between the back and cushions, and somehow forgot about it. Mrs. S discovered it a week later, and looked at me with disgust.

Out in suburban Buffalo, I felt pretty isolated. Nothing else to do in my spare time but eat. So I decided to get a guitar. With lots of time to practice, I learned enough chords (four) that summer to accompany myself on a few popular folk songs. But no matter how much time or effort I put in, I never became good at the guitar. Just good enough to get by.

In September, back at university in second year, on sleepless nights I'd head down to the dorm basement to sing and play, but mostly to sing. My voice usually drowned out the guitar sounds.

The basement acoustics were great, and the candy and junk-food machines were always restocked, ready for tomorrow. That was when my thievery turned serious. To feed my vending machine habit, I'd regularly steal money from my college roommate's handbag. I didn't recognize how much I envied this lovely, slender young woman from New Rochelle, NY, whose kind mother knitted gorgeous fuzzy sweaters, very much in style at the time, if you were a preppie (she was).

Not that I couldn't get junk food from the cafeteria. I simply couldn't let other people see me eat it and judge me. They wouldn't know that I was driven and couldn't help it, and as obsessed with getting my next food fix as an alcoholic is on getting the next drink.

But the more I stole, the more I had to eat to cover up the guilt, shame, and humiliation of what I was doing. It was one thing to rob Shirley, and another to take from my roommate.

There was, however, a bright side to the basement goings-on. Dorm residents heard me sing. Apparently, the sound wafted up from the basement into the rooms. Some wondered who was playing records so late at night. They thought I was a recording! How unexpected.

Unlike most of my behaviour, singing was the one thing I'd undertaken strictly for myself, the only way to express my true and honest feelings. I literally sang my heart out, and people must have responded to the rawness. With only one volume, loud, I sounded like a cross between rock sensation Janice Joplin, old-time Broadway song-belter Ethel Merman, and gospel queen Mahalia Jackson.

During my tormented high school years, every evening after Johnny Carson and long before the 24-hour news cycle and all-night TV channels, Mahalia sang a gospel hymn to mark the end of the broadcast day. I loved her.

And there I was, in the dorm basement, belting out gospel-sounding bluesy tunes to help mark the end of my college day. Unable to resist the praise and encouragement from girls in the dorm, I ultimately teamed up with a girl named Helen, and together we did some campus gigs.

When I went home to visit my parents in Niagara Falls that autumn, my father, in his usual disdainful tone, said, "Humph. What do you need a guitar for?" It took me till September 1983 to answer:

> *What do you need a guitar for*
> *He said almost 20 years ago*
> *I couldn't answer then*
> *Now I know*
>
> *I needed a guitar to hold*
> *Because I was so lonely*
> *I needed a guitar to play*
> *Because I had no piano*
> *I needed a guitar*
> *To amuse myself with*
> *To accompany my sad song*
> *I needed a guitar*
> *To help me express*
> *What I could not*
> *Find the words to say*
>
> *I wanted to sing*
> *Although I didn't know this*
> *At the time*
> *Deep from within, my voice*
> *Poured out ...*
> *Angry ... plaintive ...*
> *It covered the chords I played*
> *Drowned my lack of skill*
> *With its force*
>
> *People noticed, paid attention*
> *Wanted to hear*
> *My blues*
> *I put my whole heart and soul*
> *Into each song*
> *Often forgot to play chords*
> *My tempo changed*

I'd forget words
And it didn't matter
To those who heard
It bothered me a bit
And I'd quit
For a while
Hide my guitar in the closet
Or under my bed
Till I was ready to admit
How much I needed
To sing and play
How much I loved
To sing and play

What do I need a guitar for?
Now I can forgive him for asking
I didn't know either
Almost 20 years ago

Other Peeps

Once you got your tray from the cafeteria line, you could sit where you wanted, and with whom. Most ninth-floor patients were middle-aged, depressed, and quite out of it, either naturally, pharmaceutically, or a combination of both, as I'd been when I first arrived. There were also several young people in my age range, plus a smattering of thirty-somethings and seniors. When you're twenty-one, it's hard to gauge the age of anyone over thirty.

I can still picture the always immaculately dressed but joyless, white-haired, elderly woman, Mrs. G, who just sat in the lounge, day after day, without speaking or making eye contact with anyone. She'd recently lost her husband, and despite visits from her adult children and young grandchildren, seemed to have given up. Sometimes I'd watch her eat in a mindless and bored manner. I wasn't the only one who felt sorry for her.

In contrast, Celia loved to chat. Mid-forties, freckle-faced, outgoing, with a great sense of humour, Celia's face usually wore a rather patronizing and sardonic look. I soon came to understand that Celia was a fighter, a staunch NDP advocate and justice-seeker, extremely up-to-date and well-versed on the politics of the day. My fellow patients and I learned to avoid mentioning anything within Celia's earshot that could remotely be construed as political. Because like Forrest Gump's box of chocolates, you never knew what you were gonna get as the topic of one of Celia's rants. Celia often outdid herself at ward meetings, held regularly to decide what to do on activities night, or to resolve situations that inevitably developed on the ward. Mrs. G attended these meetings by default, still seated in her usual place, facing the windows. No one else ever occupied that spot while Mrs. G was on the ninth.

Philippe was a shy, anxious young man. Tall, average build, with light brown hair, hazel eyes, and a pleasant manner, he wasn't very talkative. He listened intently, though, which worked for me and others on the ward. For some reason, as if following some unwritten and unspoken code of etiquette, I disregarded my natural curiosity and refrained from asking about the all-too-noticeable blisters on his hands. Philippe was a compulsive hand-washer with OCD, and he often sat at the same table as me during lunch hour. Sometimes I think of Philippe and wonder how he's doing.

I never knew the Dutchman's first name, but he was some type of doctor, a medical professional probably in his forties – his hair had started greying. An attractive man with a suntanned complexion, Doc, as we called him, loved to measure. I could watch him for long periods of time, carefully assessing the exact dimensions of the windows and parts of the south wall, using some type of carefully calculated measuring tape, invisible to all but him. He'd periodically remove his glasses and conscientiously make sure they were clean before continuing. He behaved as if lives depended on his accuracy, and perhaps they once had. Doc had a gentle manner and was always pleasant during mealtimes. But best of all, he had a mischievous smile, a twinkle in his eye, and a sharp sense of humour.

Periodically, groups of people were brought to the ninth floor while touring the Clarke facilities. Whenever this happened, some of us under observation felt like animals at the zoo. At lunchtime one day, a well-dressed, larger-than-usual group of Clarke tourists noisily spilled out of the elevator. Doc played right along when Philippe, Eddie, and I decided to act out like really cuckoo mental patients, so the onlookers would have a story to tell the folks when they got home. As if we had an invisible director to choreograph the shenanigans, we spontaneously began to exaggerate odd gestures and movements, and to say nonsensical things in loud voices. Doc caught on right away and started measuring the table, then his own cutlery, and then ours as we were eating, which was pretty damn funny, and set us off into gales of uncontrollable laughter.

Eddie. How to talk about Eddie. Young, early twenties, sullen, dark-haired, and good-looking, especially when slightly unshaven. At times he'd go without his horn-rimmed glasses, but didn't look as good. Maybe because he had to squint to see anything. Eddie often wore plaid shirts with non-matching plaid Bermuda shorts. It wouldn't be right to call Eddie odd. We were all odd, there at the Clarke. But I never knew his back story. Eddie wasn't the kind of guy you could ask, and I must have sensed that. We got along like a house on fire, encouraging one another to get into trouble.

We were volleyball and badminton buddies at the Clarke gym, Eddie and I. We'd also spend lots of time together in what we called the music room, because it had a stereo turntable, amplifier, and speakers. That is, until Eddie's anger exploded one day and he started throwing things around. I got out in the nick of time, before he destroyed the turntable, the amp, and some of the furniture.

After this outburst, hospital staff had to accompany all patients in the music room, which kind of sucked the fun out of listening to music and dancing. Afterwards, Eddie and I didn't hang out as much, and with good reason. Certainly I was afraid of his potential violence and brute strength, but Eddie was so drugged up he wasn't much fun to be around anymore.

If you're thinking I needed an attitude adjustment about being at the Clarke, because my focus appeared to be on having fun instead of getting well, you'd be mistaken. Sometimes it was fun, especially at the beginning, when I'd emotionally regressed to a very young age. But as I began to improve and became more acquainted with reality, being at the Clarke turned out to be less and less fun. But as long as I was there, I might as well make the best of it.

Lurch was another heavily drugged individual on the ninth, an immigrant from one of the Slavic countries. That's not his real name, of course, but describes how he lumbered along, never really present. Lurch must have been well over six feet tall, broad-shouldered, with short dark hair and a lost look. I'd watch this giant totter down the hall, eyes facing downward, head slightly bent forward as if steering the rest of his heavy-set body towards some unspecified destination. Walking around and around, up and down the halls. That's what he did most of the time. He'd slide one foot slowly in front of the other, arms hanging loosely at his sides, looking for something he didn't expect to find. I'm not sure if he even spoke English. I was afraid of Lurch, so I always kept my distance.

Then there was Andrew, the engineer, a somewhat uptight man in his fifties, always immaculately groomed and always in buttoned-down plaid shirts buttoned-up tight to his neck. I think he was at the Clarke for manic-depression, now called bipolar disorder, because he was a little wired at times. Andrew and I had very little in common, so our interaction was minimal. But he was a strong presence on the ward.

One day, I'd left my door open as I puttered around on the floor in my room re-potting a plant. The leftover dirt and water had coalesced into a rich muddy mess, and served as the base for my floor sculpture. Several cherry tomatoes and a few colourful, non-edible objects were skewered on my knitting needles and artfully arranged on the muddy foundation. My lovely creation must have had some meaning at the time, everything usually did, but if so, I've forgotten. The nurses were keeping me under observation, and were well aware of my activities. But the nurses weren't my only observers.

That day, out of the corner of my eye, I spotted Andrew strut past my room several times, staring in disbelief at the muddy mess I was making. I tried to ignore him, but he couldn't resist. On what was to be his final lap, he stopped momentarily and derisively proclaimed, "Cleanliness is next to godliness." I immediately shouted back, "God created dirt too!" And that was my sole personal interaction with Andrew.

Linda was a pretty girl, a few years younger than me, with long blond hair, blue eyes, and a great figure. I think she ran away from a super-strict Christian home for girls on Dundas Street, opposite the Art Gallery of Ontario. I remember going there with her at one point, but I don't know why she had to live there in the first place. Linda would sometimes join Eddie, me, and occasionally Philippe in the music room, before Eddie ruined it. I think Linda got pregnant while at the Clarke, and then moved to another floor. Apart from being close in age and both at the Clarke, we had little else in common.

One woman on the ward was even more beautiful than Linda. Vivian was a petite woman in her thirties, with thick, long auburn hair and very blue eyes. I'd been instantly attracted to her husband when he came to visit one day, and traipsed down the hall after him. That's how I met her. When I learned she was an actress, for real, I was impressed. Viv was very intense, even more than me, and twice as dramatic, which is saying something. Everything was exaggerated. When Viv told a story, even a mundane one about shopping, it was drama higher than a Shakespearean tragedy. I befriended Viv, whom I found fascinating. She had a kind heart and a terrible upbringing, one that made my problems with Bob and Shirley seem puny by comparison. Yes, comparisons are stupid. I didn't know that then.

Eventually Viv and I grew apart. But I was still fond of her. As mentioned earlier, we bumped into each other at the No Frills supermarket soon after I started this book in 2000. Shocking how frail and grey she looked, but still beautiful, even in her seventies. That was the last time I saw her. A recent Google search brought sad news. Vivian had died a few years later.

Then there was Margaret, probably in her late twenties. She was neither particularly beautiful nor an actress, but she was really smart and extremely interesting to listen to, no matter what she said. It wasn't easy to divert my attention away from the gibble-gabble or my soliloquies, but Margaret had a charm about her that drew people in. I think she was at the Clarke for depression, but I'm not sure.

Margaret held her cards close and rarely divulged any personal information that couldn't be gleaned from a job application. I was a good listener, regardless, and that may be how I ended up sharing an apartment with her at the end of January 1968. More about that later.

I've saved the best till last. Diana (that's her real name) became a true friend, and I loved her dearly. She was perhaps in her mid- to late thirties, but would often refer to herself as an old married broad, which sounded funny in her British accent. We shared a birthplace and a wacko sense of humour. Diana was petite, with a slender build, short brown hair, hazel eyes, and a wicked grin. Her husband, Joe, loved her beyond measure.

After I gained weekend privileges, this lovely couple took me home for weekends and special holidays like Thanksgiving and Christmas to spend time with their three children: a teenage daughter, Jenny, and two little boys named John and Michael. They became my surrogate family, and we usually had a blast, as Diana would say. She suffered from deep depression, and I know she worked hard at getting better.

Diana didn't like to talk much about her upbringing, and I didn't press her. My sense is that she was badly abused. I think her treatment at the Clarke helped her a lot. Over the years, we gradually lost touch, but sometimes I think about her fighting spirit and wonder if she's still around. I've tried to track her down via the Internet, but haven't had any luck yet.

Remnants

Every so often, odd memories surface from my time at the Clarke, as clear as if they happened only a few weeks ago. Here are some of the more vivid ones, in no particular order.

Group Therapy

On several weekday mornings, I noticed people filing into a room at the end of the hall, to the right of the elevators. I thought it was group therapy and decided to attend. By the time I arrived one morning, barefoot and decked out in my pink-and-white polka-dot robe, everyone was seated at little desks, arranged in a semi-circle around the room. At the front, a male doctor was talking so I found a place to sit and tried to contribute to the conversation. I had many questions to ask and many opinions to express. I was asked, however, to wait my turn. My repeated interruptions made the doctor promise to let me speak at ten to eleven. He made sure I knew how to tell time, reiterating that I could speak when the big hand was on the ten, and the little hand was on the eleven! Annoyingly condescending, but then, I *was* behaving like a child. So I waited. And waited. And kept my gaze glued to the hands on that clock.

I heard nothing else he said. Group therapy had turned out to be a big, useless bore. The big hand inched closer to the ten, and then, bang, it hit the ten right on! But the doctor didn't stop to give me my turn. He went on and on. Someone else added their two cents' worth, which was more like 25 cents. Then, the big hand moved past the eleven and I'd missed my turn!

Clearly, a promise had been made and broken, a major anger trigger. I wasn't going to get a chance to speak. So I stood up in a huff, marched to the door, yanked it open, and stomped through the doorway. With all the energy I could muster, I slammed that door shut. So much for group therapy.

But it wasn't group therapy. It was probably a lecture or training for hospital staff, who were kind enough to let me sit in (and not listen).

TBA

While glancing through a radio or TV guide in the lounge one day, I noticed the initials "TBA" beside one timeslot. This was an acronym, I subsequently learned, for "to be announced." Thinking that this was the name of a new talent show, I decided that I would like to be announced. I managed to find a CBC phone number, called from the ninth-floor pay phone, and asked to speak to the producer or someone who worked on the TBA program. Surprisingly, someone took the call. I told the man I wanted to be announced, and that I was calling from the Clarke Institute where I'd put myself in order to lose weight. I also told him I couldn't come to see him because I wasn't allowed off the ninth floor unaccompanied.

It must have been a slow news day, because this man actually came to see me. Probably out of curiosity. I've no idea what his job entailed. He could have been a producer, a writer, a researcher, or even the coffee guy. I can still picture him sitting in my room near the nursing station. Early thirties, medium height and build, bright blue eyes, and light brown curly hair framing his round cherubic face. Soft- spoken. And nervous, very nervous. He wore a suit, white shirt, and tie underneath his trench coat, which he kept on the whole time. He did, however, remove his glasses and then put them on again, a routine he repeated frequently throughout our discussion. Maybe it calmed him. He said something about a relative in a mental hospital, which is possibly why he showed up. I recall nothing else we talked about or if I sang for him. But I was never announced.

Comfortable with Themselves

I wrote to David X on my portable manual typewriter, part of the haul Jerry retrieved from my apartment. In my room across from the nursing station, I set up a little office with a make-do desk, probably borrowed from one of the small staff-training rooms. I distinctly remember spending a lot of time on this particular letter, deemed highly important.

I told David I was at the Clarke and that I'd put myself there to lose weight and to help me sort out a few things. I explained that since I'd given up my apartment, there was lots of stuff I didn't need. Then I told him I wanted to donate it all to the kids at the youth centre where he worked and where I'd volunteered. But how to arrange this? Perhaps he could come and pick it up, or my friend Jerry could drop it off. Maybe my parents could deliver it. This last option was the one I hoped for. That way, my parents, especially my father, would get to meet David and see the kind of man I set my sights on. (I find this particularly funny now, since David X was stoned much of the time.)

The letter focused on how I felt about the kids at the youth centre. And how I identified with them, how I sensed what they really needed. And how most of those kids probably just "wanted to be comfortable with themselves." That was part of the reason I'd put myself in the Clarke, to become more comfortable with myself. That line has stayed with me all these years. Then I asked Jerry to help me repack all my stuff, ready for my father to deliver. Not surprisingly, Jerry declined. My father declined. I kept my stuff.

David X, however, said he would come to the Clarke. I don't recall whether he phoned and left a message, or whether I phoned him. Apparently he sometimes visited kids he knew on the tenth floor and said he'd stop by and see me. The date, according to Gilda's notes, was May 12, 1967. "May go for coffee with David X if he comes this afternoon."

On the appointed day, barefoot and clad in my ribbon robe, I waited impatiently in front of the elevator doors. I'd borrowed a rose from a patient's gift bouquet, generously left in the lounge for all to enjoy. I waited, clutching the stem between my teeth, but the thorns made it difficult to keep holding on. So I dropped it on the floor and guarded it zealously, lest any helpful neat freak try to pick it up. Each time the elevator stopped, I'd hold my breath until the doors opened. People got on and off, but no sign of David X.

Memory is such a curious thing, what we do and do not recall. After what had to be a crushing disappointment, I've no idea what I did or how I felt. Or even *if* I felt.

Hit the Birdie

Back in 1967, the Clarke had a really beautiful gym, in the basement, I think. It had a wooden floor and a variety of different sports equipment. I spent a lot of time there, mainly with Eddie and several others from the ninth floor. We played volleyball and badminton, and I wasn't that bad. What stands out in my memory is that when I swung the badminton racket, I actually hit the birdie most of the time. An exhilarating experience, but also quite strange. Not like the me I'd known.

I'd pretty much given up on all things athletic, thanks to Shirley and high school gym monster, Ms. P. My friends had also given up on me as a sports buddy, even before high school. Every spring, Jenny's dad set up a badminton court in her backyard. In seventh grade, Jenny invited me over to play. But because of my negative self-image and body image, I rarely, if ever, connected with that damned little birdie. I felt guilty for not being good enough or challenging enough as a badminton partner. By eighth grade, Jenny's badminton invites had stopped. She'd found other players.

And yet there I was at the Clarke gym, hitting that cute little birdie over the net time after time. The only way to explain it is that the gibble-gabble had taken a back seat for a while, and my energy was free to move and flow.

This Ain't Carnegie Hall

My hospital roaming privileges weren't reinstated until early June. Since the fire alarm incident, I'd been restricted to the ninth floor unless accompanied by approved personnel, including acceptable visitors – such as Dorothy, whom I'd met back in 1960 and who is still a dear and trusted friend. Once free to move about, I explored the Clarke basement and ground floors quite thoroughly, usually barefoot and in my ribbon robe. That's how I came across Henry, whose office was near Gilda's in the basement.

When Henry's door was open or ajar, I was welcome to stop in and chat, which I did on a fairly regular basis. I'm reminded of a line from the recent smash TV hit *Girls*,[78] when the lead character claims she's automatically interesting because she lives in New York. I felt that way with Henry. I was automatically interesting because I lived at the Clarke. He was probably an intern of some sort, for psychiatry or social work. Tall, blue-eyed, freckle-faced, with short, reddish-blond hair and horn-rimmed glasses, Henry wasn't particularly handsome, but he had a kindliness about him and a great smile. Most important, Henry knew how to listen.

My other favourite place was discovered by accident during my basement meanderings. To my great delight one day, I came upon an empty theatre. It had a stage bordered by hanging curtains and stage lights, plush seats for the audience, and other theatrical accoutrements. I don't recall if this auditorium had a balcony or not, but it wouldn't have mattered.

One of my strongest Clarke memories: I would plunk myself down front and centre on that stage floor, sit cross-legged in a meditative pose, and gaze out across the empty seats, imagining. Just imagining.

If you guessed I pictured myself doing anything musical or theatrical, you'd be mistaken. Instead, I'd envision the theatre seats filled with doctors, psychiatrists, psychologists, administrators, nurses, and others who worked in the mental health field.

And I'd have this distinguished audience in the palm of my hand, listening attentively to my lectures and learning how best to treat mental patients. And how not to. In my fantasy, I drew examples from my own Clarke experiences, and my audience was enthralled and appreciative. I conducted my pretend guest-lectures at the Clarke theatre many times over the summer. One of my favourite spaces, and a place to dream.

In some anticipatory way, my fantasy address channelled the spirit of Gestalt therapy, which I later studied. The advice offered to my imaginary, well-educated but seemingly self-unaware audience was to look at themselves and recognize how their personal life experiences and psychological filters coloured their perception and ability to understand their patients. I didn't use that language, but that's what I meant and believed. I wanted them to stop judging and assuming, and to be curious about their patients.

Too much to expect? Perhaps. But not according to the Psychological Report of July 7, 1967, based on tests I completed in April and May of that year.

[Natalie] is apt to perceive situations in terms of their relevance to feelings and drives and to expect other people to perceive situations in a manner similar to her own idiosyncratic perceptions (projection).

Well, sort of. I did expect hospital staff to at least try to understand what I meant. And I felt frustrated when most, except for Gilda and a few nurses, didn't seem to want to bother. Most simply assumed they understood me, when clearly they did not.

A few years later, I noticed a record album cover with a similar picture: a young woman in a robe, sitting cross-legged on a stage floor, front and centre, wistfully gazing out into an empty auditorium. It was the pop/folk artist Melanie, whose album was recorded live at New York City's Carnegie Hall.[79] Back then, I felt like someone copied a secret part of my life. But the scene isn't that unusual. Countless hopefuls have similarly sat onstage and dreamed their future. My own would soon take an abrupt downturn.

Sex Ed

From my first night, March 31, 1967, Gilda noted:

> *Her sexual education was and is extremely inadequate. She has only dated for one brief period in college. She admits to rejecting any advances made towards her ... and contact with men has been extremely limited.*

All of the above would be an understatement. My main early source of sex education was excerpts from D.H. Lawrence's *Lady Chatterley's Lover,* which Shirley hid in her bedside night table. Jenny and I found it while snooping through my mother's things in my parents' Barker Street bedroom. We were probably in seventh grade, which is also when I learned about menstruation and other female functions in health class at Princess Margaret Junior High.

My fellow female classmates and I were instructed to put our heads down on our desks and to keep them there until women's phys-ed teacher Miss Sutton gave the word. She asked us to raise our hands if we'd already started our periods. Was this done to protect those who had their periods or those who didn't? Most likely, it was all part of the secrecy surrounding sexuality so prevalent at the time.

In the 1950s, even married couples on TV slept chastely in separate beds, and were always fully clad in their bedrooms. This context makes it a little easier to understand the special "by invitation only" event held in the school gym for girls and their mothers. Outside, the boys had all heard about it, and kept circling around the building, whispering and jeering. I never gave Shirley the invite, so she missed the screening of "Polly Grows Up," an appalling black-and-white film showing how a happy normal family handled Polly's first period. Near the end, Polly's mom tells Polly's dad that Polly is now a woman, and Polly's dad nods his head with a very creepy smile on his face. At least that's how it seemed to me. You don't have to be a Freudian to understand that I may have projected my own fear about Robert onto that film.

By eighth grade, I was fully developed physically, and wore an under-wire bra for support. Some boys in class would mumble "wi-yer" under their breaths whenever I walked by. I struggled with the mixed feelings this created, loving the attention, but too embarrassed to admit it. Feeling a little turned on by the growls and grunts, I was reluctant to openly enjoy my sexuality. Only sluts did that. At the time, I couldn't figure out what "wi-yer" meant, but assumed my breasts were the focus.

Having my body looked at was uncomfortable, and I wondered if these boys noticed how fat I was. No doubt, I ate over these impossible and disturbing feelings. The gibble-gabble's who-you- hallelujah chorus had a vocal extravaganza with this material. (Note: I actually wasn't fat in junior high – that didn't begin till high school).

Like many girls this age, I developed secret crushes on various young men, which I shared only with special girlfriends. They, however, eventually grew past the crush stage and began to have actual relationships. I was left behind – something Shirley would not let me forget. I'd listen to my friends complain about their boyfriend du jour and could never figure out why they didn't break up. Now I know I simply never heard about the good stuff – the dating, the romance, the making-out, the companionship, and so on.

I'd attend dances at the Cyanamid plant in Niagara Falls,[80] and later at the high school gym, but usually ended up decorating the wall. If perchance some young man asked me to dance to a slow song, I'd stiffen my body and hold my stomach in to make myself seem thinner. What if he could feel the girdles?

He'd know I was fatter than I looked. He might get sick with disgust at any moment, so I'd better keep a close watch for any signs of potential upchucking. When I stopped going to school dances, I wasn't really giving up too much fun.

University was a whole other ball game. Compared to now, things were pretty tame. Men and women lived in different dormitories on campus, with curfews and lots of rules about entertaining the opposite sex. Many first-year women were there to get their MRS (an old joke, but true). But not me. I was there at the State University of New York at Buffalo – SUNYAB, for short – to get away from Shirley and Bob.

One day first semester, a young man shuffled up to me during lunch in the Goodyear cafeteria.

About my height, he wasn't bad-looking in an intense kind of way. He asked to borrow a cup or something like that. When I asked what he meant, he said he needed a double-D bra, and could I lend him mine.

Shocked and humiliated, my hands couldn't stop shaking, and I dropped my lunch tray in the middle of the cafeteria. The clatter of crashing dishes stopped everything. Heads turned, people cheered and applauded. I ran out of there, unaware of the huge coffee stain down the front of my grey sweater. Through the gossip mill, I learned he was pledging a fraternity, and a double-D bra was on a long list of items to be obtained. I also heard other girls were asked for all sorts of disgusting things, like used tampons. While appalling, I'd have been much less offended by that. I felt ashamed and vulnerable, that this guy knew my bra size. From then on, I hated him, and carefully avoided going anywhere near him.

However, that was not to be. What an unpleasant surprise to find out that this crude slob had also signed up for the well-respected Julia Pardee's acting course, the only one offered second term. I couldn't leave. No memory of what I chose for my first monologue, but clear recall of his. We all watched spellbound as this guy, Ron, transformed himself into the rough-hewn Stanley Kowalski, copying one of Marlon Brando's scenes from Tennessee Williams's 1947 play, *A Streetcar Named Desire.*[81]

Ron's talent made me willing to put aside all resentment just so he and I could work together. Or perhaps I channelled those feelings during our various George and Martha scenes from Edward Albee's *Who's Afraid of Virginia Woolf.*[82] "Daddy white mouse, do you really have red eyes?"

When Ron performed, we all knew we were watching a very special raw talent, a diamond in the rough. But none of us could predict how successful Ron Silver would ultimately become in show business, winning international acclaim for his many film and TV roles.[83]

I never mentioned this at the Clarke, but Dr. B's early notes include other things I've since forgotten, like the guy I first dated freshman year.

Her first year at University ... she began talking on the telephone with what might have been the campus Casanova. She rather enjoyed this distant relationship, and this boy encouraged her to lose weight.

I do remember the Casanova guy. Larry. One of his many former girlfriends put me on the phone with him one night. I'd never met anyone like Larry before. We soon ended up talking at the end of each day, often late into the night. To be more accurate, I did more of the listening and question-asking, and he'd tell me about his dates and the women he slept with, often in great detail. I was very impressed.

Being connected to Larry in this way helped me pretend I was cool, and motivated me to stay on a rather radical diet – black coffee, Jell-O, chewing gum, and cigarettes. That's it. That's what I lived on for about six to eight weeks. Not surprisingly, I lost a ton of weight. And somehow Larry found out about it. And encouraged me. I was hoping for an ugly-duckling-turns-into-beautiful-swan romantic ending when Larry and I finally met. But things turned out a little differently.

On what was to be the last night of my Jell-O diet, I fainted in the bathtub. The combination of stress, a lot of steam from the scalding hot water, and lack of nourishment probably contributed to this fainting spell. But it scared me a lot. Being scared was a feeling I absolutely could not tolerate and denied completely. So guess what I did. I started eating, which soon turned into binge-ing. And the lost pounds came rushing back like homing pigeons returning to roost.

I was terrified of meeting Larry in person. By the time that happened, I'd regained the lost weight and then some. So our first and last in-person get-together was anticlimactic, as expected. And embarrassing.

Dr. B tended to focus more on sexuality than Gilda, perhaps because she was a psychiatrist and more steeped in Freudian the-ory. She wrote that most of my conversation the night I entered the hospital "revolved around sex" and "gay conversation." Back in 1967, the *DSM-I* classified homosexuality as a mental illness, which wasn't removed as such until 1974.[84]

Apologies to my gay friends for the political incorrectness and inappropriateness of what follows. Concerned about my lack of sexual experience, I'd started to wonder if I was gay. While I had no sexual feelings towards any females, I loved and needed the girlfriends in my life, so I figured I still had to consider the possibility. One more question for the gibble-gabble agenda. Years before, my friend Karen and I had a running joke, saying, "Lesbee on our way" as we parted, even over the phone. Today, I'm not sure what was so funny. Was our deep affection towards one another a sign of something more? This may be part of the "gay conversation" to which Dr. B referred. It may also relate to her later comments about my "immature and bizarre" sexual fan-tasies, which I so wish she'd described. I think Dr. B was con-cerned I might be gay. It turns out we were both wrong on that score.

In contrast, Gilda tended to focus on my lack of factual knowledge about sex. Her notes reflect concerns about my igno-rance of the consequences of necking and heavy petting, and mention the literature she suggested. From then on, whenever I was in doubt about sexual matters, I turned to books and other printed materials.

Bob and Shirley at the Clarke, Take 2

In mid-September 1967, Gilda summarized her sessions with my parents in one report. She explained that I was only to see my parents in her presence at bi-monthly meetings and not on my own. This plan to help me gain independence from Bob and Shirley suited me, but my mother "refused to believe" I didn't want to see her, and my father thought the hospital was using "brainwashing techniques."

Reality didn't count for either of these poor people. They had such a hard time. The hospital tried to protect me from their influence, because contact of any kind generally set me back. My medication was usually increased afterward, and the medical records repeatedly show the hospital's strict instructions not to let my parents visit me or speak to me on the phone. This might have been more effective if I'd not made what Gilda called "30 very long distance phone calls" home myself, charged to the hospital. My phone use was therefore "discontinued." I've only a vague memory of making such calls, but it shows how attached I was to Bob and Shirley.

Gilda's report then describes how resistant my parents were to "treatment," and shows she was beginning to understand what I'd been dealing with my whole life:

I found this period a difficult one to handle with Mrs. Gold presenting a great deal of resistance ... more marked than that of her husband. She was unable to take our help or explanations of her daughter's pathology, critical of the hospital, especially the fact that we were not making Natalie diet, which she felt was the solution to the problem ... she asked several questions at once, interrupting before an answer could be given and rejecting all explanations.

I found it difficult to form a relationship with her ...

When attempts were made to deal with Mrs. Gold's feel-ings ... she was unable to discuss them except to point out our faults, and asked that we tell her Natalie was better and that Natalie's behaviour was really normal for a teenager.

Yes, my mother still saw me as a teenager, despite the fact that I was over twenty-one. Gilda then focused on my father, still falling for his BS:

As time progressed, Mr. Gold was better able to under-stand and to accept his daughter's illness, and although he had responded initially as did his wife, he became more interested in the help we could give and made di-rect attempts to elicit it.

The report details my occasional weekend visits home to Barker Street, where my father seemed to accept me, and my mother continued to try to have me "lose weight and wear a gir-dle." Apparently, I was able to "cope" with Shirley's criticism and even to laugh. But as time passed and my hospital stay lengthened, my mother turned to her family in England "for sup-port and solace," and shared their opinions with Gilda about my treatment:

[Mrs. Gold] was very clear that anyone she talked to disagreed with the way we were handling Natalie on two accounts: (1) that we were not making her lose weight; (2) that we had stopped her parents from coming to see her.

Neither Bob nor Shirley could take no for an answer. They'd send various emissaries to try to reach me at the hospital. Distant cousins and old family friends I hadn't heard of for years came out of the woodwork carrying one message: my parents wanted to see me. My mother's favourite sister, Irene, even came over from England, but the hospital supported my wish not to see her. Bob and Shirley behaved as if I'd been kidnapped or joined a cult, when in fact I was always at the Clarke voluntarily and was incredibly grateful for the support. When I read through these records now, I'm amazed it took an entire hospital to keep Bob and Shirley at bay. No problem figuring out where I got my persistence.

Gilda struggled to understand why her sessions with Shirley were so difficult:

> *I have the feeling that Mrs. Gold sees in me the things she wants for her daughter, and also the things that she dislikes in her daughter, and therefore, finds our interviews very difficult. She at various times would tell me that she can't attend the next session, that she is painting the kitchen, that she is expecting guests, etc. When I accept this, and tell her I hope she will be able to make some arrangements to come, she usually turns up (except on one occasion).*

> *On the other hand, I find her constant opposition and anger very difficult to handle, and her manner very cornering ... I have not been able to establish a relationship with her, although I have been able to establish one with her husband and with the patient.*

> *I am wondering if part of Natalie's reaction to her parents is because of feelings similar to mine. I feel that part of Natalie's pathology is because she cannot meet the high demand that Mrs. Gold makes, which makes her feel guilty and unworthy.*

Bingo. It only took Gilda five months to figure Shirley out and to understand a fraction of our relationship. Quite validating. It took a while longer, though, for Gilda to catch on to my father.

CHAPTER 11: PLAN B

At the end of grade eleven, when I was sixteen, my parents decided to send me to England for the summer. This wasn't a bribe, but a gift. In part, compensation for my being rejected as a camp counsellor. But another more important motive was involved, as I was later to learn.

It was agreed I'd stay with my mother's relatives in Edgware, a North London suburb with a fairly large Jewish contingent. All but one of my aunts and uncles lived within a few blocks of each other. My parents also hoped I'd get a chance to visit some cousins of my father's, as well as his old auntie Nellie, who lived in Sheffield. I'd never heard of these people, but I was certainly willing to travel outside London. I was also going to increase my ocean liner trips by two.

The *Mauritania*, the same ship that originally carried our family to Canada in 1948, was sailing from Montreal sometime in June 1962. In the early '60s, plane travel was a luxury and rather expensive. (Jumbo jets didn't make their entrance till the end of the '60s.) But the fact that Shirley was afraid of flying was probably the biggest influence on my parents' choice of the way I travelled.

Unbelievably and without my consent, my dear father had arranged for me to deliver a small token from the Mayor of Niagara Falls to the Lord Mayor of London. Why, I'll never know. I doubt even he could explain it. And I didn't ask. Questioning Robert was simply not an option. You could complain or whine or protest – but never question. And never, absolutely never, say no; it wouldn't have even crossed my mind to do so. The arrangement was a *fait accompli*, a done deal he'd arranged with his then pal, the Mayor of Niagara Falls. And there was no way I could get out of it. None at all.

I now understand that official pomp and circumstance meant a great deal to Robert. Just thinking about this planned little event probably gave him great pleasure. His very own daughter officially representing one of the Seven Wonders of the World. Imagine that!

My father also persuaded me that since I had journalistic inclinations, I should seize the opportunity and interview the captain of the *Mauritania* – tell him how his ship had brought me to Canada years ago. What a scoop that would be. Robert figured he could use his influence at the local paper, the *Niagara Falls Evening Review,* to publish the piece if it was good enough. This is the power my father had over me. I no more wanted to interview the *Mauritania*'s captain than I wanted to jump in the ocean. But I couldn't tell my father that. I didn't have the words, I didn't have the strength, and I didn't know that what I wanted and didn't want actually mattered. Besides, how could I disappoint this man any more than I already had by being so fatandugly?

Before leaving Canada that summer, I'm not sure what I weighed, since I played games on the scale. But I do recall the size of the dresses purchased for my trip (sixteen to eighteen), brought home from the store or from one of my father's weekly excursions to Toronto's Spadina Avenue. They didn't fit on my return.

The Second *Mauritania*

My father drove me from Niagara Falls to the Montreal docks, but I've blanked out that stage of the journey. On the ship, I shared a tiny cabin with a woman in her late seventies who smothered her feet in stinky ointment several times a day.

Automatically assigned to the top berth, I couldn't sleep because the stench wafted upward, permeating the whole cabin. After a day or so, I managed to persuade the purser to move me. He switched me to a double-bunk set-up, a room for four which I shared with two thirty-something women whooping it up on a gala adventure tour to many ports of call. Far from perfect, but a definite improvement.

Dining tables were assigned on board, and at sixteen, as the youngest person travelling alone, the crew placed me at a table with a group of men and women in their early twenties, embarking on an expensive European nightclub tour. The ultimate in sophistication to me. They'd all either finished university or worked at what seemed like fascinating jobs, at least to an impressionable teenager. Their humour was quite risqué, and as a relative innocent, I often didn't get the jokes. To them, I was an out-of- place kid whose obvious lack of cool was far from the elegant, savoir-faire style to which they aspired. They enjoyed poking fun at me, much to my embarrassment.

The first night, I tried to be polite at the dinner table and asked, "Do you mind if I smoke?" One fellow's quick retort – "I don't care if you go up in flames" – generated a lot of laughter. I joined in, pretending I wasn't hurt, but I was. The ridicule reminded me of home.

As per Robert's instructions, I reluctantly arranged to interview the ship's captain, whose name was John Treasure Jones. He invited me to his cabin, making sure, I noticed, to leave the door open. He was kind and gracious, and offered me a drink from his bar, which I accepted. I wasn't used to being treated like a grown-up, and felt fraudulent, about to be exposed at any moment. He answered all my questions in full, and then mercifully it was over. In 1993, his *New York Times* obituary noted that John Treasure Jones captained the final voyage of the renowned ocean liner, the *Queen Mary,* just before he retired in 1967.[85] Too bad I never wrote up my interview, but I had other more important issues on my mind when I got home.

Before heading for Dover, England, the ship was to dock first at Le Havre, France, where my dinner-mates would disembark. For their last night on board, they planned to stay up and watch the sunrise, and didn't mind if I joined them on deck. I brought my ukulele, and we ended up singing songs and laughing our way through the evening. Even some crew members joined us, and I recall feeling all was right with the world, hopeful that perhaps with this trip my luck would change for the better. Wishful thinking.

Cold Fish and Chocolate

Arrangements had been made for me to stay with my uncle Jack, his wife Rae, and their fraternal twin sons, about five years younger than me. They lived several blocks away from the rest of the family, but within walking distance.

Once I'd settled in, it was time to meet Grandma and her reluctant caretaker, Freda, Shirley's oldest sister, whom Grandma hated. As a spinster, Freda inherited Grandma (and Grandma's house) by default. Grandma was in her mid-eighties, almost blind, and in a wheelchair. She knew who I was and kept repeating my name, as her bony fingers grasped and clawed gently at my face. Perhaps she suffered from arthritis. I didn't ask. She hadn't seen me since I was three, during Shirley's first and only return visit, when she was pregnant with my sister.

Grandma's reputation as a cold fish seemed to fit, but it was really hard to tell at that age. She talked a lot about eggs, and like a broken record, insisted on telling me what she ate for breakfast. I wondered if this preoccupation with food was simply because eating was one of the few experiences meaningful to old people.

Over the summer, I met many of my mother's relatives, most of whom were short like she was. Auntie Dora, a rather jolly free spirit, lived away from the clan outside London, and was obese most of her life. Strangely, her name never came up when Shirley tried to goad me into losing weight. Instead, Shirley fondly recalled Dora's parties and her home-made chocolate éclairs and flans. Uncle Con, the youngest brother, and the tallest one of the bunch, was married to petite Ruby, whose lilting Irish accent couldn't remove the dour look from his face. They lived across from Shirley's favourite sister, Irene, who married widower Mick and inherited his two children. Mick's irascible sense of humour was surpassed only by his extreme fits of temper.

I liked Uncle Jack a lot. He told funny stories and puffed on his pipe to make you wait for the punchline. Twinkly blue eyes and full head of wavy grey hair with grey moustache to match, Jack looked just like my grandfather, as depicted in the framed photograph always displayed in our living room.

But my favourite, as my father predicted, was Jack's wife, my beloved auntie Rae. To this day I'm grateful for her gentle spirit and loving manner. She more than anyone tamed me. Made me realize that not all adults were bossy or domineering, judgmental or condemning. That summer, I'd venture out from Rae's during the day to explore my birthplace. I loved the Old Bailey, the law courts, where I'd line up with the other thrill-seekers hoping to witness a famous murder trial from the public gallery. But as usual, reality was much less dramatic than movie or TV courtroom scenes.

As I toured London, I also discovered Cadbury's chocolate, which supplemented whatever goodies I could sneak at Auntie Rae's. My compulsion to eat was in full swing that summer. At Rae's I didn't really need to steal, because she'd have happily given me whatever I wanted, without judgment or hesitation. That's how she treated everyone she met. With loving kindness. But compulsion is by definition not subject to reason.

Not that Rae was a pushover, either. To my dismay, she absolutely refused to let me attend a "Ban the Bomb" protest march, which was to end up at Trafalgar Square. This event was supported by statesman and philosopher Sir Bertrand Russell, and I was eager to add my voice to the political fray. But Auntie Rae, afraid of crowds and mob rule, said if I tried to go out that day, she'd tie me to the bedpost. She didn't often put her foot down, so I didn't go.

Nellie and the Stain

In late July 1962, British Rail took me to Sheffield to meet my father's cousins and his auntie Nellie, a wealthy old widow in her early eighties. Nellie's mental faculties and social graces were all intact. She always wore makeup, dyed and styled her hair in a fashionable way, and dressed to kill when she went out, in fancy hats, heels, and nylon stockings. She loved her *Players* non-filtered cigarettes, which she chain-smoked for more than sixty years. If Auntie Nellie was in a movie, she'd be the kind but crusty old curmudgeon with a deep, throaty voice and hearty laugh, who always spoke her mind and never lacked for something to say.

Her husband Philip, my father's uncle, had died some years before, leaving her and her children as the wealthy owners of a silver flatware factory.[86] I'd never heard of Nellie or Philip before. I'd never heard about any of my father's relatives, for that matter, except for his sister, Auntie Hannah.

One afternoon in Nellie's dining room, I was questioning her about how Uncle Philip was related to my father. Philip and my paternal grandfather were brothers born in Poland. Philip immigrated to England around the turn of the century. When Nellie started to tell me about my father's arrival in England, I interrupted, reminding her that my father was born in London, England. "Oh," Nellie said sarcastically. "He's told you that, has he?"

Stunned, I stared in silence first at the mahogany buffet, which stretched the length of the entire wall, then at the ornate silver tea set perched on a silver tray atop the buffet. When I asked what she meant, she wouldn't say. So I pestered her some more. All Nellie admitted was that Robert had not been born in London, England, as my sister and I had always believed (and been told), and that I'd have to ask him if I wanted to know more. She'd probably said enough for now. And with that, she wouldn't budge.

Bob and Shirley had set Nellie up to do the dirty work, to tell me the truth. To tell me that they'd misled my sister and me our whole lives, and that our father was not who he said he was. It was a crushing jolt to hear such loaded information from a virtual stranger, likable though she was. The impact was so strong, its repercussions left me confused for decades to come.

It took more than twenty-five years before my parents finally owned up to their scheme to have me learn about my father's history. Plan A had been to send me to Israel, home to many of my father's cousins. Plan B was the British route, eventually chosen because I could also visit my mother's family and see my ailing maternal grandmother before she died.

They'd counted on Nellie to clue me in and to tell me much more than she did. They didn't think to warn her I was coming, or to ask if she'd mind telling me, or to let her know they *wanted* her to explain things fully. That would be too direct and too risky. What if Nellie said no? They also didn't question how the information would affect me, especially coming from a virtual stranger.

Neither plan was well thought out. But since they wanted me to know, the only other alternative was for one or both of them to tell me to my face. Totally out of the question. Impossible. It wasn't their style, it wasn't their way, and quite frankly, I suspect they didn't know how. Now, I have compassion. Then, it was a different story.

Books about Holocaust survivors suggest that information on the Holocaust to emerge during the 1960 Eichmann trials helped create a climate of public awareness and openness to this painful subject.[87] Enough time had passed since the Second World War. Loads of hideous secrets oozed up from the bowels of the earth and seeped out of the closet like sewage, as people became more willing to discuss what had long been buried, but not forgotten.

In a strange way, I experienced some admiration for my father, who now became a hero of extraordinary dimensions, a James Bond-like figure involved in espionage and subterfuge. But the overwhelming sensations were not positive. I felt deceived. Lied to and betrayed. And despite the sympathetic and dramatic circumstances, it was too much to cope with. So I turned numb. This wasn't a choice, but my usual automatic defence to being overwhelmed.

My father had been the only adult I assumed I could rely on. I say *assumed* because on some deeper level, I hadn't really trusted my father for years, not since we we'd lived in Midland, and perhaps even before that.

Trust is such a fragile element. It doesn't take much to erode it. In Midland, I ran away at the age of seven. I don't remember what made me want to leave, where I went or how far I got. I think a policeman found me wandering somewhere by myself and brought me home to my parents. The thing is, my father spanked me on the behind, one of the rare times he used physical punishment. We were in the side hall, between the kitchen and garage, where the coats hung on the wall. As he held me by one arm and whacked, he kept repeating, "Don't you ever do this to me again!" He didn't wonder why a child would want to run away from home. And he didn't ask me. In the 1950s, children had no rights. They were to be seen, but not heard.

Still in Midland, when I was eight or nine and sick in bed with a bad cold, my father brought me a cup of what he said was hot chocolate. He'd often bragged about his special remedy for colds or flu: garlic and warm milk, with a little honey to make it more palatable. Whenever he'd mention this revolting brew, our whole family, including Shirley, would turn up our noses and say, "Eww."

Before I drank the funny-smelling chocolate, I'd asked my dad if he'd put garlic in it. He assured me, no, of course not. So I drank it. Surprise! Garlic was in it, because as soon as I finished, I spewed the whole mess up on the bed, onto the nice off-white woollen blankets I remember so well. That stain never came out, in more ways than one.

When both of these incidents happened, I promptly pushed them aside, lest they interfere with the God-like image of my father I needed to maintain. Much like the parent who doesn't want to see signs of their teenager's drug use, or the cheated-on wife who ignores evidence of her husband's infidelity, I pushed these pictures of a less-than-perfect dad from my mind. That's how denial begins, and how it continues.

But at Nellie's, this new information was harder to ignore. The shock of it reeled around in my brain. I ended up staying longer in Sheffield than originally planned. But thoughtlessly neglected to let Auntie Rae know. She worried. Perhaps I'd been kidnapped on the train or fallen off a dock. She was angry, and rightfully so, at my lack of consideration. I felt mortified, guilty, and inconsolable. To think I'd offended the one person who treated me well. The one person who was loving to me. Of course, Auntie Rae forgave me, but I couldn't forgive myself. My father had been the one I'd clung to, mistakenly or not, throughout my life. And now his reliability and trustworthiness was consciously in question.

What had been just an occasional friend, Cadbury's, became my constant companion for the duration of my visit to England.

Insincerity Times Two

I was supposed to return to Canada at the end of August, but I ended up staying in England a few weeks longer, because I didn't want to go home. I didn't want to go anywhere or be anywhere. Like a true procrastinator, I'd also put off making the appointment at the Mansion House, the Lord Mayor of London's residence,[88] hoping for some way to get out of doing what I didn't want to do. The illusion is that if you ignore something, it might disappear. If you don't think about it, it doesn't exist. But of course, like all illusions, this isn't the case.

Begrudgingly I contacted the Mansion House and managed to secure an appointment during the second week of September. Fortunately, the last ocean liner voyage was scheduled to depart Dover several days later and I was able to switch my reservations.

Looking back at it now, my official visit to the Lord Mayor of London was an exercise in insincerity. Imagine two people as different as can be, both reluctantly playing out roles they'd rather not, saying things they don't mean, and wishing they were elsewhere.

The gentleman who greeted me, one of the Lord Mayor's countless assistants, had a very fancy title and one of those moustaches that curl up slightly at the sides. He was tall and wore a grey, pin-striped three-piece suit, with a pocket watch, which he periodically removed from its little pouch in his buttoned-up vest to check, I suspect, how much longer our appointment was to last. (Picture a straitlaced version of comic actor John Cleese, of Monty Python fame, and you'd be close.)

My outfit: a black dress with a pleated skirt that was too tight and didn't button up properly in front, so I kept my somewhat grungy reversible raincoat on the whole time. Not what you'd call elegant.

Mr. Assistant escorted me around the mansion, explaining the history and architecture of the various rooms available to persons like myself. What has stayed in my mind is the sculpted white plaster ceiling. I had absolutely no interest in this topic, but asked questions out of politeness and dutifully pretended to be fascinated. After all, I couldn't disgrace Niagara Falls.

Finally, I handed over my little token to the Lord Mayor's assistant during tea, which was served on a scalloped silver tray in one of the many dining rooms. We made painfully polite conversation reminiscent of an Oscar Wilde play, amusing only in retrospect, until our time together, mercifully, came to an end.

Don't Ask, Never Tell

The weather at sea in mid-September 1962 turned horrid shortly after we left England. With cold winds and high seas, passengers were forbidden to go on deck. Instead, they did their throwing up inside, so everyone could eventually join in. Vomit is a contagious event.

Let's just say the voyage home had both comic and nightmarish overtones. But for me, this ocean crossing would have been an ordeal even if the skies had been sunny and the waters calm.

I didn't want to go back to that house in Niagara Falls. I'd gained a lot of weight and most of my clothes didn't fit. I had to wear a jacket to cover up the gaps in my clothes caused by buttons or fasteners that wouldn't do up. At the end of the summer, in the midst of a rather sophisticated London party an older cousin brought me to, I'd managed to split open the zipper all the way down the back of my white linen sheath dress (the one worn to the appointment with the Welland psychiatrist). I couldn't decide if this was more humiliating than what happened at summer camp several years earlier, when I plummeted through the attic floor into the kitchen below.

The whole time on board, I worried what Shirley would say when she saw me, and how to face my father when he picked me up in Montreal. My stomach was in knots.

When I walked off the boat, I literally had tuppence (two British pennies) to my name. My father made a joke of this as we left Montreal. I don't recall much of the drive after that. We both stared a lot at moving cars on the highway as we sped along. "Did you see Nellie?" "Yes." "Did she tell you?" "Sort of." "What did she say?" "That you weren't born in England." Silence. "That's all, that's all she said?" "Yes."

I managed to ask if it was true, and he nodded his head yes. I couldn't ask any more, not then. And he couldn't say any more. Not then. Not ever. He never really told his story, not the whole story. My sister and I got various bits and pieces over the years, but for the most part, Robert took his secrets with him to his grave.

One other thing I remember from that ride home: I asked my father if he loved my mother. "Do you love Mommy?" When I look back, it seems like an incredible question for a sixteen-year-old to ask her father, especially at that time, with the explosive new information I'd learned about his past. Perhaps it was a diversionary tactic. He mumbled his reply, which had something to do with "when a mother suckles a child at her breast." I have no idea what he was trying to say. But as soon as I heard the word "breast" I tuned out. It was too much, too sexual a reference for sure. All I knew for sure was he didn't say yes right away. He didn't really love my mother, at least not the way he used to, and he wasn't really who he'd professed to be. Anything else was inconsequential.

That night in the kitchen of the Barker Street house, Bob and Shirley told me just a little more. My father did the talking, as my mother sat beside him, in her usual spot. I avoided my usual spot opposite him. Instead I sat beside him, in my sister's seat, facing my mother.

During my father's brief story, I couldn't face him, so I stared intermittently at the kitchen sink and the window above. He'd left Poland as a young man, when he realized that Hitler was going to invade the country and that he'd be drafted into the Polish army. His two older brothers had previously fled, one to Russia and the other to what is now Estonia. His parents refused to leave with their little girl, my aunt Hannah.

My father ended up in England, having entered the country as an illegal immigrant with forged papers proclaiming his current identity. It wasn't a mere name change, but an entire fictional past he'd had to create. Eventually he met my mother, married, and I knew the rest.

Then came the warnings. I must never tell anyone about this. Ever. It could be dangerous. People mustn't know. I had to promise, on my honour. On my word of honour. It was important to say nothing. Of course, I promised. He said the secret was necessary because you never knew. You just never knew what might happen. "They" couldn't torture me for information if I knew nothing in the first place. Who were "they"? You never knew who "they" might be. So you had to be careful. Very careful. The less I knew, the better off I was, said Robert, whose history remained an unspoken mystery from that moment on.

Now I do know a bit more and understand that he didn't want to talk about it because it was simply too painful. I can't even imagine the guilt he felt at leaving his parents and sister behind in Poland. They call it survivor's guilt, which I learned about several decades later at one of Dr. Henry Fenigstein's workshops for Holocaust survivors and/or their children. There, over the course of a few months, I safely revealed the big secret I'd been lugging around so many years. What a relief to say the words, to unburden myself of this painful knowledge and finally tell my little scraps of story, and be heard.

Hannah in a Nutshell

Talking about the impact of the Holocaust on my family in Dr. Fenigstein's workshop freed me to ask questions whenever the opportunity arose. Many years later, Hannah filled in some of the blanks about what happened to my paternal grandparents.

In the middle of the night, German soldiers stormed through the small town outside of Lodz (pronounced *woodj*), Poland, forcibly yanked my grandparents and their twelve-year-old daughter out of their home, and dumped them into a ghetto area in Lodz itself with many other Jewish families. My grandfather was quickly separated from his wife and daughter and never seen or heard from again.

Hannah and her mother lived with some cousins in an attic room until September 10, 1942, the day the Germans took her mother away. That date is etched on her brain. After earning her keep with various ghetto families, young Hannah was eventually shipped by train to Bergen-Belsen, originally a prisoner transit camp but ultimately an extermination centre. The Nazis took her to a building and put her to work alongside other captive women, most of them older than Hannah.

Over the next few years, until the war ended, my aunt slaved as a factory worker in different locations, often forced to walk from one camp to another, even in the winter. She remembers the long trek from Bergen-Belsen in northern Germany to the infamous Auschwitz concentration camp in southern Poland, a distance of about 450 miles.

Hannah's life was saved countless times by the kindness of strangers and people who befriended her. She recounts stories like these in her *Shoah* video, and occasionally reveals little snippets to me during our phone conversations.

Pants on Fire

Throughout our childhood, my sister and I were unable to extract even innocent facts about our father's early life. Even his boyhood school experiences were not up for discussion. Taboo. But when he reached his mid-seventies, he became willing to reveal a little bit more about his past.

Robert left Poland on a merchant marine ship (arranged for by my grandfather, according to Hannah) and spent several years on board learning to speak English before landing in England. I have no idea how he acquired his name. He tried to locate his uncle Philip, Nellie's husband, to no avail.

Ultimately, he found work in London as a furrier, having trained as such in Paris when he first left home as an older teen.

Finally, Robert discovered Philip in Sheffield. But this extremely wealthy uncle refused to lend him money to help his parents get out of Poland. At this point, the Nazis had confiscated everything, and my paternal grandparents were penniless and wanted to leave. By the time my father saved up enough to help them, it was too late. I could only imagine the guilt my father must have felt, along with his contempt for Nellie's rich, stingy husband.

Robert's false papers were good enough to fool the British army, who may have turned a bit of a blind eye, given the wartime circumstances and the need for healthy young men, especially those who were multilingual. Robert soon became a sergeant in the British Military Police. I've still got photos of him in his uniform. During the war, he served in India and the Middle East, in places like Bahrain and what was then called Persia (now

Iran). He also said he'd worked for the Israeli underground, the Hagannah, while stationed in the area as a British soldier, but didn't elaborate on that.

His official history, the version fed to me and my sister, was that he was born in London, England, in 1914, and had lived in Palestine with his family for years, which supposedly helped explain his slight European accent.

Back in the autumn of 1962, it was up to me to tell my twelve-year-old sister the truth about our father. As she lay in her bed, I whispered across to her that Daddy wasn't really Robert Gold. After her initial shock and disbelief, my baby sister cried herself to sleep. I hadn't cried about it. Not one tear. I had, for the most part, stopped feeling altogether, except for a general sense of dread. I had to face school. And I was fatter than before, as Shirley unhappily pointed out when I arrived home from Montreal. I could see her profound disappointment as I kissed her hello on the front porch of the Barker Street house.

Fast forward to 2001, when Hannah told me during a visit to New York City that the image I had of Uncle Philip as a miserly penny-pincher couldn't be further from the truth. He didn't refuse to help my paternal grandparents leave Poland, nor did he refuse financial aid to my father. My father simply never asked. It was at that point that I realized the futility of trying to understand the lies my father told.

CHAPTER 12: REALITY ORIENTATION

Don't Wear Red

My father visited the Clarke once on his own, on May 3, 1967, about six weeks after my admission. It was a Wednesday, usually reserved for his weekly buying expeditions on Spadina. He met first with Gilda, then came to see me. This is one of my most enduring memories of my Clarke experience. He entered my room and sat alongside my bed as I huddled fetus-like under the covers. Suddenly, he began to sob. Like spontaneous combustion, I exploded, as if someone had prodded me with a hot poker. "Don't come crying to me!" I screeched. "Go to your wife!"

And then I began to wail, shocked at what came out of my mouth. That I'd said those words. More shocked that they felt true. I could sense my outrage, which made me cry even harder. Tears of fury. Tears of relief. Of self-pity. And disgust. I was the one in the hospital. I was the one who was crazy. The one needing comfort. But there he was, expecting me to comfort and reassure him. I'd forgotten. That's how it had always been.

Looking back at that scene, I wonder what would have happened if I'd just been able to let my father cry, for however long he needed. Would that have eased the burdens of his past or helped alleviate his guilt over so many things, my hospitalization included? Probably not.

That was one of the few times I'd ever seen my father lose control. I guess he felt safe with me.

The problem, or one of them, was that I didn't feel safe with him. I knew this on an unconscious level, but I dared not think it or acknowledge it.

At first, Gilda was also bamboozled by Robert. Especially when he told her he'd investigated the Clarke and learned it was "the best treatment centre in the country." Gilda liked that. She also liked that he asked for help in his dealings with me and seemed able to accept advice.

But here's a little tidbit about Robert. Usually, his true feelings more closely mirrored those of my mother. He was simply smarter than Shirley in how he dealt with people. He became "more supportive" of the Clarke because opposition wasn't working. He stopped asking Gilda and Dr. Shugar to write a letter to his doctor outlining my diagnosis, because they refused; since I was over twenty-one, my parents had no legal right to my records. He showed he could be reasonable and that he understood the situation, which was probably true to a limited extent. But this was his pattern. He'd appear to be giving in, to be on board, when he was simply saying what was expedient. I learned to do the same at the foot of this master. Gilda wrote:

> ...*In September, Mr. Gold was able to tell me, privately, that his wife did not respect me, although he did. I encouraged him to help his wife to say this in a joint session because perhaps in this way I might be able to help Mrs. Gold express her feelings toward me directly. I also feel I was the least threatening member of the team to whom he might express the feeling.*

No, no, no. This behaviour of my father's had nothing to do with Gilda being non-threatening, and everything to do with Robert's constant need to be in control.

In typical fashion, my father, by revealing Shirley's feelings to a third person, created a collusion, a secret between him and Gilda, a secret that Shirley had shared with him. Guess who was at the centre of this secret. My dad. This is how Robert retained power. This is what he'd do with me. He'd tell me something about my mother, then insist I never let her know he'd told me. Collude, triangulate, divide, and conquer.

It took almost another year before Gilda got an accurate handle on Bob. This isn't so bad, considering it's taken me the better part of a lifetime to process my own relationship with this dear but complex and troubled man. Here's what she wrote in her case summary at the end of May 1969 (when I was officially discharged from the outpatient department):

Father tried to act as if he was more liberal, but his not too well hidden horror of mental illness, in spite of his position in mental health organizations ... continually came to the fore. For example, one day when I wore a red dress, he said that mental patients should not be exposed to red...

The patient is working out unresolved Oedipal strivings with her father and is quite angry with him for ignoring mother in favour of her all her life. We saw many indications of his provocative behaviour to Natalie and his excluding his wife while she was in hospital.

Still difficult to accept. Validating, in a sad, wish-it-wasn't-so way, knowing it was so. And yet still uncertain what lessons I've learned from my father. From the subtle impact of this war vet, this tortured soul, who suffered from inner demons, untold secrets, and probably from PTSD.

Shift that Paradigm

The summer of 1967, a.k.a. the "summer of love," ushered in the flourishing hippie movement to the sound of the Beatle's chart-topping album *Sgt. Pepper's Lonely Hearts Club Band.*

Across North America, a culture change was well underway. In Monterey, California, the first- ever rock festival (the Monterey Pop Festival) featured an astounding lineup of now legendary rock performers and international icons, the soundtrack of my life. Performers included Simon and Garfunkle, Big Brother and the Holding Company (with Janice Joplin), Laura Nyro, Jefferson Airplane, Otis Redding, Buffalo Springfield (with David Crosby), the Who, Ravi Shankar, the Grateful Dead, the Mamas and the Papas, and Jimi Hendrix, who set his guitar on fire, but not for the first time. That happened on March 31, 1967, (the date I entered the Clarke) in London, England (my birthplace). Coincidence? Not really. But curious nonetheless.

Other passions also burned bright during this period of protests against the Vietnam War and against the numerous manifestations of racism. Race riots erupted in a long list of American cities.[89] But by summer's end, interracial marriage was no longer a federal crime in the US, and Thurgood Marshall became the first African American US Supreme Court Justice.

As a young Bob Dylan sang, "The times they are a-changin." And they were. On the international scene, the Six-Day War between Israel and a host of Middle Eastern states began and theoretically ended (but is still sadly far from over). The first global satellite TV program was broadcast from space. And *"Vive le Québec libre!"*, French President Charles de Gaulle's salute to separatism during his Montreal visit, created quite a ruckus.

Here in Canada, Centennial celebrations included Expo 67 – the Montreal World's Fair – and the very first Caribana Festival in Toronto. Centennial organizers couldn't have planned the 1967 Stanley Cup games any better if they'd tried. When the Toronto Maple Leafs beat the Montreal Canadiens that summer, the city's hockey fans went wild. But hockey wasn't the only drama playing out in Toronto streets.

Yorkville's counterculture scene flourished, with young artists, folksingers, poets, and other creative types streaming in from across North America, including many American draft dodgers. Coffee houses such as the Riverboat, the Penny Farthing, and the Mynah Bird gave opportunities to both the known and unknown to be heard.

To offset the public's perceptions of the Yorkville crowd as hippies and druggies and vagrants, an activist group, the Diggers, organized a peaceful love-in at Queen's Park on May 22, 1967. Over 5000 people attended, with performances by Leonard Cohen and Buffy Saint Marie, among others.[90] The Diggers also staged a series of events in late August: a sit-in on Yorkville Avenue to publicize closing the street to traffic, a love-in at Queen's Park the next day to celebrate the release of the fifty arrested protesters, and a sleep-in at Toronto City Hall several days after that.[91]

All this and more was part of the paradigm shift taking place on the continent. And of course, you know where I was during all the goings-on. At the Clarke, having to deal with what the hospital records referred to as a "reality orientation." The question is, whose reality?

Potential

For the staff at the Clarke, reality apparently meant following recommendations based on the tests I'd done in April and May, when I was out of it. Here's part of the report's conclusion:

> *...One sees Miss Gold's difficulty as basically some kind of affective state with apparently paranoid-like overtones and some apparently sub-manic loss of control.*
>
> *Situations provoke emotional responses to the exclusion of other responses, and affect interferes with intellectual controls.*

If this meant that I was emotional, mistrustful, and overreacted without thinking, then I'd have to agree.

I don't know how my sister turned out to be so level-headed. I seemed to have absorbed and copied both ends of the emotional spectrum exemplified by Shirley and Bob. Like my father, I automatically repressed and pushed away feelings. Like my mother, I acted out all over the place. (Note: acting out is a way to avoid feeling the actual feeling; the energy is focused on the drama or the misbehaviour, while the real emotion and pain isn't dealt with.) None of that behaviour involves honest acceptance of feelings, or managing or regulating them. Shirley let it all out, Robert kept it all in, and I ate mine. Thus disowned, unfelt and unexplored, my feelings ran me, not the other way around.

As for the paranoid-like overtones, it isn't paranoia if suspicions are based on reality (there's that word again). The truth is, I didn't trust most of the Clarke authorities, who I felt didn't understand me.

With a few exceptions, the notes verify that they didn't. Some tried, without success. I didn't even understand myself. We were all handicapped by the gibble-gabble.

When you grow up in a chaotic household, you become vigilant for signs of pending trouble. Everything that happens must be interpreted and figured out so you know where you stand, so you can anticipate and solve potential problems. Too much confusion can be unbearable. In my case, I turned to the gibble-gabble to help sort things out. Unfortunately, the gibble-gabble created more confusion than it solved, as I struggled to understand my experiences. Gilda again:

> *On the present tests she is not overtly psychotic but shows considerable psychotic potential. Because of the strong possibility of a chronic psychosis developing, therapeutic treatment would seem advisable, but of a highly supportive kind rather than a depth approach.*

Translation: I could become a long-term wacko. So, better to provide support instead of exploring my many conflicting issues more deeply. Apart from Auntie Rae's kindness, I'd never had support and definitely needed it. But I also needed the depth approach.

> *Although Miss Gold did not complete a vocational interest test, some suggestions can be made on the basis of other information. A job with a small company or involving contact with few people and not too much responsibility would be less threatening to her. For instance, a librarian assistant, lab technician assistant, or worker in a theatrical supply company.*

Since I'd refused to take a vocational interest test, this became the Clarke plan to help me get back on my feet. I'd been assessed as not too bright and unable to carry much responsibility, and so was streamlined into work to match this diagnosis. A diagnosis based on tests taken under the unmentioned influence of liquid cosh (British slang for chlorpromazine, an antipsychotic).

Imagine how confusing this must have been. On the one hand, a lifetime of Bob, Shirley, and plenty of teachers pumping me full of notions that I was bright and could be anything I wanted, *if* I put my mind to it and *if*, according to Shirley, I lost weight. Two potential-blocking *if*s. But at least potential featured in a future scenario.

On the other hand, official tests by mental health experts encouraged me to set my sights much, much lower. Without potential. I was facing what seemed like a bleaker future than I'd ever envisioned.

Whose Reality?

Since my arrival at the Clarke at the end of March 1967, the focus was to get me able to function in society. That meant a steady job and not blaming my parents. Here's how Dr. B explained it in her June 29 report:

> *A long stay has been planned with an effort toward reality orientation and to help her see the defences that she uses, typically of placing the blame for her failure outside herself and her poor self-image, which she defends against with rather grandiose ideation, that of becoming a great dramatic actress or folksinger. She has begun to work on the unreality of such thoughts.*

Reality orientation, grandiose ideation, and the unreality of such thoughts: phrases that belong in the category Things that Make Me Sigh. I feel stuck when I read them.

The counterculture was just beginning in the mid- to late 1960s, but mainstream show business reflected the conservatism of the times. Since I was far from conventional, I can understand how my creative aspirations would seem absurd to the Clarke staff. With the wholesome TV show *Your Pet, Juliette*[92] on CBC, and the mellow Anne Murray as the next up-and-coming Canadian singing star, my music industry chances were seen as below zero.

Actually, it was Shirley who gave me the acting career idea. "You're such a little actress," she'd say. Ever since I was a young child. "Really, Natalie, you should be on the stage." She was probably referring to my penchant for dramatic delivery, developed to capture and hold her attention for longer than a few seconds in the hope she might actually listen to me or hear me. Or as a distraction from one of her harangues. As one of the very few non-critical comments she uttered, I took it in, savoured it, and imagined myself in fabulous theatrical productions. If I mentioned this aspiration at all, however, I was treated with less-than-silent disdain. Acting was not a suitable career for someone such as myself (that is, fatandugly). The contradiction was confusing, but so were many other things. Eventually I stopped talking about a future as an actress. But I didn't stop thinking about it. And along with countless acting fantasies, it, too, became part of the gibble-gabble.

Dr. B, however, was correct about grandiose ideation. If you're okay with yourself, you don't need to puff yourself up into something you're not. A person who behaves in a grandiose way usually has a poor self-image, which is something I shared with other addicts, whatever the substance of use or abuse.

In Alcoholics Anonymous, grandiosity is seen as a major negative character trait (along with many others, such as resentment, fear, and self-will). When you lack control over your impulses, you can't sustain such an ongoing assault to your integrity and value without trying to counteract it in some way. So you create a fantasy to help you survive, which becomes the go-to place whenever you feel like a nothing or a nobody. You tell yourself one day you'll be great at something. And you pretend you already *are* great at it. And you hold on to the notion that as soon as you get your act together vis-à-vis the substance or behaviour, this fantasy will become a reality. *Snap!* Just like that!

My fantasies of greatness functioned as an organizing principle. They kept me going, gave me hope.

But at the Clarke, acting, music, and creativity as ultimate options were simply dismissed, discouraged, stomped on. No one suggested I find sustainable work and pursue creative dreams in my free time. I would have remembered something that important.

The mere idea of getting a job, with all the meaningless tasks it implied, was enough to drive me to commit a violent act in the hospital. I distinctly remember a male doctor in a white lab coat lecturing me in my room on the virtues of steady work. By this time, my ninth-floor location had changed to a spot at the south end of the hall, overlooking College Street, far from the elevators and the watchful eyes of the nurses.

Dr. McLabcoat's speech was drawing to an end. He leaned forward, looked me straight in the eye, and gleefully conveyed the bad news. "Natalie," he said, "it's time you got a decent job!" That was the moment the gibble-gabble stopped. As if some automatic switch had been turned on, I sprang into action. I jumped up from my perch on the bed and stormed out of my room. Barefoot and in my beige floral muumuu, I stomped along the hallway towards the lounge. Without thinking, I marched over to a pile of dinner plates on one of the dining tables, grabbed the top one and hurled it against the south wall. *Crash!*

Fortunately, I was an incompetent plate-hurler. My missile hit the floor with a loud clamour, missing the TV by several feet. And satisfying as the sound was, I felt shocked at this impulsive and destructive act. Just like everyone else in the lounge area that afternoon.

I kept muttering that I didn't want a decent job. To this day, I don't know if I reacted so strongly to the word "decent" (so reminiscent of Shirley) or to the word "job." Clearly, both were triggers, which when combined, were intolerable. Bits of the nonsense refrain from the song "Get a Job" played in my head – "Yip yip yip yip, mum mum mum mum" – over and over again.[93]

From then on, my mood grew more sombre, and an unwanted, disturbing reality began to gradually creep into my consciousness. It was chilling.

External Validity

Despite the creative discouragement, at the end of July that year, I got myself a job as a singer-performer at the Mynah Bird on Yorkville Avenue. Yes. Me. My long-time friend Dorothy still remembers. The Mynah Bird had been a coffee house in the early '60s. But in 1967, it featured semi-nude go-go dancers in cages. By today's standards, their outfits would be considered modest, but at the time, they were quite risqué. So, imagine these semi-clad, sexy young women writhing and gyrating to very loud recorded rock music, followed during the intermission by something completely different. Me, overweight as I was, wearing a loose, long-sleeved, coral-coloured, knee-length cotton chintz dress, with smocking across the bodice and a high neckline.

Self-accompanied on my guitar, I belted out several folk numbers – "The House of the Rising Sun" was probably one of them – to a fairly polite and somewhat appreciative audience. I don't recall how much I was paid, but it wouldn't have mattered. I was thrilled and couldn't believe my good luck. I was on my way!

To this day, I've no inkling how I found out about the gig. Probably from a sign in the window. The hospital records show two separate entries on this, dated August 3 and August 8:

Natalie has been more relaxed and in control of her moods and behaviour for five days. Obtained a 9pm to 3am job as folk-singer at the Mynah Bird, Yorkville.

Decided at "rounds" we would not permit her to keep such hours and remain an inpatient. Out for an interview Friday. Outcome uncertain. Still requires salaried 9-5 job.

Natalie got a job singing at the Mynah Bird 9pm to 3am.

*She was discouraged from doing this while under treat-
ment in hospital, and it was suggested to her that she
would have to prove herself by getting an ordinary job
and holding it.*

Discouraged, yes. Suggested, not quite. I was given a pseu-
do-choice. I distinctly remember sitting in the lounge in front of
the windows when Dr. Shugar himself approached. He said he'd
heard about my Mynah Bird job, but that I couldn't work there
and stay at the hospital at the same time. I sensed the choice
component, but choice itself was so foreign a concept, I failed to
see my real options clearly. It seemed obvious that I'd have to
give up the singing gig, but perhaps because the hospital staff
was steering me in a specific nine-to-five direction.

What would have happened, I wonder, if I'd chosen to leave
the hospital and kept the Mynah Bird gig? Would I have lived up
to my psychotic potential and ended up back in the hospital?
That unexpressed fearful thought may have fed into my decision.
We never know the outcome of unexplored paths.

Ironically, the hospital records show that after the Mynah
Bird situation, I was then usually referred to as "talented." It appears I wasn't the only one influenced by external validation.

Mudville

*Oh, somewhere in this favoured land the sun is shining
bright; The band is playing somewhere, and somewhere
hearts are light, And somewhere men are laughing, and
somewhere children shout; But there is no joy in Mudville—mighty Casey has struck out.*[94]

Besides Gilda, psychiatrist Dr. Vivien Abbott (Dr. B's replace-
ment) was one of the best people on staff at the Clarke. A Quaker by practice, she was kind, compassionate, a good listener, and
someone I truly admired. Several years later, I even explored
becoming a Quaker myself, thanks to her gentle influence. On
August 8 she wrote:

[Natalie] has been to the employment office, but has become progressively discouraged: "doesn't feel anything," "doesn't want to work," "doesn't feel life is worth living." Today, after going out and missing the direction of the employment office, she bought two bottles of 222's, with the purpose of taking them tonight. She gave them up, remained depressed because she cannot understand why she magnifies her problems or dramatizes them to such an extent.

I clearly remember this awful period of my life as one of the most distressing, second only to the time I found out about my father. Having learned from my unsuccessful suicide efforts several years before, I thought I was being clever buying two whole bottles of non-prescription painkillers.

Much as I liked Dr. Abbott, she didn't get it. In my mind, music was all I had, my sole means of honest self-expression, my main hope for a different future.

On some level, I sensed that staying at the Clarke, instead of keeping the Mynah Bird gig, was choosing conformity over hope. Conformity wasn't such a bad thing in itself – I'd just never been able to do it. As much as I kept trying to fit in, I failed. That's how I saw myself, as a failure. A failure at sustained weight loss, a failure at being able to control my compulsion to overeat, and a failure at fitting into what mainstream society touted as worthwhile.

I wasn't alone in my sense of alienation. The counterculture movement was rebelling against stultifying, mind-numbing, soul-destroying, unjust, controlling, social institutions. But I didn't quite fit into the counterculture either. Not that I didn't want to. I desperately wanted to, but I wasn't free enough, or uninhibited enough, or courageous enough to live like an actual hippie. I was terrified of street drugs, and perhaps wisely so. I knew I couldn't control myself with food, so how could I trust what I'd do under the influence of LSD, or pot. or magic mushrooms? I couldn't. So where was I to go, and who was I to become?

The hospital encouraged me to fit myself into a society and lifestyle I judged, devalued, mocked, and to which I'd never belong – that of "normal" people. I wasn't normal, never had been. Shirley convinced me of that long ago. "You're not normal," she'd say. So I decided I didn't want to be normal. But the truth was, I couldn't be. Strike one: I was fatandugly in a world ruled by Twiggies (skinny women). Strike two: I was a mental patient, ultimately to become a "former" mental patient (same stigma, maybe worse). Strike three: I wasn't smart.

Despite all this, I found a job in the Publications Department at the Ontario Institute for Studies in Education (OISE) on Bloor Street West, located at that time between Avenue Road and Bay Street.[95] I was the Publication Assistant's assistant, who looked after mailing lists, got coffee, and performed other fascinating joe-jobby clerical tasks. Gilda's September 14, 1967, report provides an accurate description:

> *Natalie was able in September to locate and find a job on her own, asking for no help from me ... She is working at OISE and earning $75.00 a week. Her mood during the early part of September when she was employed was mainly one of depression. She dislikes the routine of her job, its lack of challenge, but dislikes more the fact that she realizes she has no skills, and no way to get out of her present situation ... As she takes stock of herself, she sees herself as an unattractive, uneducated young woman with dim prospects for the future and suicide as a way out.*

I still remember walking to work daily, through the University of Toronto campus, and past Queen's Park, during those strikingly beautiful autumn days when the leaves were changing colour. Autumn was and still is my favourite season. Ever since I was young, watching squirrels and other furry creatures play in the fallen leaves would make me smile. But en route to OISE in 1967, there was no smile. No appreciation for the beauty around me.

Indeed, I kept reciting a line over and over from an old poem about baseball. "But there is no joy in Mudville – mighty Casey has struck out." As I trudged along, I believed that I, too, had struck out. The game was over, and I'd missed my chance to hit a home run. I was a loser. "Loser" wasn't as popular a term as it is today, but I was one nonetheless. I had no future, at least no future I cared about, one filled with possibility.

Like many young people, I lacked a long-term perspective. Every weekday, my depression and I walked towards what I saw as my doom.

When I look back on this period, I can't help but think with great sadness of the children attending poorly equipped schools in low-income neighbourhoods who see no future for themselves, because no one expects very much from them. I had a brief but devastating experience of being channelled into a future beneath my true capacities, of being tested with flawed instruments and under less-than-optimum conditions, and saw what it did to my spirit. I cringe when I try to conjure up the impact of a lifetime of this type of treatment, and can blame no child if she turns to any means necessary to boost herself up a little.

When she examines possibilities to get out of this situation ... she doubts her intellectual capacity ... IQ tests taken at the hospital ... the results make her feel helpless. She is frightened ... unable to take stock of her positive points and blaming others for her current condition.

By the way, as the records show, by late August or early September, the doctors had switched me from Largactil and Cogentin to small twice-daily doses of Stelazine[96] (1 mg), an antipsychotic or anti- anxiety drug, and Parnate[97] (10 mg), one of the first antidepressants, now less frequently used due to its strong side effects, such as increasing the risk of suicidal thoughts and behaviour. (I assume these effects were unknown at the time, because I cannot imagine medical professionals knowingly giving this type of medication to someone in my frame of mind.)

As for blame, Gilda was only partly correct. I certainly did blame others, such as Shirley and Bob, but mainly Shirley, because she was the most obvious and vocal about her opinions. I'd always wanted her to get off my back and leave me alone, imagining that I'd flourish once free of her intrusive influence. But ever since I'd left the Falls at age seventeen to attend university, I'd discovered that the only thing to flourish was my compulsive eating and weight.

What Gilda and the others seemed to miss, however, is that in characteristic fashion, I blamed myself more than anyone else for my out-of-control eating. After all, no one else shovelled food into my mouth. But just like a typical addict, my self-preoccupation placed me squarely at the centre of the universe, which meant that I was also somehow to blame for whatever else was wrong with the world. This, of course, is not rational. But for many years, I wasn't aware of the specific thoughts that contributed to this particular spiral of self-blame and guilt.

Ever since I was a little girl, Robert had always expected me to know better. He thought this was supportive. He was giving me the benefit of the doubt and crediting me with grown-up reason and intelligence. So when things went awry, I usually assumed I was at fault, for not anticipating the problem accurately, for creating trouble, or for some other reason yet to be discerned. And while I resented both parents, I also resented myself – for failing to fix things, for failing to lose weight, for failing to be what they wanted me to be and what I wanted me to be. These thoughts were all tied up in the gibble-gabble, on the self-hate channel, which droned softly in the background of my every waking hour.

Did I have any positive points to take stock of? Absolutely. I could accurately regurgitate what Shirley and Bob had told me my whole life, without much prompting.

First, I had such a pretty face. It was my mother's face, and the implications were (a) that I was a second-rate copycat, and (b) that I had ruined this face by having such a fat body. Second, I was very intelligent, and since Shirley had taught me to read at the age of three, I should do very well in all school subjects. This meant I should always come first in my class with top marks in everything. And third, I was a good talker, had the gift of the gab, could talk my way out of a paper bag, and so on. Fourth ... whoops, I wouldn't have been able to think of a fourth.

You might wonder why I wouldn't have included the deeply entertaining personality I worked so hard to create during my teenage years. Well, because this was self-created and known only to me, it didn't count. I could only include positives recognized by others. That was all I knew.

However, the three positives I usually counted on had been whittled down to two, since the Clarke had now disproved one of them. I wasn't that intelligent, after all.

Shirley at 17.

Me at almost 17 (appeared in the *Niagara Falls Evening Review*
announcing my entrance into the honours program at the State
University of New York in Buffalo. Must have been a slow news day).

Me at 29.

Future Tense

Since I'd started at OISE, Gilda and Dr. Abbott had worked together, thinking I might benefit from further training. Perhaps I could start Teacher's College (a not uncommon choice for women) or Ryerson[98] in the fall. In September 1967, they applied on my behalf to JVS, a Toronto agency specializing in vocational testing.[99] Here are some excerpts from their referral:

> *[Natalie] presented in the spring as an acting out adolescent with considerable disorganization of her thought processes. She has improved thus. Thinking is now quite well organized ... She is much better controlled, and is realistic now in her expectations for education and work. With this decrease in acting out, has come a moderate degree of depression and anxiety. She is being encouraged to use this more realistic mood in order to make plans to improve her qualifications. Her difficulty will rest in her reluctance to persevere along any one line of work ...*

> *The patient seems to be working through dependency conflicts with her parents. She seems to have handled her feelings in the past (of frustration) by opposing them by failing (as in her second year of university) and then experienced guilt reaction. We are currently working on this with her in psychotherapy, aiming to help her achieve and maintain independency. We see further education ... as a self-enhancing experience and expect she would strive very hard to succeed under such circumstances.*

Yes, I did oppose my parents as one way of dealing with frustration. But failing second-year university had little to do with them, and more to do with my coming apart at the seams, being unable to focus due to the gibble-gabble, having no self-discipline, and bingeing my brains out. And of course I felt guilty. Mainly for taking up so much space on the planet.

BINGE CRAZY

Over the years, I'd learned to manage any discomfort, sensation, or feeling by eating, and had unknowingly developed the following ten-step routine to cope and escape: (1) eat compulsively, (2) obsess about weight, fat and dieting, (3) fantasize about the life I'd lead when I was thin, (4) diet and succeed for a short time, while still obsessing about food – what wasn't eaten and what was, (5) binge, (6) regain lost weight plus some extra, (7) cycle into a spiral of self-hate and despair, (9) obsess about being so fat, and (10) calculate various weight loss schemes, and start again at step(1).

For the most part, that's how I dealt with frustration and most other feelings. I never told anyone.

I doubt I was even aware of the complexity of this mental-emotional cycle. At the time, no one knew about the devastating impact of binge eating disorder and in my case, the ever-present but unexplored gibble-gabble. Even today, the damaging and demoralizing aspects of BED are only just beginning to be recognized.

It breaks my heart to read through the remaining hospital records, as they verify the relevant details of my life, including the soul-destroying impact of these binges. No one really knew my behaviour was the same as that of any alcoholic or addict, and that what drove me to overeat was a complex mishmash of underlying fears and emotions, accompanied by the gibble-gabble. I never told anyone about the gibble-gabble.

On some fundamental level I'd recognized the addiction-like nature of the binges back at university, when images of Jack Lemmon and Lee Remick in the 1962 movie *The Days of Wine and Roses* would pop into my mind, accompanied by Henry Mancini's violin-encrusted song of the same name (which I never liked, other than the first line). Back when I was stealing my roommate's money to raid the dorm's candy machines, I'd sometimes think of Jack Lemmon's drunken behaviour in that movie and knew we had the same problem.

I don't recall taking the JVS tests, but the results were a vast improvement over my earlier test efforts. This beacon of hope during those bleak early months at OISE helped me accept my work situation as temporary, which made it bearable.

Now, the wisdom of age tells me that everything is temporary, and that permanence is an illusion. More Clarke records:

> *Family relationships are problematic. Mother has been rejecting of the patient due to her obesity and has never been able to accept her hospitalization. She blames the patient for family problems, especially her husband's recent heart attack, relating it to Miss Gold's disappointing behaviour.*

> *Father has been increasingly more able to accept and deal with the patient's illness but finds it difficult to face friends and relatives in Niagara Falls, and takes all signs of improvement as indicating Natalie is "better, all better." He reacts with panic to depression or Natalie working out her feelings and we therefore feel living at home will be difficult for the patient.*

Then, as a teen and young adult, I didn't know about my father's panic when I felt depressed or processed feelings. Now, it makes sense. Robert relied on me to get him through. If I wasn't emotionally available, he'd have to deal with Shirley on his own. My guess: that factor could have contributed to his heart attack, along with the foods he ate, and the past he buried.

> *Patient has a younger sister who is successful at school, has dates (patient has never had a date) and as far as we know is not presenting problems. Mother wants patient to emulate her younger sister.*

That particular paragraph has a few little twists all its own. First, my sister says she never dated during high school, but had a very busy social and athletic life. Second, years later, when I was living on my own in London, England, pursuing a musical career, Robert phoned me in a panic – the only time he phoned in my five years overseas. He wanted me to call my sister and convince her to see things his way on a particular issue.

It turns out, my younger sister had finally rebelled and broken free from the inflexible constraints of her life in Ontario, and had moved to one of the Gulf Islands in British Columbia, where she and her husband live happily to this day. She became a hippie, forsaking many middle-class materialistic values, and raised her family of four (my dear nieces and nephews) in an island community of like-minded souls.

Imagine how Shirley must have felt to see her younger daughter wearing second-hand clothes and living in a one-room shack with an outhouse, and water that had to be carried from a well on a neighbouring property. The sibling tides had turned. They expected such behaviour from me, but not from my goody-two-shoes sister. Shirley's protest and lack of acceptance of my sister's situation continued for years. She didn't attend my sister's eventual wedding in Toronto in 1981. But there you have it. One of life's little ironies.

A Mind of My Own

Every night after work, I'd return to the hospital, less and less thrilled with the place. Gradually, everything I'd found comforting began to grate on my nerves. It no longer felt like a safe haven. A sign, surely, that I was on the mend.

One night a week I attended a grade-twelve chemistry class, a do-over to compensate for failing marks in high school. On weekends, I'd often stay with Diana and her family. Once I'd started working, the parental ban had been lifted, so occasionally I'd visit my own family in the Falls. But this was usually a disaster. Despite the Clarke's efforts, Bob and Shirley still had an enormous influence over me, as Gilda so aptly describes in her October 10 report:

> *Natalie appeared for this interview after work at 5 o'clock ... When she began describing her problem, she*

*said she didn't cry as much as she used to, but as she
went on talking about it, she started to cry and said that
she only cried with me ... she was as tearful as she has
been in the past four weeks. She again expressed hopelessness, self-hatred, calling herself stupid, hopeless, and
lacking self-control.*

*We discussed the weekend with the family ... her mother
wanted her to go to Stauffer's or Vic Tanny's [Toronto
weight loss and exercise gyms] but she was unable to
keep to her diet. Although in a previous visit she said she
had started to diet, this time she had stopped and she
was overeating. She talked about her lack of enjoyment
of the food and her feelings of hopelessness when she
began to eat.*

The diet-binge syndrome was to be similarly documented in
most of the Clarke notes until the end of my outpatient appoint-
ments in May 1969. No matter how well I was doing, the roller-
coaster plunge to the bleak and bottomless pit of food addiction
maintained its vice-like grip.

*As she spoke about the weekend with her parents, she
said "I can't say anything against them. I've hurt them
enough. I feel like a rat-fink talking about them all the
time." She described both parents as saying that the
hospital was wrong in our assessment, that they had
known her for twenty years and we had only known her
for six months and therefore we thought she needed help.*

I wonder if Gilda ever told Bob and Shirley about my low-
average IQ. If so, it would have been a bombshell, and created
even more mistrust of the Clarke.

*She said that her father had made negotiations with a
lawyer friend for her to become a legal secretary, but she
did not want this job and mother said "Yes you do–and
take it."*

Every time I read and reread that, I have to stop and digest it all over again. It brings Shirley back to life with a resounding *thwack*. I lived like that. I was brought up like that. I was programmed like that on a regular basis. No wonder I believed I didn't know what I wanted. Of course I knew, for brief moments, until I'd say it out loud to Shirley, who'd then tell me up was down, or that green was blue, or that the bell would never toll for me (the wedding bell).

Eventually, I stopped telling her things, and kept them all inside. That also didn't help, because first, they got lost in the gibble-gabble, and second, Shirley would criticize me for withholding information.

> *Mother had contacted a friend ... and found her living accommodations with a widow at Glencairn and Bathurst. Natalie felt this was a good arrangement ... but that she was not very sure if this is what she wanted.*

> *She told her prospective landlady that she was going to lose weight "because my mother told me I should tell people I'm going to lose weight, so I do. I don't know what else to do." When I explored with her further what she thought other people's reactions would be to this or why she said this, she did not know ... she kept referring to "my mother says" this, "my mother says" that.*

> *She said that generally she did not know what she wanted and she wasn't sure whether she was listening to her parents because that was what she wanted or that was what they wanted. She said "I don't have a mind of my own."*

The report ends with yet another decision to postpone discharge, and to once more restrict parental access. Contact with Bob and Shirley seemed to undo whatever psychological progress I'd made. Gilda and the hospital team appeared to expect otherwise from our enmeshed threesome.

I feel that Natalie is still being dominated by her parents and has not achieved any discernible break from them. I have discussed the above findings with Dr. Shugar and the decision has been made that Natalie not be discharged on Sunday ... that parents be contacted, that joint sessions be stopped and parents be told that they cannot see Natalie at present alone.

When you think about it, a lifetime of indoctrination by Bob and Shirley couldn't be undone with six or seven months at the Clarke, especially since I didn't get in-depth treatment. And none of us was aware that I still had indelible recordings of Bob and Shirley inside my head, via the gibble-gabble. This meant that wherever I went, in essence, Bob and Shirley came right along for the ride. A cognitive approach, currently in vogue, wouldn't gain any traction in mainstream psychology until the 1970s or later.[100]

Had I ever had a mind of my own? Not really. Except for the gibble-gabble – that was mine, with major contributions from Bob and Shirley, but disguised as if they came from somewhere else, just as dreams disguise the messages they carry. That was the gibble-gabble's creative brilliance – it hid and protected its sources as skillfully as any successful investigative journalist or spy.

CHAPTER 13: LEAVINGS

Falling Through

How many songs have been written about leaving? Leaving lovers, leaving friends, leaving family, leaving jobs, leaving town, leaving home. All of them difficult, some of them painful, and some celebratory. My own leavings tended to be a mixture. Instead of heading towards some exciting new adventure, I usually left to escape from a situation I couldn't handle, with some sort of plan evolving as an afterthought.

That's how it was when I left university in Buffalo in the fall of 1965. Looking back, armed with the understanding of hindsight, I can see how disorganized thinking and emotional distress were present even then. I felt like a fraud. Nothing much made sense. I had almost no self-respect and was unable to study or concentrate. I attended only those classes I liked and skipped many of the rest.

Most of the papers I handed in were written the night before. Except for the philosophy paper in freshman year on the squirrel-tree problem. (If a squirrel is on a tree, and a person runs around the tree, is that person also running around the squirrel?) My focus was on defending my right to have an opinion, and that the problem's only relevance as an essay topic was my need for a passing grade. I ended up with a B+.

To a certain extent, this reflects typical undergrad behaviour, especially when the undergrad isn't really committed to a particular goal. But I went even further. In my logic course, I was able to talk my way into a D (a pass), instead of an F, when I'd written no mid-terms, no papers, and attended maybe two 8:00 a.m. classes during the entire semester.

While I bragged about this great accomplishment to my friends, who found it praiseworthy indeed, it bothered my conscience. Shoplifting also bothered my conscience, but not enough to stop me from doing it. One of my university acting classmates, Alice, and I spurred each other on for the fun of it, the excitement. Alice was incredibly talented, and I admired her enormously and sought her approval.

Afraid she'd stop liking me, I refrained from voicing my reservations about our little escapades, which began as a joke, turned into a dare, and snowballed into action.

Eventually, the novelty wore off, and that ended my theft of non-food items for a while. Luckily, we didn't get caught and avoided criminal consequences. But there were other prices to pay.

I was already plagued by guilt, leftovers from being around Bob and Shirley, and this extra dollop tipped the scale. I felt as if I could get away with anything, and that idea was terrifying. There seemed to be no justice. I felt like I was falling through the cracks, that there was no bottom for me to hit. Indeed, this would be my special hell, to avoid punishment and live forever guilty. I was in free-fall, floating through the universe, anchored to nothing and no one. None of this was drug-induced, unless you count sugar and junk food, which I didn't at the time.

In second year, I ran for Student Senate as an independent candidate and miraculously won. But by the spring of 1965 I had to resign, since I couldn't handle the pressure. Student politics with all its posturing and debates became too much for me. One more failure to add to the growing heap. After being in several dramatic productions and enjoying every moment, unlike my time in the rest of my courses, it became clearer that what I really loved to do was act. So I thought of applying to acting school, maybe in Montreal or New York. Or maybe I'd head to New York to pursue singing. In the meantime, I'd have to get a job and earn some money to pay my way.

Once I left university, US immigration wouldn't let me stay in Buffalo, so back I went to Niagara Falls. If I'd been thinking clearly or paid attention to all the warning signs, I would have chosen any other place but there. But I wasn't thinking clearly. I'd read that people needed to face their problems, not run away from them. I took this literally and returned to Barker Street, hoping to finally resolve my difficulties with Shirley and Bob.

You Can Go Home Again, but ...

Both parents were unhappy about my return. Shirley had grown accustomed to my absence, and while Bob was disappointed I didn't finish university, he was ready to help. His contacts got me: (a) a job at Niagara Falls radio station CJRN, writing radio commercials, mostly for local businesses; (b) my first car, the aforementioned used British Anglia[101] which my sister nick-named Boris; and (c) connected to the Shaw Festival in Niagara-on-the-Lake,[102] to help out at the box office on some evenings and weekends.

**Me in my new used car (a British Anglia named Boris),
Cindy leaning on the car, Shirley in the background. At
the Barker Street house in Niagara Falls in 1966.**

This was the summer of 1965, and I was at the Shaw as a volunteer, since profit-making was still illusive for this start-up company. I got to meet my dad's friend, lawyer and founder Brian Doherty, along with Festival President Calvin Rand[103] and Assistant Artistic Director and playwright Sean Mulcahey.

This was very exciting, and certainly a step up from acting class at university. I vaguely remember the closing night cast party at someone's home in Niagara-on-the-Lake,[104] when we all sat around the baby grand piano and sang.

Being at the Shaw and mixing with the theatrical crowd helped me tolerate home life with Shirley and Bob. Nothing specific stands out, other than the same old. I was working, earning enough to pay for a small apartment in the Falls, but Robert nixed this notion, and that was that. No daughter of his was going to live in her own apartment in the same city. Like Shirley, he worried what people would think.

When Calvin Rand suggested I apply to run the box office at the reopening of the Studio Arena Theatre in Buffalo,[105] it seemed like a lifeline. Through his contacts, I got the job and left the radio station in Niagara Falls with no regrets. It had been fun, but writing copy for tombstones or drugstore sales had grown stale. Thrilled to be part of something special, I found the daily commute to Buffalo tolerable. As soon as I'd saved enough to move there, I'd be gone from Barker Street.

Opening night of Eugene O'Neill's *A Moon for the Misbegotten*[106] was a glitzy event, but the after party in the theatre lobby, attended by the star, Colleen Dewhurst, and her then-husband, actor George C. Scott,[107] lacked the intimacy and camaraderie of the Shaw.

My parents knew nothing about this new job. Just as well, because it didn't last long. The other box office person, a man in his mid-forties, had overseen the theatre's box office for years before its reinvention as a non-profit venue and naturally resented me, his know-nothing supervisor.

Glamour aside, running the box office was a big bore. I made many mistakes and to my relief soon got fired.

Toronto-Bound

Being sacked helped me realize I'd have to face my problems with Shirley and Bob from a different geographic location. Since I wasn't ready for prime time in Montreal or New York, Toronto was the next best thing. Although another year would pass before the Beatles' "She's Leaving Home"[108] was released, this song eerily describes my getaway from the house on Barker Street. It may not have been a Wednesday morning, but it was still dark as I carefully closed the bedroom door (so as not to wake my sister), tiptoed downstairs, and quietly loaded Boris's trunk with my important belongings: records, turntable, transistor radio, books, clothes, and some toiletries.

The carefully crafted note I left on the kitchen table was for Shirley, a plausible reason for her friends as to why I left for Toronto. She'd be glad to see me go.

As I drove off towards my future, I did feel free, just like the girl in the song. Really free. All the way to Toronto on the QEW, the landscaped boulevard and the vibrant autumn leaves seemed to welcome me. A good omen. Everything would be fine as long as I kept moving. But eventually I had to stop and find a place to stay. And it had to be cheap. After all, I had a mere $18 to my name (a fact recorded in the Clarke records and not my memory). Asking friends was out of the question. I hated the idea of being a burden to anyone. Correction: I hated the idea of being a burden to anyone anymore.

Somehow I found the Elmwood Hotel for Girls on Elm Street in the heart of downtown Toronto.[109] A heritage building and luxury spa since 1982, back in 1965 it was a dingy, red brick, four- story hotel, where women could share a room for as little as $5 a week. Originally built in 1889, the Elmwood housed the YWCA before being turned into a home for unmarried women, which is what I was, to Shirley's dismay.

At the Elmwood, I had two roommates – an older woman who'd been there quite a while, and a nine-months-pregnant girl from a small northern Ontario town, who planned to give the child up for adoption. We each had a single cot and a place to hang a few clothes. A disgustingly filthy kitchen was available at the end of the hall, and there must have been a communal bathroom, as well. I've blocked it from my mind.

Next day, I applied for a waitress job at Tops Restaurant on Yonge Street. I didn't get it, but the manager, Joey, did provide my first night's entertainment. He was promoting an upcoming championship match with Toronto-born heavyweight boxing champ George Chuvalo.[110] Even I had heard of Chuvalo, who'd fought Floyd Patterson earlier that year at Madison Square Garden.[111]

That evening, Joey picked me up at the Elmwood and drove first to the Paddock Tavern[112] to collect Artie, who had the posters. Then the three of us drove around the city, stopping so the guys could tack them up on telephone and hydro poles. En route, Joey discussed real-estate values and pointed out the homes of well-known Torontonians. Eventually, the guys dropped me off at the Elmwood before moving on to other more exciting establishments. An odd first night in Toronto.

How innocent I was back then, to go driving around at night with two men I didn't know. I felt safe with Joey, since he said I reminded him of his sister. But also, I had fatness to protect me. More important, I had blind faith that no one was going to let me die on the street. In the squeaky-clean 1960s provincial city of Toronto, people didn't live on the street to the extent they do now. If they were around, law enforcement probably made sure they were well hidden. Besides, developers and redevelopers hadn't yet gentrified low-income neighbourhoods, so plenty of places like the Elmwood were available to those of us with little money.

Within a few days, I'd found the junior clerk-typist job at Vickers & Benson ad agency and a new place to live in the Bathurst-Eglinton area. I had my own bedroom in someone's house, plus use of a spotlessly clean bathroom and main floor kitchen. A few giant steps up from the Elmwood, to be sure.

CHAPTER 14: OUTPATIENT

Out of the Frying Pan

By mid-November 1967, Gilda and Dr. Abbott saw a light at the end of the tunnel and envisioned me living outside the hospital. Two months later, that happened. Another patient, Margaret, had found a rather spacious two-bedroom apartment above a store on Yonge Street near Manor Road, a few blocks south of Eglinton. I was to move in with her. With these plans in place, in mid-January 1968, I was officially discharged as an inpatient of the Clarke.

Admitted:	*March 31 1967*
Discharge:	*January 20 1968*
Admitting diagnosis:	*schizophrenia*
Final diagnosis:	*acute dissociative reaction and adolescent behaviour problem*

No longer under Dr. Shugar's supervision, I began the next fifteen months as an outpatient, seeing Gilda and Dr. Abbott about twice a month each (until Dr. Abbott's departure). It seemed like only yesterday that I'd left for university, left for Toronto, and left my cake out in the rain.[113]

And now here I was, leaving the Clarke, hoping to leave my loathsome OISE job, and planning to apply to the fall 1968 Radio and Television Arts (RTA) program at Ryerson to escape my life of monotony. Everyone involved in my case at the Clarke was on board with this arrangement, and expressed optimism about my changing relationship with Bob and Shirley, as noted by Gilda in February:

Natalie shows independence and less guilt in handling her parental relations. She is able to have them up to her apartment, was pleased she did not over-react to her mother's remarks, and is able to limit her time with them without feeling guilty.

*She also permits some gifts and she is able to graciously
accept their need to give and to direct this need to things
she wants, e.g., an old lamp rather than things she
doesn't want, e.g., a girdle.*

*During tense moments with them, she recognizes a ten-
dency in herself to shut off, thinking of something else,
etc., which she still seems to need to defend herself.*

Yes. I either shut off or distanced myself in other ways, such
as bingeing. Gilda always reported the binges I mentioned during
this early part of 1968, but obviously not the ones I felt too
ashamed to mention. Her observations and mine show how much
we both wanted to believe I was making progress.

*[Natalie] finds her "binges" spaced farther apart and
their intensity decreased when they do occur. From her
description of her eating habits, she is developing a
healthy eating pattern ...*

*Parents came on weekend. Natalie had not wished to see
them, then felt guilty. Had a compulsion to eat. Was able
to resolve it by giving to herself in the form of buying a
dress. Natalie feels that this indicated an improvement in
her self-esteem and in the process of achieving independence.*

This above shows how easy it is to switch from one compulsion to another, unless the underlying issues are dealt with. I did-
n't transfer my dependency from food to spending money. I always preferred the familiar, relatively less expensive, but ultimately more satisfying food to anything else. To paraphrase an
old saying, I'd rather binge than switch.[114]

*Weight level continues to go down. Binges are infrequent
and Natalie is under the understanding that each binge
means not that she is off her diet, but that her goal is
postponed for a couple of days. She has a goal about*

weight loss and hopes to get down to a size 14, which is appropriate to her build.

That second sentence should have read "... Natalie is under the *mis*understanding." Had this been my first, second, or even third time dieting, the goal-postponement approach could have been a valid perspective. But again, bingeing and extreme weight fluctuations were seen strictly through the lens of weight loss, and not as the chronic, complex, and multifaceted underlying eating disorder elements they are. Dieting would never be an answer. In mid-April 1968, Gilda wrote:

Last night [she] had a minor binge ... Why? (1) Parents coming this weekend. (2) Getting nervous, lost 39 pounds.

I'd joined TOPS (Take Off Pounds Sensibly), a non-profit weight loss organization,[115] and attended weekly meetings for several months. This precursor to Weight Watchers, with its focus on dieting, food, weigh-ins, and mutual support, is still going strong today. My nervousness at weight loss, however, morphed into a strong apprehension as I anticipated my next inevitable screw-up.

My all-too-familiar pattern was to lose weight, freak out at the changes, and ultimately return to frequent binges until the weight was regained and homeostasis restored. I'd been-there-done-that countless times before, so why would this time be different? It wasn't.

In July 1968, Dr. Abbott left, so the head of the outpatient department and Gilda's supervisor, Dr. J, took charge of my case.

Who's Petty Now?

It should be no surprise that my apartment-mate Margaret and I didn't get along. Margaret was a few years older and twice as sophisticated. She'd already acquired a lot of neat stuff, including cooking utensils and actual furniture. I bought an armless, black leatherette couch, which Margaret insisted I keep in my room (I now suspect because it wasn't real leather).

At first, everything was peachy. Margaret took pleasure in preparing gourmet meals. She'd cook, I'd clean up after, and that seemed fair at the beginning.

It turned out that Margaret knew someone on Ryerson's board of governors who put in a good word for me at her request. I felt beholden to her even though I'd returned the favour. Through my good friend Dorothy's professional contacts, Margaret began a new career, which she enjoyed and excelled at right away. But the added work pressure pushed our tenuous relationship into a new imbalance. Our ability to get along had been based on my giving in to her wishes. She'd win by saying the issue wasn't important. I'd agree, then cave.

Ultimately, I realized I'd been repressing my anger towards Margaret, afraid to confront her. I'd also ignored angry feelings toward my OISE supervisor, who'd grown intrusive, controlling, demanding, and martyr-like. I ended up with neuralgia pain on the right side of my face, which I now connect to this resentment. Both women, in fact, were "in my face." The wisdom of the body.

Somatic psychotherapy is based on the idea that unprocessed emotional energy can affect the body by creating pain, and ultimately illness if not dealt with.

In early summer, Margaret decided to leave earlier than planned to live on her own. She sold me a few pieces of furniture and wanted to include two large metal garbage cans. I didn't want them. Margaret said, "Let's not be petty," so I bought the garbage cans. Just like that. Heaven forbid I become petty.

Margaret always got her way, and in this instance, I helped her.

My friend Jenny from the Falls moved in temporarily while sorting out her divorce plans. But since I'd been accepted into the RTA program at Ryerson, I needed a cheaper place to live.

Dog House

A trendy young couple rented me a bedroom on the second floor of their old remodelled home on MacPherson Avenue, also centrally located in Toronto. They could even accommodate my black leatherette couch upstairs in the back room. What's more, when they weren't there, I could use the main floor of their beautifully furnished home. But the pièce de résistance was the four dogs, three large and one small, whom I adored. Apart from several miniature turtles and goldfish, Shirley had refused to let my sister and I have real pets like dogs or cats, because they were much "too dirty."

My landlady ran a small but trendy downtown boutique, and her husband worked for a large corporation. Both excellent cooks, they often prepared lavish meals, which they only wanted to sample once. The leftovers were stored in the fridge for me or until they had to be thrown out. So suddenly, I was able to host small dinner parties, serving delicious cuisine on lovely dinnerware in an elegant dining room, a lifestyle I'd never imagined or even wanted.

Into the Fire

If you were over twenty-one, Ryerson classified you as a "mature" student. Otherwise that word would never have applied to me or my RTA classmate Marilyn. Being a bit older than most of the kiddies drew us together almost instantly, creating a bond that solidified when I discovered her off-beat sense of humour. Marilyn lived quite close to the dog house, so I'd often go over to her place after school and marvel at how she'd rearranged the furniture into yet another fabulous-looking configuration. Shortly after school started, we both got parts in a one-act play.

Gilda's report of Friday, November 15, outlines her concerns and the psychiatric session she arranged for the following Monday:

Up until this point Natalie seemed to be making an excellent adjustment on all levels – social, school and recreational. She acted in a play which had won and is to be entered into the finale ... Although her weight has not gone down too much, she had a minimum of binges, was going out socially with boys although not on a date basis, and seemed to be enjoying life.

However, when I saw her, she presented some of the symptoms that she had while in hospital. She said that following the play, she felt empty, that she has increased her eating and has binged twice in the last week. She seems somewhat tense and was asking for the purpose of life, what she was going to do, etc. She said she was having difficulty getting down to business and studying.

It is not the content of her presenting problems that worries me as much as her manner in presenting them. She seems much more excitable, close to tears, and although her symptoms are not what they were when she was in hospital, I feel that a psychiatric evaluation is necessary at this point.

The play, by the way, was called *Chamber Music*, a one-act, theatre-of-the-absurd piece about eight women in a mental institution, who imagine themselves as famous female historical figures.[116] Winning the school's one-act competition meant rehearsals during second semester. So this ironic reminder of my all-too-recent former-mental-patient status, and deep dark secret, was top of mind throughout my first year of school.

At the end of November, Dr. J noted that while I enjoyed most of my courses, my "work habit and study routine difficulties" hadn't improved since starting Ryerson that September. I was skipping classes, behind in assignments, and sleeping excessively. The diagnosis: not clinically depressed, but simply "the old problem of persevering in hard work and making a disciplined routine as a student." That's like saying an addict has no self-control. I just needed to buck up and study was all. Except that I had no idea how to do that.

Throughout the hospital records, psychiatrists Dr. B, Dr. Abbott, and Dr. J all claimed I lacked perseverance. Only now do I know how mistaken they were.

Someone with obsessive-compulsive tendencies automatically perseveres at their repeatedly disruptive behaviour, whether it's hand-washing like Philippe, or binge eating, like me. It's an attempted but misdirected solution. But once the underlying feelings are owned and the connected thoughts examined, the ability to persevere can be channelled in a healthier, more constructive direction. I know this from experience. So I'm correcting the record now. I have and always have had perseverance and tenacity. But I couldn't harness it because of my food addiction,[117] a destroyer of self-trust and self- efficacy.

Lucy in the Sky

Like most people, I've never forgotten my first sexual encounter. But I'm probably in a minority when it comes to having it recorded in hospital records. Memories floated back after reading the brief, handwritten note from my follow-up psychiatric session of Monday, November 18, 1968:

> *Patient is looking lively, feeling better. Had pleasurable heterosexual relationship this weekend. Symptoms seem to be under control.*

After seeing Gilda on Friday, I'd taken a chance, phoned David X out of the blue, and told him I was now back at school. He seemed pleased to hear from me, so I invited him over to the dog house. The next night upstairs in the back room, we shared some wine he'd brought and one of my landlord's gourmet meals. We sang, played guitar (he was way better than I was), and then began necking on my black leatherette couch. I recall saying some idiotic, irrelevant things, lines memorized from a book or movie because they sounded cool. (They weren't.)

At some point we moved into my bedroom and had sex. I'd love to paint a more exciting and sensual picture. But that wasn't my experience. First, I wasn't present in my body. From the moment we'd started kissing in the back room, I'd gone into my head, into the gibble-gabble, to try to manage the very strange sensations I felt from this unexpected encounter. Apart from some mild necking and petting, I'd never been touched all over by a man before. And now, here I was, not only being touched all over, but being touched while naked by an equally naked man. And, to top it off, it was David X!

That he'd come over to my place and had dinner with me on its own was a lot to process. Now he was in my bed. I wondered: was he doing this to be nice, or so he wouldn't hurt my feelings? (Probably.) I also wondered: was he just acting out of pity? (Again, probably.) Strangely, what I didn't wonder was if he was stoned, which he was, or if he'd had too much to drink, which he had. Those types of thoughts would simply not have crossed my mind back then.

It was all happening, albeit not exactly how I'd imagined. But he was here. And we were doing it! A rather CNN-like commentary started running in my head, noting how it felt to be touched wherever he touched me, and how odd it was to have a naked man on top of me and inside me, and wondering what to make of the peculiar sounds of intercourse, the strange pain, and even stranger physical positions. I kept thinking, *So this is what it's like!*

But the weirdest thing was that throughout it all, the Beatles song "Lucy in the Sky with Diamonds"[118] also kept playing in my head. A song I'd never really liked, and now, here it was, seemingly of its own accord, on continuous replay.

He fell asleep shortly afterwards, but I lay awake the whole night trying to make sense of what had happened, that song playing in the background of my mind all the while. I felt high. Psychologically high. I was no longer a virgin! I'd had sex with David X! Hallelujah. Finally, I knew what sex was about, I thought.

In the morning, while getting dressed, David said he'd been much heavier when he was younger but lost the weight. Clearly, he *had* noticed how fat I was. I asked him if he wanted coffee or breakfast, but he said no and let himself out.

And that was how I handled the emptiness and emotionality Gilda so aptly described. I tried to fill it with excitement and then sex. But as any recovering addict will tell you, that doesn't work. You can't fix emptiness by filling it with anything.

My hindsight-full guess is that I needed to grieve: the end of the play, with all the fun and camaraderie involved; the end of the Clarke and the relative safety it provided before my new status as a former mental patient; leaving home; leaving university; and all the other leavings and losses I'd experienced, including the loss of Shirley and Bob as authorities in my life.

The Clarke had helped me break from them physically and given me permission to keep my distance, but I hadn't healed emotionally. The emptiness was a sign, a clue, a warning that some deeper work needed to be done. But none of us knew that, then.

In early December, Gilda wrote that I hadn't heard from my "boyfriend" for several weeks, and that I was sending him cards in an effort to make contact. That would be an understatement. Yes, I sent him cards. I also sent little notes, walked back and forth in front of his apartment as often as I could, and phoned frequently (hanging up when he answered). I felt so distraught that he hadn't called. So one evening, I spoke up when he answered the phone and chattily asked if he could come over and show me some blues chords – like he'd promised, though I didn't add that bit. He suggested I get a book. And that, as the saying goes, was the end of that.

I actually did buy a book about blues chords, which I still have. But it didn't help keep my blues away.

Afterglow

Within eight months or so, I began years of intermittent sexual promiscuity. Intermittent here means during the diet-weight-loss phase of the diet-binge cycle, when I had more time for a relationship, given that I wasn't stuffing my face with food. I was always surprised when a man wanted sex with me. No matter how often reality showed otherwise, Shirley's admonition that no man would want to touch me was crazy-glued to my psyche. This meant I often didn't pick up on cues or signals from men that were obvious to those I was with.

For years, strangers even had to point this out, like the mother of five kids I once sat next to on a plane. As a singer-performer, on my own and when I worked with various bands on and off throughout the '70s, I received more than my fair share of offers. But I didn't really believe sex was happening until it was over.

And when it was over, whether a one-night stand or something longer lasting, I'd begin a binge- cycle and eat myself into oblivion. Sometimes I'd start bingeing as a way to end a relationship. I couldn't say no to anyone, let alone a man. I couldn't say what I wanted or didn't want. None of that had changed. But bingeing made me less responsive to the guy's needs, less able to discern his moods, less interested in what he wanted. In most cases, he ended up doing the dirty work. He broke up or called it quits. And then I could sing more blues songs.

At times, these hook-ups involved making love, not just having sex. But in those instances, the after-binges were ten times worse. While I was clearly desperate for a man to love me, I also couldn't cope whenever I sensed this might be happening. It felt too overwhelming, like being owned. The idea of belonging to anyone felt too much like I might disappear. So instead, I disappeared myself with food in a misdirected, self-destructive effort to keep myself safe.

At the same time, I was busy reading up on how to be a great romantic partner. My main source, Helen Gurley Brown's *Sex and the Single Girl.* The book was revolutionary in its time, and author Brown (who often referred to herself as a "mouseburger") made it (a) okay for women to remain unmarried and (b) even more okay for women to have and enjoy sex in or out of wedlock.[119]

Like millions of other North American women, I also devoured the monthly contents of Brown's *Cosmopolitan* magazine.[120] I tried very hard to live up to this successful little mouseburger's suggestions, usually with comic consequences. At the most inopportune moments, some random thought from the gibble-gabble would escape and come tumbling out of my mouth. Once it was out there, let's just say it usually cast a rather dim shadow on the proceedings.

Shell Shock

The dog house fairy tale worked until the fights began. Big, loud, knock-down, drag-out battles between the husband and wife, which escalated when she drank too much. So she drank more. I never knew when one of these brawls would erupt, but when they did, I hid in my room until the noise died down. By the end of my first year of RTA in April 1969, the brawls had escalated into physically violent clashes.

Furniture heaved around, dishes or other breakable objects smashed against walls or floors, clothes tossed out of second-floor windows, and glass shards in the bathroom. Dreadful screaming and crying. Apart from the awful ruckus, I worried about the dogs' safety as I cowered in my room.

One final blow-up put me into a shell-shocked state during exam time. I shut down completely. No information coming in, none going out. Fortunately, after explaining the situation to my teachers, I was given a chance to rewrite a few exams and did okay. But I had to get out of that house, fast.

Fortunately, Vivian (the actress I'd met at the Clarke) came to the rescue for a few weeks, until my "zany" new summer job "with a homosexual" (as Gilda put it) took me out of town for a while.

Farewell Gilda, Hello Jack

I ended my first year at Ryerson with 71%. Not great, but not horrid. Gilda noted I still tended "to give up on subjects" I disliked and to "over-excel" in others. She also stated that I wouldn't have written as many papers without her "intervention." How right she was.

The thing about institutions like the Clarke is that the people who work there often leave. It's a good thing when it's someone you don't care for, like Dr. B. And a difficult thing when you do, like Dr. Abbott. And now Gilda. I'd known this was coming for months and felt sad about it, and a bit scared. Gilda did so much for me. I trusted her, and she'd never let me down, despite her rather conventional views on work. She gave my life a reboot and I'm forever grateful to her for that. Notes from our last few sessions recap my Clarke history, my struggles with Bob and Shirley, and my new path. They also highlight changed perceptions.

> Natalie is above average in intelligence ... and has a flair and talent for musical and theatrical fields. She recently had a song published ... is an accomplished folk singer who has been booked for several engagements at coffee houses in Toronto ... and has some income from the sale of her song.

I'd forgotten about this song until rereading the hospital records. During school holidays, I'd worked as an office temp at Michael Jacot Productions[121] where I met Kit Hood, a young film editor just over from England. His then schoolteacher friend, Linda Schuyler,[122] bought my song to use as the theme for a documentary film[123] they were making.

"City Without a Song," written in the fall of 1967, during those first awful months at OISE while I was an inpatient at the

Clarke, was recorded in a studio. I remember seeing black-and-white images of children running on a concrete playground, but I don't know the film's title or if it was ever released.

> *Patient in for her last appointment ... She is doing extremely well and felt she got a great deal out of contact here. She expressed a great deal of regret in leaving me, brought a gift but said that she will contact the private psychiatrist that I have suggested ...*

This was Gilda's last note, dated May 29, 1969. My time at the Clarke had come to an end, but not my struggle for mental health. Gilda referred me to psychiatrist Dr. Jack Birnbaum,[124] who offered group therapy with individual consults when necessary.

Jack had some Gestalt training, and it was through him I first learned a little about Gestalt's experiential, non-analytical approach. I had no idea at the time just how important Gestalt would become in my life.

Ten years later, it was Jack who sent me back to the Clarke.

CHAPTER 15: UP TO THE BOTTOM

The thirteen years between my leaving the Clarke, hitting bottom, and finally getting onto a recovery track were jam-packed with loads of experiences that don't belong here. However, some are worth mentioning since they relate to binge eating disorder and how easy it was to fool myself that I was improving when I was not.

Even when the binges reduced in frequency or didn't last as long, and even when I managed to stay at a somewhat lower weight for a while, I had not really dealt with many of the underlying issues. So my compulsion to overeat – or my addiction to food and eating – was simply waiting in the wings for an opportunity to manifest.

Other areas of my life, however, moved along.

Yorkville Revisited

The summer after first year RTA, door-to-door research surveys and temp office work killed time till that "zany" job with costume designer Roger the Dodger[125] kicked in. Hired for a TV shoot in Ottawa,[126] but knowing nothing about sewing, fabric, or design, I became Roger's Girl Friday, also known as a gofer: you go for this, you go for that. An old joke, but accurate. We all (including Roger's dog, Charlie) got to stay at the swanky Chateau Laurier hotel.

The Ottawa gig lasted several weeks, and on my return to Toronto, I found a semi-furnished attic room in a house off Avenue Road, on Boswell Avenue, for a great price. The snag: my housemates were five young working guys. The payoff: picturing Shirley's reaction. Hey Ma, I'm living with five guys!

While seemingly bold, daring, fun, and a bit glamorous at first, the opposite was true. Much as I enjoyed the frequent visits from the squirrel who often perched on my attic windowsill, my housemates kept the kitchen and bathrooms in a perpetually disgusting state. And despite the proximity of five young men, whose presence I mistakenly assumed would remind me to stay on a diet and lose weight, I still snuck food into my room and binged. Now that I think about it, this may be why the squirrel and I became so well-acquainted.

By the time school started again in the fall of 1969, I'd found two rooms on the third floor of a Hazelton Avenue house in Yorkville – a large main room with a mattress on the floor and a tiny kitchenette down the hall. Plus a shared bathroom. My parents visited once, and Shirley agonized that her daughter was now a "hippie." I wasn't, but facts had never mattered to my mother. I loved the location and spent a lot of time at the outdoor café on the corner of Yorkville and Hazelton, drinking coffee and playing scrabble or cards with other Yorkville regulars. Like the five-guy house, the Hazelton house was walking distance to St. Paul's Avenue Road United Church,[127] home to the University Settlement, where I'd volunteered to lead teen groups since May, as hospital records noted.

However, unlike the five-guy house, the Hazelton tenants often held some fairly wild parties, so you never knew who was roaming around the halls in the mornings. For this reason, I made sure to lock my door when I went to the kitchen or bathroom. But sometimes forgot my key. Since the two rooms I rented formed an L-shape, you could almost reach from one window to the other. I have a faint memory of crawling across this third-storey expanse to gain access, thinking how much I didn't want to die.

So when RTA classmate Dana offered the spare room in the flat she shared with her long-time friend Sandy (also in RTA), I jumped at the chance.

Sitcom Anyone?

The two-storey flat at 217½ Church Street perched somewhat precariously above a used office equipment store just below Dundas Street West. Close to Ryerson. Three bedrooms occupied the top floor, and below, a sloping hallway led to a bathroom, kitchen and large living room, which had enough space to accommodate my black leatherette couch.

Dana's boyfriend, Michael, also moved in, but their families weren't to know, so everyone else's family had to be kept in the dark, too. In the 1960s, it wasn't socially acceptable, at least to our parents' generation, for single men and women to live together, even as friends, and certainly not as an unmarried couple.[128] This was a fun secret, unlike some of the others I had to cart around. I told Dana about the Clarke before moving in, and that I was in group therapy. I liked Dana a lot and didn't want to pretend I had my act together. In retrospect, this would have been obvious.

As students, none of us really had our acts together. During second year, I was in another one-act play, this time with Dana, that had wonderfully absurd scenes and funny lines. I could phone Dana right now, say one of my lines, and she or Michael (they eventually married and raised a family) would instantly know who it was.

I also got fairly busy doing music gigs at coffee houses and pubs around Toronto, including a regular event called "Poetry n' Things." Well-known poets like Al Purdy, Doug Fetherling,[129] and Ted Plantos[130] read their work, with a musical interlude featuring a performance by some pretty amazing singers and musicians, including several talented American draft dodgers. I felt honoured to be included, belting out bluesy songs like "Nobody Knows You When You're Down And Out," which for a long time was my signature number. My material was drawn from many musical genres, but whatever songs I performed, they all came out sounding bluesy.

What I loved about living at the Church Street flat was that you never knew what was going to happen. Being so close to Ryerson, friends stopped by for coffee between classes. Sandy's boyfriend moved in for a short time. And some of Dana's old friends took the flat next door. We'd visit via the back roof, accessible through the kitchen windows. On our side of the roof, you had to be careful not to step on the fake black coffin left there after a film shoot. I often thought our living situation would make great sitcom material. But whenever I said so, my flatmates would simply roll their eyes and laugh. It became a running joke. Despite the camaraderie, I still binged. Sometimes I ate other people's stuff. The result: if you looked in our fridge, you would see almost everything initialled by magic markers, including individual eggs. The message: keep your grubby paws off. Clearly, I was not the only one pilfering, because eggs were the last items I would have touched, given the binge-like need for instant gratification. But the labelling worked as a deterrent and funny reminder.

By the end of second year, it was once again time to leave school, making me a two-time dropout.

I hadn't been able to study, and my old transcripts show I didn't write most of my finals, just like university in Buffalo. Except that I wasn't coming apart at the seams. I just couldn't mentally focus enough, probably due to several factors – my sugar-brain, the gibble-gabble, and too many as yet unresolved issues from my past. Good thing Gilda didn't know about my failure. I couldn't have tolerated disappointing one more person.

Despite group therapy with Jack Birnbaum, my compulsive eating still hadn't really been adequately addressed. I'd tried several more diets, including Dr. Stillman's highly restrictive low-carb, low-fat, high-protein diet (the first of its kind), where you ate low-fat protein six times a day and drank eight to ten glasses of water. No surprise I lost weight quickly. But bingeing in a movie theatre on more than a pound of skim-milk cheese (one of the few allowable foods, along with shrimp) triggered a bender that lasted until I had regained what I'd lost. The pattern persisted.

I stayed on at the Church Street flat for another year. During that time, while I received a lot of support for my music from friends and audiences, my search for an agent or manager in Toronto was less successful. During one audition, a not-so-charming fellow unknowingly did a Shirley imitation. The first comment out of his mouth when I finished my song was "Have you always been that fat?" The second was that while I had "something," he didn't know what to do with it. I understood both remarks. I simply did not fit into anyone's vision of a female solo artist, especially not in the Toronto of the late 1960s.

So, since my flatmates were graduating and making other life plans, I decided to come up with one of my own. In June 1971, I bought a one-way ticket to London England, to pursue a musical career, and ended up staying there for five years.

London Revisited

In a way, Dr. B was correct. I never made it as a great actress or a great singer. But I was good enough to work professionally and semi-professionally throughout the 1970s, in Canada and abroad. I even got my British Equity card, and a membership in the Canadian actors union (ACTRA).[131] Good enough is capital-S Something. But the reality of road trips and living in vans taught me what I needed to know about showbiz.

Reality also taught me what I needed to learn about the importance of structure and routine. I became more than good enough at office temp work in the hundreds of jobs I did in Toronto and London, where I developed the self-discipline and good work habits I sorely needed. The work gave me freedom, the responsibility to do whatever mindless or challenging task the day brought, and a modest income while I pursued a music career.

More important, I learned to see the positive in every situation – an important life lesson. I honed my office skills and excelled through sheer repetition. When equipment broke down, the repairman taught me how to use it. I learned to make small talk. To stop judging others. And to appreciate most of the people I worked with. I could keep my integrity by charging only for the hours I worked. I also learned how to focus – how to turn off the gibble-gabble.

I remember writing letters to friends back in Canada from the Binklebonk (Barclay's Bank in London) where I was a clerk-typist hooked up to a Dictaphone machine. Whenever I made an obvious typing error, I'd stop and glance at the rest of my work, and always find an earlier mistake. It was as if some inner guidance system alerted me to pay attention to what went before. Sort of like Zen and the Art of Temping. This track-back approach is used today to help addicts learn about their triggers. To look at what happened just before the urge or craving. Life always teaches us what we need to know, as long as we're willing to learn. And pay attention.

Along the way, I met some interesting and wonderful people, some of them well-known at the time.[132] I asked questions and gained knowledge about whatever business I was sent to, surprising most of the folks I worked for. Temps usually kept their noses to the grindstone, but my curiosity, suggestions, and involvement earned appreciation. Despite all this, I still remained on the diet-binge roller coaster.

Fat Acceptance

By late autumn 1971, I'd found a rather classy flat to share on Prince of Wales Drive, opposite Battersea Park. Quite a posh place, actually, and a major step up from the three tacky places I'd stayed in when I first arrived in June. I'd also joined some sort of diet club, the name of which escapes me, but it was a national organization with meetings across the country. No, it wasn't Weight Watchers.

At the time, this diet group differed from all others because on a daily basis, you could choose something sweet or salty from a list of calorie-counted treats in the diet booklet. The whole concept was based on non-deprivation.

The do-not-deprive theory is still alive and well today, and can be effective for certain people, but not those addicted to sugar or with strong sensitivities to other foods. I had no idea back then that a sugar addiction even existed, so I was thrilled to hear one speaker say that it did not matter where calories came from – they were all the same. Apparently, a daily allowance of twelve hundred calories' worth of chocolate was just as effective for weight loss as the equivalent in regular food. Imagine that! Although if you were a quantity fan, this wouldn't amount to very much chocolate on your plate.

One woman described how she had lost weight even though she consumed mainly sweets and junk food for several weeks – calorie-counted, of course. However, when her hair started to fall out and her skin turned into zit central, she decided to find a more balanced approach to eating. She still enjoyed her daily treat, of course.

It sounded good to me, and for the next six or seven weeks, I managed to stay on the treat diet and lose weight. Thrilled, I thought I'd finally hit upon the magic formula! Until I found myself binge eating on the long bus ride to what turned out to be my last meeting. En route, I realized I was playing some sort of terrible game with myself, and that Shirley was right – there was definitely something wrong with me. My farewell speech to the group left that bit out, but I did mention my decision to stop tormenting myself, to accept my body, and to work on improving myself as a person. At the time, I might even have believed what I was saying.

Fast forward several months to early 1972, when I received a phone call from a producer of the *David Frost Show*, inviting me to participate as an audience member in a TV show about weight loss. At first, I thought this was a mean joke, because David Frost (who had not yet been knighted by the Queen and therefore wasn't *Sir* David Frost) was a renowned British television personality who interviewed world leaders, politicians, and major international celebrities. A British version of the well-known American TV journalist, commentator, and talk-show host, Phil Donahue.

The producer told me that someone from the diet club had given her my name and phone number because I was giving up dieting and accepting myself as a fatty. It was probably stated more tactfully, but that was the gist. Of course I agreed to do the show. Very exciting.

If you've ever been part of a televised studio audience, you know the preparation that goes into every detail and that almost every second is timed and choreographed, with very little left to chance.

Selected people are seated within easy camera access, which is how I ended up in the centre section, several rows from the front, alongside several male experts – a physician, a psychiatrist, and an academic with several important credentials. In my lavender-coloured angora wool beret (a hat I wore everywhere), I glanced around excitedly at the packed house.

The show began with a look at weight loss methods and interviews with various experts, including one handsome hunk, a former weightlifting champion and authority on exercise. Eventually, the topic turned to fat acceptance, and it was my turn to speak. I blithered on about how there was too much emphasis nowadays on how people looked, and not enough focus on what they were really like, as people, on the inside.

When I finished uttering these pearls of wisdom, deafening silence rose up to greet me, instead of the standing ovation I'd fantasized. But a split second later, from the back row a woman with bleached- blond hair jumped out of her seat, both arms flailing in the air, and with the evangelistic zeal of a fundamentalist preacher intent on saving the world from Armageddon hell, shrieked, "I used to be fat and ugly, and now I'm thi-i-i-i-n!" She drew the word "thin" out so it reverberated with apocalyptic warning. I thought but didn't say, *Yes, now you're thin and ugly.* David Frost, to his credit, was able to calm her down quickly, and the show continued. A bit of an anti-climax, as far as I was concerned.

At the end, Mr. Frost asked the experts beside me to sum up and give their final comments. The psychiatrist said that the one person who had made the most sense, and with whom he agreed, was the woman in the purple hat. Hey, that was me! Finally, an accolade, understated though it was.

The truth is, at that point, I really did want to accept my weight, whatever it was. The constant fluctuation was unsettling on so many levels -- physically (especially on my digestive system), mentally, emotionally, and financially (binge food wasn't cheap if purchased in large quantities). The big problem was that I could never stay at any particular weight or size for longer than a few weeks. After a binge session, which might stop abruptly or taper off, I'd usually end up eating a lesser amount for a while. That not only felt good and moral and right, it would also inevitably lead to a bit of weight loss.

Feeling encouraged by this loss, I'd start taking more control of what I put into my mouth. This control gradually increased, until I became a nutbar about consuming fewer and fewer calories. For example, while sharing a flat in London's Holland Park area, I clearly remember walking a long way to buy a particular brand of tinned ravioli that was perhaps fifteen calories less than the brand sold closer to home. I also remember heating that tin, unopened, by immersing it in a pot of boiling water (not a clue where that idea came from). Everyone in the flat heard the explosion, and was shocked at what we saw as we entered the kitchen -- bits of ravioli suspended everywhere, hanging from the ceiling, dripping from the windows, walls, cupboards, and counters, and splattered all over the floor and the table, including someone else's dinner. I've never had ravioli since.

The Parking Lot

That same year, I spent the summer touring American Armed Forces bases in Germany with a British country-western band called Nashville Skyline, an homage to Bob Dylan's album of the same name. As lead female singer, I did solos and also duets with Michael, the male lead and head of the group. Michael and I had "chemistry," which sparkled on stage and exploded into arguments most other times. The other male band members (bass player, rhythm guitarist, and drummer) chose not to take sides, and preferred to get plastered instead.

Barbara, the back-up singer, was the other member of the band. A tall, long-haired, long-legged, shapely farm girl from Lichtenstein, with countless outfits composed of hot pants, mini-skirts, knee-high boots, and glittery halter tops, Barb was great as backup, but couldn't carry a tune on her own. But no one cared. Certainly not the soldiers for whom we performed, who took understandable pleasure just seeing her onstage. And there was my obese self, wearing the same floor-length dresses I'd worn to do temp office work. They were okay, but far from glamorous. (A friend in Toronto had made them for me before I left.)

No matter how much the crowd liked my songs, and no matter how loudly they cheered and whistled, standing next to Barb on those stages steadily deepened my shame. Comparisons were obvious and unstoppable. I didn't know it at the time, but except for office work (which I felt I'd earned), I had no place within me to receive compliments or praise, so any appreciation from the soldiers didn't register in my brain. I did have plenty of shame receptors, though, which increased tenfold during this adventure.

The shame-topper happened when we had some time off before our next gig. Everyone wanted to go swimming at a nearby beach. Everyone except me. I decided to stay in the van, unfortunately parked in the centre of a vast asphalt parking lot on what may have been one of the hottest days of the summer.

While I certainly didn't have a bathing suit, I could have chosen to sit on a picnic bench under a tree, but I had some journal writing to do to help me cope with the most recent altercation with Michael. I'd also secretly bought a large stash of German chocolate I'd never tried before and wanted to eat it in peace and privacy, without having to share (typical binge-eater behaviour).

Because the van was full of expensive musical equipment, it's easy to understand Michael's reluctance to leave it unlocked, but less easy to fathom why he wouldn't hand me the keys so I'd have the option of joining them later. He said the van couldn't be locked from the inside, so if I wasn't coming with him and the others right away, I'd have to be locked in.

The guys promised they'd only be an hour, tops, since we still had some distance to drive and needed time to set up before our performance that night. So setting aside my slight claustrophobic tendency, I chose to be locked in the van with my chocolate. A far better option, I thought, than watching Barb and her little bikini frolic in the sand and the water, and listening to my bandmates do running Monty Pythonesque commentaries on the bodies of every woman they saw.

So there I was, in my heavy denim jeans and denim shirt, sweltering under a hot tin roof in a sugar-induced haze and a sizzling pool of envy, self-pity, self- blame, self-doubt, and self-loathing. The van's tiny side windows only opened about three inches, so very little air flowed in.

The guys didn't return for three hours, during which time suicide crossed my mind several times.

If I'd stayed in that overheated van much longer, I wouldn't have needed to act on it. This isn't what people usually refer to as a "near death experience," but it was mine.

The power of shame has few limits, whatever its origins. It has pushed most of us who have wrestled with an eating disorder to extraordinary lengths. One of my most regrettable shame-driven choices was to let myself be locked in that van.

Despite their many flaws, the guys in the band never once said anything or shamed me about my weight or size, not even Michael. And they probably would have picked a fight with anyone who did, although they didn't need a reason to pick a fight. The shame was mine. I fat-shamed myself. "Fat-shaming" is a relatively new term, now accepted due to the obesity epidemics in many industrialized countries. Folks (the well-known and the unknown) can be held accountable (or shamed) online for it. But no one could have held me accountable, because I never spoke it.

Nor was I aware how deeply shame was entrenched in my psyche, and how it informed so many of my choices. Originally planted by Shirley, I unconsciously took over and regularly watered the fat- shaming seeds, so that they blossomed secretly in the background no matter where I went or what I did.

For years, I remained unaware of shame's influence. It hovered silently behind the scene even when I finally reached goal weight, which I'll get to shortly.

Does It Look like a Duck?

When I came home to Canada in 1976, I picked up where I'd left off: temp work, singing gigs, and an ultimate return to group therapy with Dr. Jack Birnbaum, hoping once again to get a handle on my compulsive eating.

On March 28, 1979, Dr. Paul E. Garfinkel,[133] then a staff psychiatrist at the Clarke Institute (who ultimately became an eating disorder expert and head of CAMH), wrote a three-page letter to Jack, thanking him for "allowing me to see this most interesting patient." That's me. After an initial conversation, Dr. Garfinkel decided to include me in his body image study. And I agreed.

In his letter, Dr. Garfinkel did a great job of summarizing my life up until that point, focusing on my history of "bulimia"[134] (the term then used for binge eating) with weight fluctuations, "transient" weight loss attempts, sexual history, details of my family history, and a summary of my progress as a Clarke inpatient.

He described me at 150 lbs as "mildly obese." He specified what I usually ate when "in control" (what I call dieting), and noted my behaviour when "out of control" (what I call bingeing, and what he called "bulimic").

When out of control, she eats fairly large quantities steadily for several hours. The quantities, however, are considerably reduced in comparison with several years ago.

It's worth noting here that my "reduced" binges were viewed as progress, and had been seen that way even before I left the Clarke ten years prior, not only by me, but also by the professionals who worked with me. We all thought this signified eventual success and that I was heading in the right direction. How fooled we all were!

The unfortunate truth is that although I did make advances in many other areas of my life, any so- called improvement on my eating disorder was a misdirect. You know the phrase "If it looks like a duck, walks like a duck, and quacks like a duck, it's a duck"? Well, that does not apply here. My reduced binges looked like progress, sounded like progress, but quacked like a duck. So the idea of forward movement was a myth.

In fact, as Dr. Garfinkel's letter points out, in certain ways, the compulsive eating got worse and went underground:

> *The triggers ... are not hunger sensations, but thoughts of a drive to eat in response to strong emotional feelings, both pleasurable and unpleasant ... these bring out a sense of her being out of control. While the bulimic periods have decreased in frequency ... there has recently been the onset of night eating, i.e., since last fall she often gets up from sleep, not totally awake, and eats ... almost once per week.*

I *was* totally out of control. Just like someone who loses their temper in a flash, like Shirley. That's sometimes what a binge is. You lose your temper, using food. You bite, chomp, munch, crunch, chew, and swallow instead of throwing things, slamming doors, or yelling (also not advisable, but included here to show the strength and ferocity of many of my anger-based binges).

More important, I'd almost forgotten the night eating. It probably started before I returned to Canada, but I'm not sure. I'd awake in the morning to find empty cartons or packaging, with only a vague memory of having eaten the contents the night before. Since I lived on my own (except for my pets), and since the likelihood of someone sneaking into my place just to consume my food was below zero, it had to be me who ate this stuff. Frustrating. Scary. And baffling.

It was one thing to lose control during the day, but what chance did I have at night? Clearly, to use Gestalt terminology, lots of unfinished business lurked beneath the surface.

[She] has experienced rare vomiting, on three or four occasions following binge eating. This has been associated with diarrhea and is not self-induced.

These clinical notes don't convey the real picture. I wouldn't have told anyone the real picture, or accurately described the contents of a typical binge, any more than I would have walked naked in public.

First, I would have felt too ashamed. Equally important, it's often hard to remember everything eaten during a binge, especially if it lasts more than an hour. And especially if a lot of sugar and junk food is consumed, which can fog up your brain. If you were an accomplished long-term binge eater, which I was, you could polish off an incredible amount of food in ten minutes.

Disgust alert! Don't read this paragraph if you don't want to be appalled and repulsed. A number of times in my binge-eating career I ate so much stuff so quickly that my body literally couldn't take it anymore. And the two delightful experiences of diarrhea and vomiting erupted at the same time. I remember using two pails, one for each end, because I couldn't get to the washroom in time. I felt wretched, like the lowest of the low, distraught with self-contempt and self-loathing. In pain physically, mentally, and emotionally.

The very first time my body exploded this way, I was living in London. I thought for sure I'd hit bottom and would remember sinking into this repugnant cesspool. But I didn't remember. Because there was a next time. And even if an image of the two pails had come to mind, it would have been swept aside by the sheer strength of the obsession and compulsion to overeat. Progress? Nope.

After the third or fourth time doing the two-pail thing, I began to wonder if I was possessed. I wasn't, at least not in the demonic way this word is used. But in another way, I felt like I was at the mercy of some inner wrongness I didn't understand, but kept trying to understand. I assumed that understanding would automatically lead to change. It doesn't.

I don't recall the interview session with Dr. Garfinkel, the satiety or personality tests (which may simply have been interview questions) or the EEG[135] (a brainwave scan) he ordered because of the night eating and bingeing.

But I clearly remember the body image study. I had to strip down to my underwear and stand there while head-to-toe photographs were taken. Afterwards, these images were projected onto a large screen, and adjusted in various ways, as I identified those that looked most like me. I know I felt embarrassed and humiliated at the time, even though I'd lost forty or fifty pounds and my remaining weight was evenly distributed. It was, however, the same forty or fifty I'd lost and regained countless times, over and over and over again. Nice, but no big deal.

The diagnosis: "bulimia within the context of a personality disorder largely of an hysterical type." Whew! I got stuck when I first read that in 2006. Personality disorders (PDs) are sets of enduring traits that don't change over a person's lifetime. And yet, in his letter, Dr. Garfinkel praised the "marked improvement" I'd made over the years. The characteristics of someone with a hysterical PD tend to match those of many addicts, regardless of their substance of abuse: overly dramatic, reactive, and self-centred.[136] So in that sense, he was correct.

But back in the 1960s and 1970s, women were often diagnosed as "hysterical," given Valium or other tranquillizers and sent on their merry way.[137]

In the end, Dr. Garfinkel "agreed" with Jack that as little emphasis as possible should be put on "weight and eating habits."

The idea was that once I got other issues sorted out, my eating habits would improve over time. Kind of a harm-reduction approach, emphasizing the progress and the positives.

After a while, I stopped going to Jack's group because I no longer found it helpful. Binges and weight fluctuations ebbed and flowed as they always had. The night eating and two-pail sessions occasionally reoccurred.

When I returned to Canada from England in 1976, I destroyed whatever few photos I had of me at my heaviest, for example when I wore maternity clothes (and wasn't pregnant) and when I wore a Canadian size 24. From that time forward, like many who have been labelled "obese" or who are sensitive about their weight, I avoided being photographed (only one of the shots below were posed). Three of the pictures below were taken during two major relapses during my recovery process (mid-1980s, and mid-1990s), when I regained about half of the 70-90 pounds originally lost.

Me singing at friend
Dorothy & Bob's wedding,
1969.

Me in London, England, probably
1974.

Me, mid-1990s.

Me, while visiting my sister
on Canada's West Coast,
mid-1990s.

Me in mid-1980s.

CHAPTER 16: A NEW DIRECTION

The Turning Point

Another two years passed before I found the help I needed. After finishing up a great "executive assistant" contract in 1980, I'd started a new career path with a company that would train me as a computer programmer. I was finally off the office-ghetto track and on my way!

As the three- and six-month probation periods went by, despite the long hours and exhausting mental focus, I believed I was home free. I wasn't. On or about the nine-month mark, I got fired. It catapulted me headlong into the abyss of despair.

That fateful May of 1981, if binge eating had a skid row, a Bowery, or a filthy gutter, I was in it, or speeding towards it. The month itself was spent mainly in a blur, a sugar- and binge-induced stupor. I ate until I threw up from cramming so much down my gullet, or until I passed out coming down from the sugar rush. I shopped for food, ordered in, and stared at the TV while I gorged. That's what I did. Friends who were used to giving me "my space" stopped calling.

Too many two-pail experiences brought me to my knees, not in reverence, but in agony. I could not stop bingeing. This wretched nightmare seemed endless. There was no night, no day. When I awoke from a restless sleep and I saw it was seven o'clock, I didn't know whether it was morning or evening. I kept thinking I'd hit bottom and that now I could change. Except no change was imminent, and one miserable twenty-four hours rolled into the next, indistinguishable from its predecessor.

The who-you-hallelujah chorus button was on repeat, as flashbacks of my countless failures came to mind. Even music, my other go-to for comfort (besides food), now came with its own pain attachment. Ever since a disastrous mid-winter tour in 1979 to Newfoundland with a pop band – in the back of a van – I'd consigned any professional musical ambition to the junk heap. So music was no longer available to provide relief. And neither was food, but I kept on eating, anyway, because I simply could not stop.

Amidst the fog and food, one moment stands out. A brief black-and-white TV ad on one of the American channels showed a woman standing in front of an open refrigerator, weeping. The voice-over mentioned a twelve-step program that could help. I've never seen anything similar in the more than three decades since. At the time, I didn't have the wherewithal to write down a phone number. But shortly after, I must have looked it up and made the call. A woman phoned back and told me, among other things, where and when there was a meeting nearby.

After several weeks, on June 3, 1981, with great trepidation and doubt, I wandered into a garishly bright church basement in Toronto. Little did I know that from that day onward, my life would never be the same.

Goal Weight at Last

It took me about a year in the twelve-step program (henceforth referred to as just "the program") to reach goal weight, something that had never happened before. Some doctor somewhere had once told me that 133 pounds would be about right for my height. So I'd chosen that as the magic number. With 220 as my highest "known" weight, a safe estimate is that I probably lost between seventy and ninety pounds. But I can't be absolutely sure because I refused to get on a scale when I joined the program, and didn't until June 3, 1982, my one-year anniversary date.

This was a Very Big Deal. I'd never reached any specifically set goal before, especially not one related to weight, and I had no idea how to be with it. My reaction was a mixture of excitement and terror. What did this mean?

Quite early on, I remember thinking if this is how I looked at 133 pounds, how would I look at 122, or 111? (This is how anorexia can begin.) If you wonder why I picked these particular numbers, all I can tell you is that I'd dabbled in numerology, where increments of eleven are considered master numbers. This is where my head was, and one of the ways I mentally coped with such a major change.

This may sound strange, but where losing weight is concerned, there is a difference between those who were once slim and those who have never been. I'm not saying it's easier, but the former do have a familiar place to return to, a memory bank of physical and psychological experience, while the latter do not. So if you've never been at a low weight, getting there can be scary. Of course, I must have passed the 133 mark for a few moments en route to obesity without it consciously registering. But once I actually reached that number, no familiar reference point was anywhere in sight.

So as the pounds came off and my pants got baggier and baggier, I kept wearing them. Until someone said something to me. Then I had to shop for new clothes.

At the time, I didn't know how terrified I really was. My food addiction and binge eating had succeeded in keeping most emotions at bay, including fear. So I didn't know how to recognize it.

What's more, being fatandugly was part of my identity. So now, who the hell was I? I didn't know. Was I thin and ugly, like the woman on the *David Frost Show*? I hoped not, but I wasn't sure.

So I got busy. Busy being thin. Except that I didn't think of myself that way, even at goal weight. I considered myself no-longer-fat. With this new status, I allowed myself to go where I'd never been before. To places like the gym to participate in various workout classes. First, though, I had to check out who else was in the class to make sure I was no longer the fattest. Sometimes it was hard to tell. While I may not have accomplished much in the way of exercise, that wasn't really the point. The point was to simply be there in a non-fat way.

I took my no-longer-fat self to other places I'd avoided in the past due to shame. Such as social events, parties, and dances.

There, too, my focus became comparative fatness or thinness. I can't really say I enjoyed these functions – I had to learn how to do that – but I did mentally appreciate being there without standing out in the old fatandugly way.

Me in June 1982, after losing 70-90 lbs.

Me in 1989 with Toronto City Hall in the background.

Me with Shirley in front of Barker Street house, 1991.

Me in 2006.

The Myth of Thin

As you've read in earlier pages, throughout my life I believed with all my heart that once I lost weight and got thin, my life would turn into wonderland and all my dreams would come true. This "thintasy," fostered by Shirley, helped me tolerate being painfully obese in a world where obesity was much less common than it is today. Shirley promised "the world will be your oyster." I didn't know what an oyster world would look like, but I did imagine what would happen if I was thin.

First, I'd be able to walk into any store and try anything on (all stores would have my size) and everything would fit perfectly and look sensational.

My second fantasy was that any guy I wanted would automatically be attracted to me. Moreover, I would have no heartbreak and no annoying relationship issues (after all, thin people always lived happily ever after).

Third, I would get whatever job(s) I wanted, and as a thin person, would somehow automatically acquire the skills to do them.

And finally, everyone would like me. Having worked so hard on my capital-P Personality and having thought about things so deeply, I wouldn't just be another of those shallow skinny bitches. My suffering would pay off.

Such imaginary experiences engraved in my brain helped me envision a future I could look forward to without worry or pain. So being thin was this magical power that meant true happiness in every way. Forever.

This, of course, did not turn out to be the case. When I finally reached goal weight, a bolt of happiness, with its corresponding fashion, romance, job, and people success, did not come along for the ride. What a shocker! Now, a new scientific study[138] has proven that physical weight loss on its own does not translate into happiness.

In fact, the study, which involved almost two thousand people who lost a significant amount of weight, showed that although their physical health usually improved, factors affecting their mental health (for example, depression) often got worse! And no wonder.

When I reached goal weight, the first surprising disappointment came in the clothing department. While all stores carried my average size, the outfits I liked were often out of stock. And many of the clothes I did try on either didn't fit properly or felt uncomfortable -- for various reasons having nothing to do with weight. That was a huge and unpleasant discovery.

I was even more disappointed in the romance arena. While being thin helped me feel more confident about how I looked, I hadn't learned through experience how to deal with the trials and tribulations of dating. What's more, being thin didn't automatically make me attractive to all men. (I am now grateful for that, for I would definitely not have been able to handle that kind of attention.)

When it came to jobs, again I did feel more confident when applying, but I often had to start at the bottom and slog away to acquire skills (like everyone else!) Another irksome discovery.

And, as you probably can guess, everyone did not like me when I got thin. This was possibly the hardest pill to swallow, no matter how many people-pleasing tricks I pulled out of the hat. In other words, being at goal weight was certainly preferable to being obese. But it was far – very far – from the be-all and end-all I had imagined.

The authors of the study concluded that when people are encouraged to lose weight for physical- health reasons, they might be better served if they also had mental-health support to help them manage. I was extremely fortunate to have such support from the program, and from the various therapists I worked with over the years.

We already know that maintaining a weight loss of any significance is usually more difficult than losing the weight. Surely, mental wellness and emotional wellness are key factors that should not be overlooked when people face losing weight.

Psychotherapy or mental-health support during and after weight loss can help prevent putting those pounds back on again, along with their accompanying misery. And acknowledging the myth of "thin" for what it is – a lot of wishful, highly unrealistic thinking – can make it easier to navigate such an important passage.

Fathead

"In my own mind, I am still a fat brunette from Toledo, and I always will be." (Gloria Steinem)[139]

At the time, I had no idea that losing a lot of weight could be so confusing. Once I reached my target weight, I knew at some level that I was an average size (or what passed as an average size back in 1982). But it was easy to forget.

Here's an example of how my own fathead worked. One fine spring day while walking along Dundas Street in Toronto's Chinatown and feeling pretty spiffy in one of my favourite new outfits, I bumped into someone I hadn't seen for several years, when I was at least seventy pounds heavier. We chatted for a while, but the other person made absolutely no mention of my appearance or considerably decreased size. The result: I came away from that conversation wondering if I had actually lost weight, a thought so troubling I had to phone someone to confirm my weight loss as a fact.

Later I realized how much I relied on what other people thought (just like Shirley had wanted) to tell me who I was and how I was, and that my attachment to this external focus could not be permitted to continue. As part of the fathead syndrome, my confusion was not that unusual.

The fathead period of adjustment showed up in other ways. For example, I often got confused about my 5'4½" height. Thanks to my excess weight and in part to Robert and Shirley, I often felt bigger and taller than that. However, after losing seventy to ninety pounds, I felt smaller (which I was) and shorter (which I wasn't).

Puzzled by this misperception, I'd invite my friends to do a "who's taller" comparison. As a formerly heavy person, drawing attention to my physical body in any way was something I avoided like the plague, lest anyone notice my hugeness and wonder how I got that way. But at goal weight, standing back-to-back with various kind and obliging friends as someone appraised our heights, I was always dumbfounded to discover we were the same height or that I was actually taller. This directly contradicted my own perceptions of being shorter. And smaller. And sent me into a bit of a panic. I felt a bit like Alice, whose self-perception changes after she's fallen down the rabbit hole.[140]

What size was I, anyway? While I often felt smaller, I grappled mentally whenever I was able to fit into a "small" size anything, an unexpectedly uncomfortable experience for Robert's formerly "big" daughter. Feeling small or smaller also made me feel more vulnerable, since I lacked the heft that accompanied excess poundage. A very scary prospect indeed as I traipsed around Toronto. And confusing. What did I actually look like? I could no longer trust my own eyes.

What complicated matters even more is that after I reached goal weight, I actually grew half an inch taller, to 5'5." This happened after I started seeing a chiropractor to alleviate the constant internal crunching noises whenever I moved. As mentioned earlier,[141] my slumped posture, which began in my early teen years, had made it physically impossible for me to stand up straight.

Chiropractic treatments not only remedied this, but also prevented a slipped disc and helped ease some of the physiological tension caused by the many new fears associated with a changed body. A preventative maintenance program with a chiropractor has been part of my self-care routine ever since.

So even though I knew on a cognitive level that I was, in fact, a bit taller, I still felt shorter and smaller than others when this clearly wasn't the case. The anxiety of my new relative size was by far the most disturbing aspect of having a fathead.

Food First

Most of the ideas in this chapter were first encountered and learned in the program. Many have since been supported by research and adapted by eating disorder treatment centres across the globe and are a major part of any treatment approach, with a few exceptions, which I'll point out as we go along.

The Eating Part

Here's what I learned quite early on about eating. No dieting. Eat moderate planned meals (with snacks, if required) on a regular basis. Eat nothing in between. Drink enough liquids (water, coffee, tea). And avoid troublesome binge foods. And if you wanted to weigh and measure certain food groups to keep yourself honest, that was okay.

Back in 1981, the idea of not dieting sounded quite freeing and almost revolutionary, which may have been one of the reasons I liked it. A diet, as we know, has come to be known as a restrictive plan you stay on for a while and eventually go off. Or fall off. Then you feel like a failure, again. In contrast, not dieting means finding a plan you can stay on and live with. While there may be changes and adjustment over time to manage health or situational concerns, or new learning about yourself, there's no "off" button when you're not dieting.

So when you make a mistake and slip or binge (which everyone inevitably does), you still carry on with the plan. When the next mealtime rolls around, you don't skip it. I used to do that a lot. To compensate for a binge, I'd miss a meal or two, which then set me up to be extra hungry, which in turn led me to overeat at the next meal (or even beforehand). Overeating, itself a trigger, led to yet another binge, and the misery cycle would continue.

Over time, I discovered how important it was after a binge to get back to the regular mealtime routine as soon as possible. To keep getting back on that horse. And somehow find a way to accept the consequences of the binge and learn something from it.

For me, not dieting also implied that I didn't have to eat "diet food" anymore. That meant using no products, such as salad dressing, with the word "diet" or "low-calorie" or low-anything on it ever again. Back then, it also meant no cottage cheese or tuna – foods I associated with failed diets that had led to weight gain and misery. Some of these items were eventually integrated back into my plan, but it took a while.

Being able to choose the foods I wanted to include within the three meal allotment felt wonderful. Nobody told me what I could and could not eat. Like many others hung up on weight and food, I had already consumed books on nutrition and had enough solid information to guide me to (relatively) healthy balanced choices.

Contrast that with today's glut of food-related information everywhere, which seems to increase exponentially. Books, print, and online articles in newspapers, magazines, and blogs, along with features on radio and television shows arm us with the latest up-to-date theory, fad, recipe, diet, warning, and research findings related to food and its consumption.

Choosing what to eat in our mixed-media climate can be overwhelming. Back in my dieting days, I was mainly concerned about caloric content and fat grams. Front pages did not feature headlines about obesity or offer weight loss advice, nor were there entire TV shows devoted to that topic. Now, many more ways to eat "healthy" (which involve restricting or limiting food choices) are available to obsess over.

As well as the "lows" (low-cal, low-fat, low-carb, low-salt, and low-glycemic), and the "frees" (sugar-free, fat-free, meat-free, dairy-free, gluten-free, wheat-free, GMO-free, free-range, and free-trade, not to mention pesticide-free, hormone-free, anti-biotic-free, and MSG-free), you've also got pressure to buy organic, local, or both.

Add to that the plethora of fast-food and junk-food outlets with their huge advertising budgets, omnipresence at schools and universities, and portable menu options, and you've created temptations that are hard to resist. And inner conflict.

For today's binge eaters, food choices can be agonizing. To cope, some resort to a very limited menu, while others fear any limitation lest they rebel and overeat even more. To help eliminate the guesswork, some successful multibillion-dollar businesses offer meal plans with easy-to-count options, or an increasingly wide selection of convenient frozen or prepackaged entrees or meals.

Nowadays, most eating disorder treatment centres have adopted the regular meal concept. The first principle is to nourish and stabilize the body. Providing a steady stream of nutrition lays the physical and mental groundwork for all the other healing that needs to take place. But this is easier to say than do.

It is fairly well-known that people with anorexia don't eat enough to sustain their bodies in good health. But neither do some obese individuals, whose bodies are operating in nutritional-starvation mode. Their dieting periods have been so restrictive that their bodies have decided to hold on to the extra pounds in preparation for the next famine. In their attempts to lose the excess weight, they eat less and less, but their bodies soon adjust to that amount. Understandably, they fear gaining even more weight if they increase their food intake and eat regular moderate meals. Since 2007, I've seen many such clients in my psychotherapy practice. Usually, after trying regular meals for a while, they feel more balanced and stable, mentally and physically.

But in 1981, I knew instinctively that eating three moderate meals a day (plus one specific snack) would get me where I wanted to go in terms of my weight, as long as I didn't binge. That's the tricky part.

The Not Eating Part

The main idea here is to identify particular binge foods and avoid them. This is the more controversial piece. Some argue that eliminating binge foods is part of a restrictive regime and creates or increases guilt and a sense of deprivation. Others say that if certain foods trigger overeating, for physiological or psychological reasons, then they need at best to be regarded with caution. Still others claim that some foods are actually physically addictive, like alcohol to the alcoholic or heroin to the heroin junkie, and should be eliminated.

The idea of avoiding binge foods is one that is not yet widely accepted by national organizations such as NEDIC (Canada's National Eating Disorder Information Centre) or NEDA (the National Eating Disorder Association in the United States), or even BEDA (the Binge Eating Disorder Association, also in the United States). At most treatment centres I've heard of, everyone who lives in or who attends a day program is generally required to eat everything, including snacks and sweet treats, unless they're allergic or have medically diagnosed conditions. Restriction and deprivation are out. All-inclusive menus are in.

This seemingly rigid non-restrictive stance has been adopted because so many people along the disordered eating spectrum are actually afraid of food and eating, since both can make them get fat (or fatter). Many have also tried to follow various rules and diets for so long that the number of foods they let themselves eat is very small. Understandably, widening the choice would seem a much healthier alternative. But as is often the pattern with change, the pendulum may have swung too far the other way.

Back in 1981, avoiding binge foods didn't make any sense to me at first. Given half the chance, I could binge on anything. Sure, I had my favourites, but when these weren't available, it almost didn't matter. Like most binge eaters, when I felt like I had to eat and keep on eating, that's exactly what I did. In that sense, all foods were binge foods. Anything edible went down the hatch, along with some barely edible items, like semi-thawed frozen food, food retrieved from the garbage, and crazy concoctions created from whatever ingredients were available.

However, some foods themselves actually foster and/or create cravings. Thanks to research, we know now that junk food has been specifically developed and designed to do just that.[142] You can't eat just one, or only some. You don't have to be a binge eater to always want more. As program people suggested, I listed off a slew of foods like that – sweet, salty, chewy, crunchy, smooth, cold, warm, and aromatic. They mainly fell into the dessert, snack, or junk food categories.

People also tend to binge on certain foods with emotional or childhood associations because doing so brings comfort in some way. Maybe they were deprived of those foods as a child, or maybe these items were always available.

At one of my earliest meetings that summer in 1981, I heard one woman identify bread as her primary binge food. To her, the idea of giving up bread forever was too difficult. Impossible. She simply couldn't do it, and it wasn't for lack of trying. One simple concept, however, made it possible. She didn't need to give up bread forever, she just needed to avoid it for just one day. Today. When she awoke one morning, she figured she could live without bread for that one day, and she did. In fact, she kept on giving up bread, one day at a time, for the two years since she'd been in program. And ever since, for the past thirty-five years. Sounds easy, doesn't it?

In some ways, doing things "one day at a time" is easier than carrying "forever" or "never" along for the ride. But in other ways, individual days can bring with them some excruciatingly tempting moments.

The woman's story impressed me. It was a new and different way to think about things. Most of the items on my particular binge food list had next to zero nutritional value. I could definitely avoid them for one day. But I wasn't too sure I could keep it up on an ongoing basis. Whoops. I'd forgotten not to think outside the "today" box.

Some people with disordered eating not only become afraid of food and eating, they also fear enjoying what they eat. I've seen all three in my psychotherapy practice. The main worry: enjoyment might make them want to eat more and lead to weight gain. In fact, the opposite is true. Enjoying what you eat and feeling satisfied with what you eat means you are less likely to overeat. Unless, of course, something else is going on.

I'm all in favour of moderation, when and if it can be managed, and I support an individual's right to "experiment" or "conduct research" to find out what binge foods can and cannot be handled. Some circumstances may work, and others may not.

Addictive Foods

At some point during that first summer in the program, a man named Gord suggested I read a book called *Sugar Blues,* by William Dufty, because it had made a huge difference to him.

Gord was certainly an unusual character. A former gutter drunk who had been homeless and destitute for years, Gord ultimately joined Alcoholics Anonymous, sobered up, got his act together, and had been sober ever since. He discovered, however, that he began relying more on food and overeating to avoid dealing with his problems, and noticed he couldn't stay away from the doughnuts and cookies usually provided, along with coffee, at his AA meetings. In fact, his obsession and cravings for sweet things made him feel as if his sobriety was in jeopardy. After reading Dufty's book and getting off sugar (and white flour), he discovered that the sweet cravings soon disappeared, and his desire to overeat other foods lessened.

Note that some people with addictive tendencies often switch their addictive substances or behaviours when they get off their substance of choice. The sober alcoholic might turn to food, or sex, or gambling. The recovering binge eater might start relying on shopping or booze. That is, "unless and until" (to borrow a Dr. Phil phrase) they do the necessary mental and emotional work so that they can heal.

I liked Gord, which was rare in itself, because I didn't like most people I met when I first joined the program. So I bought Dufty's book and decided to include sugar as a binge food. Note: when Dufty refers to sugar, he is talking about refined sugar and white flour, the highly processed stuff, as well as the various sugar derivations, such as high fructose corn syrup, or HFC, found in most processed foods. At Dufty's suggestion, I read labels and became willing to do whatever it took to stay off the sweet stuff.

Dufty is not talking about the natural sugars found in fruits and vegetables, which our bodies need and process differently. I mention this now because as a therapist, I see individuals who have taken the

no-sugar idea to extremes. Because of their natural sugars, one young woman had eliminated all fruits and most vegetables from her diet, especially those higher on the glycemic index. She'd found that idea on the internet, and taken what was to be a two-week sugar detox plan to extremes. Fortunately, she realized she needed help.

I can honestly say that my brain changed after I'd been off sugar and white flour for a few weeks. Imagine turning on the radio and getting mainly static, no matter where you turn the dial. You can hear faint sounds from the various channels as they converge, but no single station comes in clearly. That was my brain on sugar. That was my only known normal.

After a few weeks away from sugar, the mental static was gone. While many channels still came in together, they were each somewhat discernible. And gradually, over time, I became able to hear one or two stations clearly. These were thoughts I'd suppressed for years at last coming to awareness. Usually tangled, many of them conflicting and/or irrational (such as the who-you-hallelujah chorus). But there they were in my conscious awareness and ready to be worked on.

I began to write out what I "heard." Notebook after notebook full of stream-of-consciousness gibble-gabble drivel. But occasionally, a particular thought or idea made me sit up and take notice. A kernel of truth amidst the clutter. I'd struck gold!

Gradually, I made new inroads into understanding what made me tick and why I'd needed to abuse food and abuse myself with food for so many years.

As I've mentioned throughout this book, there is now ample scientific evidence[143] that sugar can not only be addictive, but also harmful to certain people. It's certainly gratifying to be validated by science.

Not everyone, though, has the same reaction to sugar as I do, just like there are those who can use cocaine or alcohol and not get addicted. I know some individuals who can have sugar and sugar products occasionally. It's a grey area for them, so they are careful with it. Others can eat sugar with impunity and not crave it or care about it that much. These are the folks who can eat a square or two of chocolate a day, and can walk around for weeks with a partially eaten chocolate bar in their handbags and not have it gnaw at their brains screaming "Eat me!"

Everyone is different, and eating disorder treatment centres need to come to terms with this fact. Insisting that a sugar addict eat sweet desserts may help them in the short term, especially when they are locked up in a residence for treatment, but it doesn't help them in the long run, when they are out on their own.

To date, there doesn't seem to be a blood or urine test available to see if people are particularly vulnerable to a sugar addiction, but I sure hope someone develops one. Soon.

I do not want to give the impression that once I got off sugar, I stayed off it happily ever after.

Because that would be far from the truth. In fact, over the past three decades, I've conducted plenty of my own "research" and experimentation on the matter. And suffered the accompanying consequences (see "Relapse" later in this chapter).

For example, one day, in a particularly defiant mood, I decided to hell with it. I would eat one licorice Twizzler that beck-

oned to me at my corner convenience store. After careful moni-
toring, what surprised me was that I had no adverse reaction at
all. A happy thought crossed my mind: maybe now I was one of
those lucky "normal" people who could handle sugar occasionally. (Note: being a so-called "normal eater," whatever that may be
-- if it even exists -- is a common yearning or fantasy of many
who binge eat or compulsively overeat.)

So the following week I had another strand of licorice. And
several days later, yet another. You'd think at this point I'd catch
on to the increasing pattern of use, but self-deception is very
much part of the addiction process. So I blithely continued, until
blam! I was headlong into a doozy of a binge, not just on sugar,
but on whatever else I could get my little paws on.

I would like to tell you that this licorice incident was a one-
off and that I smartened up and never ate a sugar product from
that point on. Again, that would not be true. Stubbornness is another one of the characteristics addicts everywhere share, and I
was no exception. I kept doing my "research" until I finally had
to acknowledge that indeed, I am a sugar junkie. (Incidentally,
the upside of stubbornness is perseverance, and I also have plenty
of that.)

My experience with sugar isn't unique. One young woman
who struggled with sweet foods thought she might be a sugar
addict, but didn't want to give it up if she didn't have to. I suggested she try staying off it for a little while, just to see what
would happen. She decided on a two-week period. Without sugar
(and white flour), she experienced peace of mind for the first
time in her life, which blew her away. Despite this, she felt she
needed to conduct a further investigation, so she ate sugar products and then stopped, then started again, and so on. Eventually,
she came to place a higher value on the sweetness brought by
peace of mind than on the brief anticipatory excitement leading
up to the high she'd get from sugar.

Peace of mind. Five decades ago, before I got myself down
to the Clarke Institute, I had no idea what this meant. I equated it

with interminable numbness and boredom, and no feeling at all. (That wasn't peace of mind, by the way, it was depression. The who-you-hallelujah chorus had been turned down so low it was barely discernible, thanks to all the junk I was bingeing on.)

Years later I'd hear people in the program talk about serenity and think, *Who cares?* All I wanted to know back then was how much weight people lost.

But once I'd been off the sugar for a while and had stopped bingeing, the who-you-hallelujah chorus came to life, accompanied by other noisy thoughts in my brain. That's when I saw serenity, calmness, or peace of mind in a different light.

Now, peace of mind has risen to the top of my "what I want" list. Whenever I'm tempted to do more "research" on sugar, I know that peace of mind is what I'll be giving up. The choice is that simple. Because once I start eating sugar, and/or indulge in a binge, I do not know when I might stop. Maybe in ten minutes. Or an hour. Maybe not for several days. Or weeks. Months even. Experience has shown me it's impossible to predict.

Since peace of mind has such a high priority, when wrestling with a challenge, I'm now willing to do what it takes to bring it back when it's gone. Peace of mind has, for the most part, become an integral part of my version of "normal."

Life in Between

The whole point of avoiding binge foods and eating regular moderate meals is what happens in between those feeding times, as you live your life. Stabilizing your meals and avoiding binge foods means that any cravings and/or desire to eat (or eat more) are not based on hunger or an addictive-type of inducement, but on a range of other things.

That is the real work – finding out what makes you want to eat, otherwise known in the addictive world as "triggers."

I well remember when this idea became crystal clear. One afternoon at home in my little apartment (I wasn't working since being fired less than eight weeks before) about an hour after my usual lunch (which had been the same thing every day since I'd started the program), I felt "hungry" and wanted something more to eat. This seemed odd. I wondered why I wasn't hungry after the same lunch the day before and the day before that. I decided to phone someone from the program.

The woman I called heard me out and then asked if I'd been to the bathroom lately. She also wanted to know if I was tired or if I was thirsty. Her questions seemed very odd, until she patiently explained that each of those three circumstances had created in her a desire to binge. So those were the three questions she always asked herself first whenever she had food thoughts or cravings in between mealtimes.

When I got off the phone, at her suggestion I decided to find out whether any of those three conditions applied. Two of them did. I did have to go to the bathroom and I was thirsty.

My almost total lack of awareness of my body's needs was the root cause of my wanting to eat at that particular time. Being out of touch with my own body probably started long before the blossoming of my binge eating (when I was ten or eleven). I learned from an early age to do as I was told, regardless of my own needs. I didn't obey, of course, but I got the message that my own emotional needs were unimportant.

As the compulsion to eat picked up steam and gradually took over my thinking, and as I gained increasing amounts of weight, detaching from my body physically and psychologically completed the picture. By the time I became a teenager, all the normal bodily cues that people experience, including the need to eliminate, quench thirst, and sleep, got channeled in my brain into one major command. *Eat!* Of course, all the girdles I wore didn't help the situation. They dug into my skin, causing great welts, which I taught myself to ignore.

After asking for help that afternoon and then paying attention to my own physical needs, I was quite surprised when my hunger disappeared. Gone. That moment has stayed with me all these years, because it was the first time I understood that beneath my cravings, unknown factors were at work.

Of course, the next time I got a feeling of hunger in between meals, I checked out those three conditions first. When they didn't apply, or when they did but my desire to eat was still operating, I had to reach out again to get some help. And that became the new healing pattern.

I began to see any in-between-meals craving as a signal that I needed to pay attention to something triggering me on a physical, emotional, and/or mental level. Decades later, I am still learning, and still paying attention to those somethings.

In the old days, the word used was "introspection," but nowadays we are probably more familiar with the term "mindfulness" or "self-reflection." My own preference, a Gestalt term, is "awareness." But the word matters less than the actual process, which differs considerably from the endless ruminations, mental meanderings, and analytical claptrap of my younger days.

As a recovering addict, you'd think I would know all my triggers by now. Nope. As I change and grow older, and as the world around me changes, so do the challenges and learning situations.

My tendency now is to work on problems or issues as or before they arise, to prevent any potential overeating or binge eating notions from bothering me. This proactive approach, and one that's taught to all addicts, reminds me of a phrase borrowed from one of those old cowboy westerns, when the leader tells his posse they're going to "head 'em off at the pass." I'm heading the food thoughts off at the pass, before they become problematic.

People on the disordered eating spectrum tend to have certain triggers in common, while others are specific to each individual. Think of all the external cues in our media-rich environment related to desirable food – the sight, smell, and sounds associated with the pleasurable and fun pastime of eating. Simply watching a TV ad or noticing someone eat something while walking along the street can trigger a desire in the observer to do the same, which is why ads are so effective.

While we can avoid or shut out those obvious food-related external triggers to a certain extent, at least on a temporary basis, dealing with what goes on internally (that is, emotionally and mentally) is much more difficult.

Once I got off the diet-binge cycle, reactions to internal events were probably the most difficult triggers to uncover. Thinking a particular thought (or combinations of thoughts), or being unable to identify a particular feeling (or combination of feelings) usually strengthened the desire to binge myself into oblivion.

While sorting through the daily experience of living, without using excess food, I learned a range of temporary tools and actions to help keep myself away from bingeing or overeating. These would fit under the "behaviour modification" heading, and were all things I tried because they had worked for other people.

For example, since I lived on my own, I learned to set out my entire meal on a tray and not return to the kitchen for second helpings, even if I had to sit on my hands during the twenty minutes or so it can take for cravings to pass. I learned not to eat a meal while preparing a meal, which meant not licking my fingers or the spoon or any other utensil, and not sampling or tasting things ahead of time. Other tricks included: eating meals only when sitting down, putting food on dishes (rather than scarfing it from jars, tubs, or boxes), and planning far enough ahead to ensure that the right kind of foods were available in my fridge and cupboards.

I still do all those things today. It's amazing how our brains love habit and routine, especially if you have obsessive, compulsive tendencies. You can learn to make it work *for* you rather than against you.

Putting any one of the above behaviours into practice felt weird at first, but it really didn't take long for a habit to form (between twenty-one and twenty-eight days). For some like myself, doing something once was the hardest part. Doing it a second time was already establishing a pattern.

The Power to Choose

Those who aren't part of a twelve-step program[144] typically cite the support network and shared experience as the most important aspects, which have since been incorporated into most treatment regimes. And that's a good thing. Support and shared experience mattered to me, and they still do.

But there's one thing a twelve-step approach has that many others don't, especially those sponsored by most government agencies in Canada and the US. And that's the spiritual component. However, recognizing the role that spirituality can play in healing, some eating disorder treatment centres now offer an optional spiritual element for those who want one.

When I was a little girl, Shirley taught me to say the following prayer every night before I went to sleep:

God bless Mommy, God bless Daddy
God bless all my aunties and uncles
And please God, make me a good girl. Amen.

Well, that didn't happen. God apparently did not make me a good girl, at least according to Shirley. So eventually, I stopped praying and asking, and gave up on God. However, I didn't stop searching for some undefined spiritual something.

By the time I walked into that church basement in June 1981, I already knew I was powerless over food, and I didn't find it a self-fulfilling prophecy to say so. That's the major complaint of people who misunderstand the first of the twelve steps, which is: "We admitted we were powerless over food ..."

The word "powerless" hit me like a ton of bricks, but in a good way. Since powerlessness had been my lived experience for so long, it was easy to admit I lacked control over food. Lacked control? I was badly out-of-control much of the time.

Back then, I was unaware how being out-of-control with food served as a counter-balance to the amount of control mustered when trying to diet, and that the two were inextricably linked. Picture a tug- of-war using an elastic cord, with control on one end, and on the other, the poster child for out-of-control: binge eating. Pull too hard on the control side, and *snap!* Back you spring to the other. This control/out- of-control cord operates in my clients, as well. The more control they exert in various areas of their lives, the more psychologically devastating their eating binges, regardless of how much they actually consume.

The basic idea in the program is that you admit you are powerless and need help, you come believe that help and healing are possible, and you consult with a major power source for that help.

Turning to a spiritual source for help is not new. But in twelve-step, you get to envision a power greater than yourself any way you want. That was new to me, and unexpected. This power greater than you can be whatever you think will work for you, with one exception: it cannot be another human being, such as a family member or a close friend. For example, one woman chose an image of the late comedian George Burns (from his role of God in the first movie version of *Oh God*) as her higher power because he looked friendly in his baseball cap.[145] Others, such as agnostics or atheists, may choose the group as a whole to function as their higher power.

I had no idea what I wanted for a higher power. All I knew was that since the age of ten or eleven, my personal gods had unconsciously been food and eating. Despite their powerful destructive impact on my life, I kept turning to both the substance and the behaviour to get me through my troubled days and nights, despite the consequences. Now, maybe there was another possibility.

No way could any human being help me stop eating, nor would I ever take orders from one. But a power greater than myself? That was worth trying, because I was so desperate. That was worth trying, because other similarly desperate people had done so with success.

One night, in my tiny kitchen, standing in front of the open fridge door, I rolled my eyes towards the ceiling, as if to say, "I know this is ridiculous but I've gotta give it a shot." And then out loud, in a highly irreverent tone, I called on my higher power for help. "Yoo-hoo, up there," I said, pausing for a nanosecond, "if you're there." Another pause and eye-roll, then, "Please remove these obsessive thoughts of food from my brain." Then to show I really meant it, I took some action by closing the fridge door and walking out of the kitchen.

It wasn't till the next morning, upon waking, that I realized no food thoughts or images had entered my mind for the rest of the night. That sure freaked me out. For a few seconds, I wondered if I was losing it again.

Do you remember the old TV series *The Twilight Zone*[146] and its eerie music whenever something weird happened or was about to happen? Well, that's the sound that played and replayed in my brain the morning after the food thoughts had disappeared.

Despite my concerns, the fact was I had asked for help and received it. However anyone else wants to explain it, I wanted to see this as a higher power at work. So I did.

By the way, asking a higher power for help in this particular way was not my idea, but something I'd heard from a woman at a meeting. And while she was much more reverent and formal in her approach, I copied the essence of her story, adding my own modifications. And I got results!

Was I actually communicating with my higher or highest self, the spirit of the universe, or the great creator? Or with a figment of my own imagination – a kind and nurturing parent, a fairy godmother or godfather, a guardian angel, benevolent ghost, dead saint, or an ancient ancestor I somehow tapped into? Perhaps. To be honest, it felt a bit like magic. And while that appealed to me, I kept what happened to myself for quite some time.

Shortly after that evening, I came up with a very loose definition of a higher power: loving energy, an all-knowing and all-understanding life force, a universal consciousness, a creative energy source. Nothing destructive or harmful about it. Sometimes for convenience I could call it God, because I knew what I meant and didn't mean by that. (What I *didn't* mean is the God of religion.)

My higher power, which is both inside and outside of me, knew and understood whatever was going on, which meant I didn't have to hide anything or try to figure things out anymore. What a relief! The gibble-gabble didn't have to work so hard.

The visual metaphor I used was the energy that made plants grow towards the light. This concept worked for me then, and it still does.

Through my higher power, I became empowered to resist the temptations I could not resist on my own. I became empowered to get honest with myself, first about the food I'd consumed and my history with it, and then about my behaviour in other areas of my life. In doing so, I became empowered to do many things I'd been unable to do before.

That empowerment gave me the greatest gift someone suffering from being out of control can have – the power to choose.

The power to choose actually sidesteps the control/out-of-control struggle, rendering it unnecessary. The power to choose offers the freedom to live without what might be described as an inner clench.

Choice trumps control every time. For me, control means I'm bossing myself around, telling myself what to do and not do, which creates a situation ripe for rebellion. It also means fighting a compulsive drive to eat and getting stuck in the yes-I-will/no-I-won't or the do-it/don't-do-it debate and their ugly aftermaths.

But choice means I can ask my higher power to help me resist binge eating. And to help me accept and tolerate the discomfort that not bingeing might bring about.

The power to choose also means that because I'm human, I'm free to make mistakes. In fact, I'm probably programmed to learn by trial and error. And once I accept that process, I'm free to stop beating myself up for such imperfections and to treat myself with some compassion. Those are all choices, too.

Relapse

It was bound to happen, as it does for most people dealing with any type of addiction. I'm talking about relapse, which has been identified as a normal and expected part of the recovery process, whether seeking help at a treatment centre or in a twelve-step or harm-reduction program. "Relapse Prevention" is what managing a chronic addiction is all about.

For two and a half years after entering the program, I'd managed to stick to my food plan, avoid my binge foods, and not binge. With the help of my higher power, of course. And then in mid-December 1983 – *bam!* Just like that, I tumbled headlong into a very dark and confusing abyss.

I actually don't remember exactly how the bingeing started. Probably with something compulsively eaten in between meals, which then escalated into an unstoppable ravenous gobbling of whatever was in my fridge and cupboards. Once the "eat" switch was activated, it couldn't have been long before I went out to buy and then devour massive amounts of binge food, including sugar-based products, which I hadn't touched for thirty months.

The sudden introduction of processed sugar into my system was such a shock, it set off massive alarms and turned off any inhibitory buttons, sending me over the edge into endless eating. I was gone. Stuck once more in an unrelenting cycle that took on heightened virulence and strength.

I don't know exactly how long this first relapse lasted. Perhaps ten days. Or two weeks. Most of it is a blur. I do know, however, that the bingeing and the sugar failed to alleviate the pain I was in, its primary task. I remember sitting in my chair crying, then making strange sobbing sounds, like a wounded animal. That's the single image I've retained from this experience.

The curious thing is, my life was good. I was thin, and on a new upward career path, one that was to serve me well for the next twenty-five years. I had more friends and was more "sociable," to use a "Shirley" phrase, than ever before. I even had a man in my life. So all the external markers of success were present. But not the internal ones, the ones that really count.

Hindsight reveals that many factors contributed to this relapse, but the top two were my relationship with this man and honesty. Or dishonesty. I wasn't used to being honest in relationships, or with myself, and certainly not with a man.

Note: you can't be a full-fledged addict and be honest with yourself at the same time. The two are mutually exclusive. For most of my life, I had lied to myself a lot to justify binge eating. The biggest whoppers I told myself were either that I didn't care anymore ("Who cares?") or that it was pointless to try anymore ("What's the point?"). Both were always the final straws before I let go and binged, since they led to the inevitable conclusion "Might as well eat."

The picture that comes to mind is of standing on the edge of a very high diving board, brought there by circumstances, feelings, thoughts, and events. But what catapults me over the edge and plunges me into the cesspool of binge eating is always my own permission to give up, fostered by the idea that I no longer care what happens to me, or that nothing matters anymore. Pure BS, for sure, which had been operating for years on an unconscious level.

The truth may be that I don't want to care at that particular moment, or that I'm tired of caring, or that I wish I didn't have to care, *and* that I actually do care. And that's what I tell myself now whenever the I-don't-care refrain rears its ugly voice. Similarly, my answer to what's-the-point is sanity and peace of mind.

Over time I've learned to challenge the BS and see it for the destructive easy way out it offers. Now, when I don't want to deal with something, I give myself permission to set it aside for a while, which eliminates the need to binge. A conscious choice is involved, rather than an automatic reaction.

The other factor contributing to my first and most devastating relapse back then was confusion, an ever-present state I found very difficult to tolerate. So many things confused me. I've spent the rest of my life sorting these confusions out.

And where was my higher power during this relapse? No doubt I was probably asking the same thing in my sugar stupor. "Where the f*** are you?" But I don't remember any specific moment of doing so. What I do suspect, however, is that there were probably many moments during this period when higher power help was available. I just wasn't open to it. For example, I'd ignore the phone when it rang or stay away from meetings where some light may have had a chance to break through, if only for a few seconds. But more important, I was probably too angry at myself for the relapse and at my higher power for letting it happen.

Now, of course, if I'm determined to stuff my face with food, my higher power does not physically intervene and grab the food out of my hands. But minor mishaps during a binge – like dropping food on the floor or burning it during preparation – could be seen as little signs of interference or little pauses to give me a chance to stop. Sometimes I've grabbed on to these moments, and at other times ignored them so I can frantically continue to eat like a dog with a bone.

During this first relapse, I didn't fully comprehend that asking for higher power help with a binge involves being willing not to eat and being willing to face the real problem when every fibre of your being screams "Eat!" So I may well have asked, but I sure wasn't ready not to binge.

In the six months after relapsing, my ability to stay on track was shaky, to say the least. But each time I had a food slip (an extra something that didn't lead to a binge) or an actual binge (brief though it was), I had to work purposefully and diligently to understand what happened and to learn from it. That, too, has become an important pattern throughout the rest of my life. I suspect that in the months leading up to my first relapse, I'd probably gotten a bit of a swelled head and so eased up on the effort.

I'd love to be able to write that after this rough patch, I never relapsed again, but that wasn't the case. Each time I fell down and wanted to quit the program, I didn't. For weeks and months on end, I'd tasted what life was like when food occupied a quiet place and binge eating was the farthest thing from my mind.

Eventually, I came to see any type of setback, food-related or not, as a blind spot. Like a red flag or warning signal, I'd missed something and needed to find out what it was. This process suits my super- curious nature, certainly. It also shows me how persistence pays off.

Current treatment programs tend to use the term "symptom" to describe these red flags. For example, excess weight is a symptom of overeating, which itself (along with undereating or purging) is a symptom that something is out of whack. I agree.

There's one more thing I want to include when talking about relapse. And that is the shame that accompanies it, along with the guilt and remorse. Once you've found help, be it in a twelve-step program, a treatment centre program, professional therapy, or any combination thereof, the expectation is that the behaviour will stop. And it usually does. For a while – even a long while.

But inevitably, in most cases, you hit a snag, or snags, and you either fall directly into the food or you topple into a full-colour stereo replay of your favourite justifications and ultimately pick up the food (or your substance of choice) once again.

Getting back on the horse is tricky at the best of times, but it is made even more difficult when shame, guilt, and remorse are involved. Because that trio tends to perpetuate the struggle and prevents a clear view of the factors that contributed to the mistake in the first place.

Over the years, I ultimately learned to stop feeling ashamed after a slip or binge, and to stop beating myself up about it. Beating myself up, the job of my "inner bully" (abuse unknowingly copied from Shirley) was a go-to pattern I applied to most situations, so it was difficult to stop when it came to binge eating.

Fortunately, I had non-judgmental people to confide in, who taught me an effective post-binge process. Namely, to itemize exactly what I'd consumed, preferably in writing. Once on paper, I could see if I'd over- or underestimated what I'd eaten (more times than not, it was the latter). But most important, the writing helped me get honest with myself and freed me to move on to the real work -- finding out what the hell had happened. Or what I'd missed.

Here's the irony. Binge eating essentially functions as an avoidance mechanism. There's a problem or set of problems I don't want to deal with, and the best distraction of all is binge eating or any other addictive or self-destructive behaviour. Once I give in to that, I now have to cope with two problems

– the original one and the binge. If I then get into a shaming, self-blaming, guilt-remorse loop after the binge, I end up with three problems – the original one, the binge, and its various physical aftereffects (bloating, gas, extra weight), and the shame, blame, guilt, or remorse. And, I'm even farther away from being able to deal with the original problem. Could anyone consciously design a better avoidance system? Maybe, but this one is highly effective for countless folks who suffer from disordered eating.

By the way, a group setting is not the place to recite the contents of a binge, which is best handled on a one-on-one basis. As a therapist, when clients need to get honest with me about what they've eaten and find no judgment, shaming, or condemnation, they are much more likely to move forward.

The Experiment

Sometime in 1984, at a vulnerable point during a post-relapse, slip-sliding phase, I decided to try an experiment based on well-known American author Geneen Roth's concept of intuitive eating. This non- dieting approach would replace my three structured meals.

Intuitive eating has grown increasingly popular among treatment providers nowadays, especially for those suffering from anorexia and bulimia. It involves learning to trust your body to help you decide what to eat when you're hungry. According to her book,[147] Roth had trained herself over time to be binge- free and bulimia-free. Very impressive. The two basic guidelines: you eat when you're hungry and stop when you're full; and you are free to eat whatever and whenever you want. This sounded fantastic!

So despite some skepticism, and even though I was still in the program, I decided to try her approach. How thrilling to stock up on all the junk I loved. The full freezer and cupboards were supposed to give me a sense of security and calm. The theory: knowing ice-cream was available anytime I wanted would eventually eliminate the need to gobble it all up in one panicky session. Moreover, the excitement of eating ice-cream and the ensuing guilt would wear off to the point where ice-cream would occupy a pleasant but quieter place in my life. I could have ice-cream whenever I wanted, as long as I stopped when I'd had "enough," or when I felt full.

Guess what happened. Within a short while, it became evident that intuitive eating might not be the way for me to go.

First, this was a handy-dandy excuse to ignore my addiction to sugar. In fact, the constant availability of ice-cream not only failed to diminish its excitement, thanks to the wide varieties and flavours available, there were also plenty of other amazing sweet treats choc-full of high fructose corn syrup to take its place (not to mention the salty crunchy stuff). So boredom never had a chance.

Second, without the structure of planned meals, I had no idea when I was physically hungry. On some days, I grazed my way along, nibbling on a constant supply of snacks. And third, I couldn't stop eating when I felt full, because feeling full turned out to be a major physiological trigger to keep on eating more! There was no "enough," no beginning or end, and my weight rose accordingly, with no end in sight.

The only difference between my faulty version of intuitive eating and binge eating was the absence of frantic desperation. Eventually, with the help of my higher power, I got honest with myself and back to the three-meals-a-day, sugar-free structure.

Note: while intuitive eating didn't work for me, it can and does work for others. Its effectiveness probably depends on a range of factors, from the length of time someone has been bingeing to the types of psychological and emotional issues that need to be confronted.

Looking back, I'm not at all sorry I tried it, and hats off to those who can do it.

Archeology

So now it's time to get down to the nitty-gritty and identify certain underlying issues that drive people to various kinds of disordered eating. Some function simply as triggers, while others carry a more pervasive impact. (See Appendix for a detailed list of possible triggers.)

Digging deep is a process that differs for each person, and often involves taking a look at what noted psychiatrist Carl Jung[148] calls our shadow – those denied darker characteristics that have been operating beneath our awareness. Exposing our shadows to the light helps make us whole. The Gestalt term "disowned parts" includes positive characteristics we may be blind to and gives us a fuller life and a much wider range of choice. After digging deep, we ultimately come to know ourselves on many different levels and in many different ways.

Is this a path I wanted to follow? At first, yes, because it was the way to lose weight. And later, no, because it's so difficult. But I chose it, because I'd experienced the alternative – a half-life of unmet dreams, fueled by unnamed energies, untamed impulses, and misery.

To provide an idea of the depth and breadth of issues that may need to be confronted, a fairly lengthy but by no means exhaustive list of over ninety items is appended at the end of this chapter. Some people will need to focus in a major way on only a few, while developing the skills and mind-set to sort the rest out on their own, with perhaps some occasional professional support. Others will have to work longer and more diligently if they want to recover.

Since books grounded in many different modalities have been written on most of these subjects, it would be foolish for me to reinvent the wheel here. But I will offer personal examples from some of the major categories: physical, emotional, intellectual (cognitive or mental), spiritual, personal characteristics (personality traits or qualities), relationships, and socio-cultural factors.

Please bear in mind that the process of personal growth is organic, and neither linear nor straightforward. You may need to work on X before you can focus on Y. In my own case, I had self- protective blinders on so that I recognized only a few issues at any one time. Resentment? Nope. Fear? Hell no. Dishonesty? Absolutely not. And so on. I figured that with all the therapy I'd done up to that point, I was pretty much okay, and that after I lost weight, I'd be good to go.

From what I've observed these past thirty-plus years, such blinders weren't unique to me. Gestalt therapy provides the theory of self-regulation[149] to explain this phenomenon. Very simply put, only when the most pressing need has been addressed and completed can the next one rise to the top for attention.

Given my history with binge eating and mental illness, I had plenty to work with. But if I took on too many issues at once (and bit off more than I could chew, which is typical binge-eater behaviour), I'd feel overwhelmed and be unable to concentrate on anything.

So over time, as I gradually came to comprehend that many things needed work, I learned to slow down and deal with one issue at a time.

The personal growth process unfolds differently for each person. For example, I can still recall the moment when awareness of my dishonesty began to take root. Hearing honesty or dishonesty mentioned so often at meetings kept it top of mind. One afternoon, at home in my little apartment, I suddenly noticed that the pen I was using came from a previous workplace. No big deal. Everyone takes pens, don't they? But bit by bit, I began to spot other items I hadn't paid for, but had brought home from various office locations. An ashtray and stapler here, a box of paper clips there, and so on. Quite a little stash when I gathered it all together.

But after I dealt with the easy and obvious stuff (the visible material things), memories of little white lies I'd told began floating into focus, followed by a steady stream of the whoppers I'd spouted when living with Shirley and Bob. Then I began to recall dishonest actions, like stealing money from my college roommate to raid the candy machines at university, or stealing chocolate from a neighbourhood convenience store as a kid. So much for the perception of myself as honest.

Like slowly unravelling a tangled ball of yarn, coming to terms with my dishonesty helped me see and eventually accept the impact of the lies I told Shirley and Bob, then the mountains of lies I told myself, and gradually pierce the accumulated layers of self-deceit.

That's why self-honesty is so important when facing down an addiction or eating disorder. Self- deception comes easy when we want to justify taking that first bite (or drink). We know it can lead us into deep trouble, so we seem to turn to the trickster or saboteur part of our personalities to come up with the lies that will make what we're doing okay.

Physical

On a physical level, apart from losing weight and eating in a reasonably nutritious way, the main work I had to do was learning how to live in my body. I had grown so used to detaching and dissociating from my body, and so focused on viewing my body from only one perspective – how I looked – that I needed to learn how to re-inhabit myself.

Reclaiming my body in itself was a slow and gradual process, including sensory awareness, various forms of movement and exercise, learning to physically ground and centre myself, and focusing attention on how I felt on the inside. No simple tasks at all, and ones that have taken years. My Gestalt studies and training were essential in this regard, as were my still ongoing preventative chiropractic visits and sessions with a cranial-sacral therapist (a massage therapist who practices a form of osteopathy).

Emotional

For years, emotional aspects have been given less attention in mental health treatment, and are only now coming into their rightful place in the recovery process. North American society generally gives short shrift to emotional intelligence, and pays for that with increased mental and physical illness. That's because until lately, it's been difficult to measure and evaluate emotions and their intensity, which are basically subjective. Even though we learn ways to discern emotions in others (by looking at their facial expressions or body postures), our interpretations are also subjective.

However, now that brain imaging is possible, researchers are figuring out how to collect and evaluate more objective data on emotional reactions and responses.

Looking back, I had no idea how angry I was, or how fearful, sad, or any of the myriad other feelings I'd pushed away with food. The credit for teaching me about emotions belongs primarily to my Gestalt training. Over the years, I learned that emotions happen within my body, and my brain interprets them. But by using food and bingeing to avoid feelings, I missed their messages, one of their primary functions.

The way back to sanity was to learn how to identify my emotions from my body's clues. Emotions tell me how and what I feel, and equally important, what I want and don't want. Knowing this gives me the power of choice.

While feeling was the emotional work, it went hand-in-hand with a cognitive and behavioural piece. Our bodies and minds are connected and need integrating before we can function as whole people; hence the value of chiropractic and sacro-cranial treatment. To identify any feeling, I had to first focus on it in my body: where was the feeling located? What happened to my body during this feeling? For example, I noticed that I'd clench my teeth when a particular feeling occurred. The next step was putting a name to it. Was I feeling sad? Disappointed? Angry? Eventually, I came to associate clenched teeth with anger. Then I needed to be curious about it. What was the feeling of anger trying to tell me in that particular moment?

Often I hadn't a clue. So I'd write about it, stream-of-consciousness style, and more often than not, eventually I'd realize what was bothering me. Perhaps something recent, or some memory from the past, or both. While a recent event can trigger a past memory, something from the past that hasn't been dealt with can intensify the impact of something in the present.

Often, I'd notice several ideas or thoughts swirling around amidst the gibble-gabble. Sometimes I talked to someone about what was bothering me and then wrote about it. Other times, I did the reverse.

But always there was something for me to see. A tiny piece of the jigsaw of my life would fall into place, if that isn't too trite a way to explain it.

People who have been traumatized as children or adults often carry deep wounds that can be easily reactivated. In these situations, once aware, it may not only be unnecessary to keep returning to that particular pain, it may actually be harmful to do so. Once felt, and the fact of it acknowledged, the challenge becomes how to avoid getting stuck in the feeling but still be able to recognize its activation, resist its pull, and find constructive ways of expression.

My own emotional progress was exceedingly slow. Once I noticed a feeling and figured out what it was, I had to trust it as accurate. Anger, for example, was fraught with anxiety, dread, conflicting thoughts, worries, uncertainty, my rebellious nature, and thanks to Shirley, my early decision to never be like her. So whenever I experienced a feeling somewhere on the anger spectrum – from rage at one end to slight irritation at the other – my reaction was usually a delayed one.

For example, several weeks after a conversation with a friend, I'd catch myself mentally stewing over something she said. After recognizing I felt angry or annoyed, I'd then debate whether or not to tell her. Eventually, perhaps three or four weeks after the initial exchange, I might mention it towards the end of a conversation. Usually, I'd say I had a bone to pick or some similarly obscure phrase. Speaking up was usually a victory in itself, even when my friend couldn't recall what she'd said or meant. That's how I operated for years, even in the program and even while journaling, talking to others, and seeking higher power help.

However, while waiting for the subway one afternoon, a mere ten minutes after a Gestalt therapy session, I realized I was annoyed at something my therapist had said. Progress! It had taken about eight years of effort to shrink that delay between the triggering event and my awareness of feeling angry.

I've focused on anger here because it's often a very difficult emotion to accept, especially for women, whether or not they have an eating disorder. Society has many unflattering names for women who show anger. But the difficulty in expressing anger effectively is not limited just to women. Many people have limited ideas about what anger looks like. Clients may have experienced an angry parent as a child and made a decision similar to mine never to be like that.

Intellectual

That's where the intellectual, cognitive, or mental element comes in. By far, this required the most arduous and painstaking effort from me. It meant examining my attitudes, beliefs, values, opinions, judgments, perceptions, patterns of thought and experience, and any other mentally based component.

Here's an example. One of my most treasured beliefs was that fairness should prevail. So when it didn't, I was always thrown into panic and confusion. It turns out, on some level, I believed it was my fault. Totally illogical, but true from an emotional standpoint. In doing this, I thought I was taking responsibility, when in fact I was simply self-blaming. Ultimately, I traced this idea further back to the basic belief that I was bad, and that if something didn't go as it should, it was probably my fault. (Note: this is not an unusual belief for people who were emotionally abused as children.) Putting these two interwoven beliefs together was far from an overnight task. I don't know how long it took. But suffice it to say, a lot of effort was involved.

Actually, the struggle to accept the notion that life isn't fair belongs in several categories: cognitive (what I believed about it), emotional (how I felt about it), and spiritual (learning to accept what is).

Spiritual

Spirituality involves much more than developing a relationship with a higher power and accessing the support it provides. There are practical things to do, such as pray. Yuck. That was my initial reaction, until I heard the Serenity Prayer,[150] one of the few non-revolting things from my early meetings, and one that is closely linked to all twelve-step programs:

God, grant me the serenity
To accept the things I cannot change
The courage to change the things I can
And the wisdom to know the difference.

Essentially, the Serenity Prayer has a calming "sort" function, which helps simplify and clarify what I can and cannot change and what I need to do in each case. Here's an example of how it worked for me.

One crisp autumn day, while my newly thin self was waiting for the bus, the weather suddenly changed. The sky darkened, rain started to fall, and cold gusts of wind began to blow right through my unlined corduroy coat. (Since losing at least seventy pounds, I've been much more sensitive to the cold.) Standing at the bus stop, cursing the stupid bus and the effing weather, I realized that both were something over which I had absolutely no control. So I began to recite the Serenity Prayer over and over again, almost mantra-like, and got a little calmer.

When the bus finally arrived, it was almost empty, so I took one of the unoccupied single seats at the front, usually reserved for disabled people or seniors. Still silently saying the prayer, I noticed an elderly woman get on the bus at the next stop. Without thinking, I jumped up and happily offered her my seat. *Happily.* To this day, I have no idea why, because it was completely unnecessary. To her credit, the woman graciously accepted and I moved a few seats down. An absurd scene, and one I've never forgotten.

What struck me as bizarre was that I was usually a bit of a pushy pig on Toronto transit, especially when it came to getting a seat. In this instance, however, it seemed as if I'd had a temporary character alteration. And the only new factor seemed to be that prayer.

The bus incident confirmed the prayer's effectiveness and solidified my decision to keep on using it. I'd ask old "Yoo-hoo-up-there" to help me accept difficult people and situations. Surprisingly, I learned that acceptance does not mean I approve of the person or what he or she did. It is simply an acknowledgment of what is (or was). If the weather is stormy and I don't like it, then acceptance means here's a fact: the weather is stormy; and here's another fact: I don't like stormy weather. Acceptance is coming to terms with what is and not fighting it. Much easier to say than do.

I still need to use the Serenity Prayer, and I do so gladly, because it provides me with a simple and direct link to my higher power.

Personal Characteristics

Personal characteristics, traits, or qualities are the focus in twelve-step literature (in steps four through ten) for what needs to change. After dishonesty, the next three are resentment, fear, and self-will.

At first, I assumed these traits had nothing to do with me and probably applied more to alcoholics. But because others were looking at how these qualities showed up in their lives, I thought I'd take a quick peek.

So I shortlisted the people, places, and things I resented: bureaucracy, animal cruelty, ignorant people, poverty, and so on. Surprisingly, Shirley and Bob were absent from my initial effort. I figured I'd done plenty of work on them already and didn't resent them anymore! This, of course, turned out to be a blind spot, as I soon discovered.

As for fear, it took me years to recognize how terrified I really was just walking around Toronto in a smaller body. Once I did, I signed up for a women's self-defence course and got permission to be impolite when confronted with potentially threatening situations. That meant it was okay not to get on an elevator with a creepy guy. It also meant that if anyone approached me with a pine paddle about an inch thick, I'd have the confidence to smash it in two with the side of my hand.

Other fears, however, were less easy to identify and solve, and I could not have confronted any of them without the support of my higher power and the courage my higher power provided. For example, renewing a lapsed driver's licence meant learning to drive on Toronto's 401 highway, one of the widest and busiest in the world.[151] The examiner probably sensed how nervous I was, but I doubt he knew of my constant silent prayers to my higher power to keep everyone safe on that multi-lane thoroughfare.

Here's a more current example of fear: the fear that publishing this book might keep potential clients away, and wondering who would want to see a therapist who was a "former mental patient" and who has taken so long to get her act together. (Apparently, the who-you-hallelujah chorus hasn't gone totally silent.) The truth is, it's a risk. So if you're reading this, I've come to terms with the worst-case scenario and am prepared to deal with whatever happens.

As for self-will, what that really means is "my way." Like most other addicts, and possibly most human beings, that's how I wanted the world to run. That's how I wanted my life to run. And when things didn't go my way, which was most of the time, my emotional reaction was astounding. Throughout my life, up until that point, how many binges had I indulged in when things did not go the way I wanted them to, or the way I thought they should? Countless.

The remedy for self-will is to check in with my higher power. So I ask the question I need to ask and wait for some intuitive guidance. If none is forthcoming, then I go ahead and do what I want.

However, if information does come my way, usually in some synchronistic or coincidental form, I appreciate the help and tend to see it as emanating from the universe.

If I choose to act on that information, then I alone am responsible for my choice and my action. Heaven forbid I should sound like one of those crackpots who imagines God told her to do such-and- such, or the poor psychotic souls whose voices tell them to do terrible things. While I had the gibble- gabble in my brain, it was always too vague and distracting to guide me any-where but in circles, and its incessant droning actually prevented me from action and blocked my access to a spiritual connection.

The point is that I became willing to consult my higher pow-er and willing to concede that my way may not be the only way or the best way. Such consultation eventually enabled me to seek support and counsel from friends and colleagues, as I do to this day.

Personal Relationships

When it comes to relationships, here's another story about Shirley, who changed after I slimmed down. By the time I reached goal weight, you'd think that Shirley would be pleased. To the contrary, she just shifted her criticisms to other aspects of my physical appearance. My lipstick was too pale, my hair too long, my earrings too something. All of those could have been expected. But no one could have prepared me for the shift in her attitude towards me and what I ate. Whenever I'd visit, she'd constantly tell me to have some more of this, or another piece of that, and got quite offended and a little worked up when I said I'd had enough and no thanks. She even pushed sugary desserts on me, even though I'd informed her that sugar was harmful to me. It was as if she'd forgotten our past completely.

There's a name for this – sabotage – and it happens frequent-ly to people who have lost a lot of weight, or made any signifi-cant change, for that matter. Family members and loved ones es-pecially, much as they genuinely want you to be happy and healthy and reach your goals, often have a difficult time coping with such a major shift within the family system. Your physical and psychological transformation has altered the family balance, however dysfunctional it was, and their place within it.

Most saboteurs, including friends, are usually unaware that they are trying to get you to return to the former familiar and much more comfortable status quo.

Once over the initial shock, my role was to learn how not to react or overreact to Shirley. Over time, the numerous OTGs (opportunities to grow) during home visits gave me plenty of practice. So when Shirley started emptying her fridge into parcels of food for me to lug back to Toronto, usually via Greyhound bus, I joked about her role as typical Jewish mother. "No thanks, Mom, I'm pretty sure they sell cottage cheese in Toronto." But I had a lot of resentment, blame, and anger to let go of before I was able to lighten up with Shirley in this way.

As for my father, his reaction to my losing weight was general approval, but no big deal. I sensed he felt less ashamed of me, but I never checked it out.

Socio-Cultural factors

Socio-cultural factors might be more difficult to pinpoint, so I'll go with the most relevant to anyone with a weight-related or appearance-based issue: the media's astounding influence on self-image, body-image, behaviour, expectations, ideas of romance, relationships, and so on. Recently, I spoke to a friend about her failed marriage, and how she had tried to be June Cleaver, the perfect wife, mother and homemaker, as shown on the 1950s TV show *Leave It to Beaver*.[152] Since she couldn't possibly live up to that image, she turned to food to help her cope.

Some of my own ideas about romantic relationships, as mentioned earlier, were definitely influenced by *Cosmopolitan* magazine. But also quite possibly by *Archie* comic books, whose characters seemed to be constantly throwing drinks in their friends' faces. I actually tried this once at a party, shortly after I left the Clarke. Needless to say, the guy thought, quite rightly, that I was nuts.

The sheer number of issues and their possible combinations makes me smile at the simplistic notion I had that there was just one main cause of my overdependence on food. One central reason I kept on bingeing despite the horrid consequences.

Of course there isn't just one cause. However, there is one overarching aspect to binge eating that needs emphasizing. It works! Binge eating is highly effective in helping you avoid your own truth, or complex set of truths.

Here's the Thing

When I entered the Clarke in 1967, not only were eating disorders unheard of, no one, including me, knew that honestly facing my addiction to food and eating had to be dealt with before I could function more fully in society. So even after I left the Clarke as an outpatient, I'd go along for a while until a crisis occurred, which would inevitably catapult me into the food and despair.

I couldn't get a real grip on my life until I got off my particular drug (the food) and behaviour (the binge eating). Since that began in June 1981, despite several major relapses, numerous slips and binges, and with a lot of help and support over the years, I've built a good life for myself. A life, in fact, that has been spent almost blessedly free from diets and food binges.

The terrible events of 9/11 for some reason woke me up to several important changes I wanted to make. I returned to the Gestalt Institute of Toronto to complete the four-year training program for therapists,[153] which I'd started in the mid-1980s. After that, I went back to university to study psychology for a third kick at the can, graduated on the Dean's List four years running, and went on to complete a post-grad program in addiction and mental health.[154] My strong motivation throughout this nine-year period, based on an authentic inner value, finally enabled me to do what I could not do before. And so, I write this book informed not only by my life experience, but also by education and training.

If anyone who suffers from obesity, mental illness, or binge-eating is reading this, you may need to do some intensive work on yourself if you want to heal. Most people don't want healing. They just want the symptoms – such as the pain and/or the weight

– to go away. I include myself in this category. If I could have recovered any other way, I would have. But "the road less travelled," to borrow from the author M. Scott Peck, is the one I needed to trudge.

For many years, I was under the illusion that mental hospitals are places to heal, when they are not. Healing takes time. Hospitals are there to treat crises and to provide immediate care for those in distress. The system can't afford otherwise. It couldn't back in 1967, and it can't now. Nor can most institutions.

The field of psychology came into being initially as a form of social control. The idea is still to patch people up, provide some help to get them to function within society's rules, but not to deal with the pain. Emotional and mental distress appear to be too much for mental health workers at all levels to contend with to any in-depth degree. Drugs are offered to stop the pain and to render clients manageable, while most emotional symptoms go unhealed and unattended to. It would be like giving pain medication to someone with a tumour, while leaving the tumour intact.

With mental illness, if you don't address and deal with the pain at the source, it will surface in other ways. It might develop into a physical ailment or disease, or simply result in living only a half-life. If you get physically sick, at least your treatment is covered in Ontario.[155] However, if you're just surviving rather than thriving, that's an incredible loss of human potential and very sad. We all lose out.

A current treatment option is to provide what's called "psycho-educational groups" to those with various mental health issues, especially addiction and eating disorders. The theory is that with enough of the right kind of understanding and how-to information, people can change. Well, that's true for some. But like many methods – from mindfulness, relaxation, and yoga to the more prevalent CBT (cognitive behavioural therapy) or more effective and more expensive DBT (dialectical behaviour therapy) to twelve-step programs – they are effective *only if* people do the inner work that's required.

This means doing what's necessary on a daily, sometimes even hourly or minute-by-minute basis. That's a big *if* in this culture of quick fixes and pill-popping solutions.

Weighty Matters

At the Clarke and at Jack's group therapy sessions, nobody got it, including myself for many years. Nobody understood that my weight served a distinct range of functions within my family. My weight *embodied* the relationship with my parents. People usually look at weight as a simple physical issue, based on bad eating habits and unhealthy food choices. However, research is now showing that a range of factors – genetics, income, living conditions, awareness, education, past trauma, media habits, access to healthy foods, big business, and social milieu, to name a few – may also be in play for some people. But in other instances, weight itself can be a solution to a complex set of unacknowledged problems.

I keep reading about simplistic measures, such as a tax on soft drinks, presented by well-meaning professionals in various walks of life, to stop or ameliorate the current obesity epidemic. Some of these may help a percentage of the population. But really, obesity is complicated.

In my situation, for example, being fat put a deep wedge in the relationship between Shirley and me. Painful though it was, this wedge enabled me to bond with my father against Shirley. It also created an issue of mutual concern to Bob and Shirley, and thus served as a bond between them, since they both felt the same way about my being overweight.

In addition, the fights Shirley and I had about my obesity both absorbed and expunged some of the negative energy in that household. In part, this destructive energy emanated from a toxic mix: Robert's repressed rage and guilt and whatever else his demons pushed down; Shirley's frustration, guilt, and unexplored grief; and my own tormented confusion. I have no doubt that at least some of my excess fat was there to both absorb this energy and protect me from its toxic impact.

Like many overweight women, I saw my fatness as making me unattractive enough to keep all men at bay. In my case, this included my father. At the same time, this failure to attract boyfriends pleased Robert and created a sense of relief for me, as well as sadness and yearning.

Am I making too much of this? Perhaps. But I've been telling people, and I firmly believe it, that there is more than meets the eye to the pattern of chronic weight loss and gain, as it implies ambivalence in a number of areas. Add to that my own unacknowledged fears and feelings, and the overeating and weight fluctuations begin to make sense.

Weight can also be a symptom of unresolved issues in society, like the changing roles of women and men, the shifting of patriarchal values, the dishonesty of advertising images, and so on. Fat, as psychotherapist and author Susie Orbach[156] has said, can be a feminist issue, but it can also be related to the environment, genetically modified foods, highly processed foods (like high-fructose corn syrup) that are made to be addictive,[157] big agribusiness, and to all sorts of toxins and chemicals so pervasive in the food, soil, air, and water in industrialized countries.

Weight can be seen as *the* problem – that's how Shirley and I saw it – or as one of many problems, or as a solution, or as a result of other unseen and unresolved factors. It's not just a matter of counting calories, fat grams or carbs, or of changing your lifestyle, or finding the perfect exercise regime, although all these can be beneficial. Solving the weight puzzle can involve an archeological expedition to your very core; and be an invitation to take a deeper look at yourself.

The Loving Truth

During a recent visit with Auntie Hannah, now eighty-six, in New York, she told me something I'd always suspected – that my father never really loved my mother. How did she know? My father had told her directly.

In 1945, after the Allies freed her from the concentration camp, Hannah was sent to Sweden to recover. About a year later, at age fifteen, she went to stay with her revered big brother, Robert, his wife, and new baby girl – me, at six or seven months old.

The way Hannah tells it, like the rest of the family, she was shocked that Robert had married beneath him. During her brief stay, she asked him why he married someone like my mother. He told her he'd promised Shirley's dying father that he would always look after her, a fact I'd known for years.

According to my aunt, Robert said it was all camouflage – the marriage, the tattoo of Shirley on his arm, and so on – to solidify his new identity and mask his undercover work for the British during the war. As someone who spoke many languages, my father had hinted at these activities from time to time, but always refused to discuss them.

No one who knows Hannah would ever doubt the accuracy of her long-term memory. So no question my father said those things to her. Even so, my sister and I found the news jarring, since we'd both believed our parents had fallen in love when they first met.

If this information was true, if I hadn't already forgiven my mother long ago, she would now be completely exonerated. Most of her craziness could be funneled through this very sad lens. While married to a man she loved and adored, the feeling wasn't mutual. If the information was true, then how sad for Robert as well.

The thing is, I'll never know the truth. And at this point, it no longer matters. Finally. Whatever anger I once felt towards my father is gone. If he was a spy or an agent for the British, or if he wasn't; if he fell in love with my mother when they first met, or if he didn't; if he made up stories, or tried so hard to do what he thought was the right thing, when it may not have been – so what. I'm done with the puzzles.

There is one thing, however, I can be sure of. Shirley and Bob did their utmost to love their children the only way they knew.

A Sunlight of My Own[158]

As I explored the countless issues that emerged after I stopped the diet-binge cycle, I grew hopeful and learned to trust. First, I learned to trust my higher power, and then I learned to trust my-self, along with a few other people. I developed some integrity (I could trust myself to honour a commitment), and courage, and discipline, and so much else.

My point is that I needed to get off some substances – sugar and junk food to be able to do the cognitive and emotional work necessary to heal.

Now, I'm happy to report, the gibble-gabble is, for the most part, gone – it no longer is the background noise of my life. Actually, those thoughts probably aren't really gone. Neuroscience research in cognition and memory has shown that memories and thoughts don't die, they simply shrivel and weaken from misuse as their neural connections dwindle and atrophy over time. But they can always resurface. *Snap!* Just like that.

With the disappearance of the gibble-gabble came the fading of the obsession and preoccupation with weight, fat, and food. Peace of mind is now my new normal. Now, most of the time, I can channel my obsessive-compulsive tendencies to focus on and complete tasks with a clear brain. When my thinking gets foggy, that's a sign to do some emotional work. Since Gestalt taught me that emotions reside in my body, I monitor the shifts and subtle changes that tell me how and what I feel.

One of the main criticisms of twelve-step programs is that by claiming powerlessness, as we all do in the first step, the individual's responsibility is diluted. But the opposite is true. I am responsible for everything I've done, not done, do, and will or will not do. Period. That includes looking after my mental and emotional condition.

Just as someone who's had a heart attack pays attention to their health and signs of stress, I do the same with my own vulnerabilities, as a preventive measure. I'm tempted to go on and tell you more about my imperfect, zigzag recovery from binge eating disorder. But perhaps I'll leave that for another time. After all, I'm not finished yet, and my story isn't over. I'm still learning.

Bob and Shirley's 50th wedding anniversary, June 1990.
Top row from left: granddaughter Shira, me (in my blonde phase),
grandson Dan, Cindy and her husband Paul. Bottom row from left:
Bob, Shirley, granddaughter Niki and grandson Toby.

APPENDIX: UNDERLYING TRIGGER ISSUES

The following list of potential trigger issues has also been divided into several main categories. Some items clearly belong in only one section, while others could easily fit into several. For example, shame is under the "emotional" heading, although it can be a physical sensation and have strong cognitive and social components, as well.

Physical

1. Living in your body and being a body (vs. detachment/dissociation from your body)

2. Appreciation and respect for your body and what it does

3. Self-care: paying attention to daily physical needs for food, water, sleep, exercise, etc.

4. Experiencing all your senses, paying attention to the messages they convey

5. Paying attention to grooming: personal hygiene, wearing clothes that fit comfortably

6. Awareness of comfort/discomfort, amount of space you need, physical limitations

7. Noticing changes in your energy level

8. Posture, alignment, movement, flexibility

9. Sexuality, sexual preferences and how to ask for what you want and need

10. Proactive stance on health concerns

11. Trust in your intuition and gut instincts, recognition of the guidance they provide

12. Competitive sports/athletics, professional dance

13. Pregnancy, miscarriage, abortion

14. Living with chronic pain, undiagnosed condition, physical disability

Emotional

15. Learning how and where feelings/emotions manifest in your body

16. Self-regulation: developing your ability to accept/tolerate your own (and others') feelings (such as: anger, resentment, sadness, disgust, happiness, joy, fear, disappointment, uncertainty, emotional confusion, boredom, worry, excitement, overwhelm, frustration, rage, grief)

17. Learning what you want and do not want

18. Differentiating between wants and needs

19. Learning how to express feelings non-destructively

20. Learning assertiveness, how to say no

21. Learning how to be alone with yourself

22. Learning how to handle conflict within yourself and others

23. Learning how to recognize anxiety and depression

24. Developing courage, taking risks, and trying new things

25. Coming to terms with past emotional abuse and trauma

26. Becoming aware and letting go of shame, self-blame, remorse, guilt, and self-doubt

27. Recognizing procrastination and when you're stuck

28. Taking responsibility for your emotional growth

Intellectual, mental, or cognitive

29. Becoming aware of the thoughts and ideas you use to trigger binge eating and learning how to challenge those thoughts

30. Recognizing blind spots, warnings and triggers

31. Becoming aware of past and current thoughts, attitudes, beliefs, and values about the more troublesome aspects of your life

32. Becoming aware of your opinions, judgments, and comparisons and their impact on you

33. Becoming aware of the expectations you have of yourself, others, and the world

34. Becoming aware of the social constructs or qualities you value (e.g., fairness, freedom, thoughtfulness, sincerity)

35. Learning the difference between healthy and unhealthy thoughts, beliefs, and attitudes

36. Letting go of illogical thinking: all-or-nothing thinking, black-and-white thinking, generalizations, over-exaggerations, comparisons, etc.

37. Being able to change self-destructive thoughts, beliefs, attitudes to healthier ones

38. Changing self-perceptions: body image, self-image, self-worth, self-respect, self-esteem

39. Learning the impact of perfectionism and finding a saner approach

40. Discovering your identity (e.g., mine was "fatandugly" for many years)

41. Acknowledgment of your strengths, talents, and skills

42. Developing the ability to set goals and pursue them in a sane manner

43. Expressing creativity; undoing creative blocks

44. Accepting responsibility for your mental state

Spiritual

45. Finding and/or defining a power greater than yourself (of your own understanding)

46. Developing a relationship with that power

47. Consulting your higher power, especially when in doubt

48. Valuing the power of choice

49. Differentiating between the power you do and don't have

50. Practicing spiritual principles, such as acceptance of what is, gratitude for all that you have, and forgiveness

51. Letting go of the demand to understand everything that goes on

52. Recognizing when you need help, and having the humility to ask for it

53. Peace of mind

54. Respect for all living creatures and appreciating nature

55. Developing spiritual practices, such as prayer and meditation

56. Learning spiritual principles, and living by them

Personal characteristics, traits or qualities

57. Recognizing and accepting your negative qualities and how they contribute to binge eating

58. Identifying the impact of your most harmful negative qualities in all areas of your life, and how to minimize this impact

59. Learning how to transform negative qualities into their polar opposites

60. Recognizing and accepting all your positive qualities and the impact of binge eating on them

61. Learning how these positive qualities have affected your life, and/or how you've negated them

62. **Some negative characteristics**: arrogant, blaming, closed-minded, dishonest, envious, ego-centric, foolish, grandiose, hostile, indecisive, jealous, lazy, mean, negative, opinionated, people-pleasing, quarrelsome, resentful, self-centred, thoughtless, unreliable, vengeful, wasteful

63. **Some positive characteristics**: adaptable, assertive, bold, compassionate, courageous dependable, expressive, fair, generous, helpful, humble, independent, joyful, kind, loving, merciful, open-minded, patient,

quick-witted, responsible, sincere, tactful, understanding, vibrant, wise

64. Recognizing and developing qualities you lack

65. Control: wanting to control or manipulate others, fear of being controlled or manipulated

66. Self-will: wanting your way, demanding to be the centre of attention, attention-seeking

67. Dependence and super-independence

68. Wanting everyone to like you

69. Acknowledging what needs to change

Relationships

70. Accepting people as they are, without trying to change them

71. Family roles, sibling rivalry, birth order, blended and extended families

72. Family secrets

73. Learning to recognize and avoid toxic and codependent relationships

74. Setting boundaries

75. Breakups, makeups, hookups, dating

76. Friendships, social connections

77. Marriage, divorce, separation, single parents, adoption

78. Competitiveness, entitlement

79. Rejection, exclusion, ostracism, bullying

80. Being truthful with others, social skills

81. Making amends when you are in the wrong

82. Playing victim, persecutor, or rescuer

83. Blame vs. accountability

84. Having a support network

85. Grieving, loss, and bereavement

86. Gender issues, sexual orientation

87. Childhood sexual abuse, sexual trauma/assault

88. Work challenges, job interviews, being hired/fired, difficult bosses/employees

Socio-cultural factors

89. Awareness of attitudes, beliefs, opinions and feelings on controversial social issues and the part this plays in your eating disorder: e.g., justice, fairness, racism, discrimination, prejudice, stigma, poverty, inequality

90. Looking at how feminism and the changing roles of women and men in society has affected your self- image and body image

91. Examining your views on how the world should and shouldn't be (politics, the environment) and how this may fuel your use of food to cope

92. Awareness of attitudes towards and interactions with the media (including social media), and its influence on your attitudes, opinions, and beliefs

93. Awareness of your experiences with the health care and educational systems, religion, nationality, cultural background, the police, etc. and how this has influenced your beliefs and attitudes about yourself, others, and the world.

ACKNOWLEDGMENTS

I am deeply grateful for much in my life, including the opportunity to write this book (which I originally called a book-thing, out of fear). So I want to thank the people who plodded through the earlier versions, and helped me accept that *Binge Crazy* was indeed viable. They include: Dorothy Aaron, my faithful and generous long-time friend, who has been a loving support since were were teenagers; Dr. Arlis Barclay, a godsend of encouragement and friendship right next door; and Maryan Gibson, friend and now trusted editor, whose initial opinion was crucial (having worked in publishing for years) and who referred me to Arrow Publications. My appreciation, as well, to readers of the later editions: Rosalyn Wosnick, Lana Biro, and my beloved sister, Tsiporah Grignon. The generosity of time, patience, positive feedback, and kindly offered constructive criticism from all these lovely people has made this so much better. Without their input, *Binge Crazy* would be less clear and certainly more verbose (if you can imagine). From Arrow Publications, my sincere appreciation to publisher Pat White for taking a chance on my book, and to Tom King, for all his efforts behind the scenes." Last, but not least, I want to thank Mrs. Gilda Katz, wherever you are, for reaching me when no one else could.

BIBLIOGRAPHY

I couldn't possibly identify all the books that have shaped my thinking and recovery, whose lessons are reflected in my writing. So, I have chosen the most influential (and dog-eared).

AA. (1976). *Alcoholics Anonymous: The Story of How Many Thousands of Men and Women Have Recovered from Alcoholism* (3rd ed.). New York, NY: Alcoholics Anonymous World Services, Inc.

AA. (1980). *Twelve Steps and Twelve Traditions* (11th ed.). New York, NY: Alcoholics Anonymous World Services, Inc.

APA (1952, 2000, 2013). *Diagnostic and Statistical Manual of Mental Disorders (1st ed., DSM-I; 4th ed., text revision, DSM-IV-TR; 5th ed., DSM-5).* Washington, DC: American Psychiatric Association.

Appleton, N. (1985). *Lick the Sugar Habit.* New York, NY: Warner.

Association for the Advancement of Gestalt Therapy (AAGT). http://www.aagt.org/.

Avena, N. M. (2013). *Why Diets Fail (Because You're Addicted to Sugar): Science Explains How to End Cravings, Lose Weight, and Get Healthy.* CA: Ten Speed Press.

Avena, N. M., Rada, P. & Hoebel, B.G. (2008). "Evidence for Sugar Addiction: Behavioral and Neurochemical Effects of Intermittent, Excessive Sugar Intake." *Neuroscience & Biobehavior Review*, 32 (1), 20–39. http://www.ncbi.nlm.nih.gov.

Beattie, M. (1990). *Codependents' Guide to the Twelve Steps: How to Find the Right Program for You and Apply Each of the Twelve Steps to Your Own Issues*. New York, NY: Fireside.

Berton, P. (1997). *1967, The Last Great Year*. Doubleday, Canada.

Bill B. (1981). *Compulsive Overeater*. Minneapolis, MN: Compcare Publications.

Binge Eating Disorder Association (BEDA). USA. http://bedaonline.com/.

Birch, L. L., Fisher, J. O., & Davison, K. K., (2003). "Learning to Overeat: Maternal Use of Restrictive Feeding Practices Promotes Girls' Eating in the Absence of Hunger." American Journal of Clinical Nutrition, 78 (2), 215-20.

Birnbaum, J. (1973). *Cry Anger: A Cure for Depression*. Don Mills, ON: General Publishing.

Birnbaum, J. (1979). *Discovering the Pleasure Principle: Feeling Up Naturally*. Don Mills, ON: General Publishing.

Borysenko, J. (1990). *Guilt is the Teacher, Love is the Lesson*. New York, NY: Warner.

Bramson, R.M. (1981). *Coping with Difficult People*. New York, NY: Ballantine.

Canadian Mental Health Association (CMHA). http://www.cmha.ca/.

Carlat, D.J. (2010). *Unhinged: The Trouble with Psychiatry – A Doctor's Revelations about a Profession in Crisis*. Toronto, ON: Free Press.

Collier, D.A. & Treasure, J. L. (2004). "The Aetiology of Eating Disorders." *The British Journal of Psychiatry* 185, 365.

Curtis, O. (1999). *Chemical Dependency: A Family Affair.* Belmont, CA: Brooks, Cole.

Davis, C. & Carter, J.C. (2009). "Compulsive Overeating, as An Addiction Disorder. A Review of Theory and Evidence." *Appetite, 53*, 1–8.

Doidge, N. (2007). *The Brain That Changes Itself: Stories of Personal Triumph from the Frontiers of Brain Science.* Toronto, ON: Penguin.

Dufty, W. (1975). *Sugar Blues.* New York, NY: Warner Books.

Dychtwald, K. (1981). *Body-Mind: a Breakthrough Approach to the Secrets of Self-Awareness.* New York, NY: Jove Books.

Endangered Bodies UK. London. http://endangeredbodies.org/.

Epstein, H. (1979). *Children of the Holocaust.* Bantam.

Fagan, J. & Shepherd, I.L. (1970). *Gestalt Therapy Now: Theory, Techniques, Applications.* New York, NY: Harper Colophon Books.

Forward, S. (1990). *Toxic Parents. Overcoming Their Hurtful Legacy and Reclaiming Your Life.* Toronto: Bantam.

Frayn, D. H. (1996). *The Clarke and its Founders: The Thirtieth Anniversary: a Retrospective Look at the Impossible Dream.* Toronto, ON: Clarke Monograph Series (6).

Friday, N. (1977). *My Mother/My Self: The Daughter's Search for Identity.* New York, NY: Dell.

Gardner, H. (1993). *Multiple intelligences: The Theory in Practice.* New York, NY: BasicBooks.

Gestalt Institute of Toronto. (1987). *Peeling the Onion: Gestalt Theory & Methodology.* Toronto, ON: Gestalt Institute.

Goldberg, N. (1998). *Writing Down the Bones: Freeing the Writer Within.* Boston, MA: Shambhala.

Goldbloom, D.S. (2008). "Building on History: The Centre for Addiction and Mental Health in the 21st Century." *Honouring the Past, Shaping the Future: 25 Years of Progress in Mental Health Advocacy and Rights Protection: Psychiatric Patient Advocate Office 25th Anniversary Report.* Psychiatric Patient Advocate Office. 17-19. http://www.sse.gov.on.ca/mohltc/PPAO/ en/Documents/pub-ann-25.pdf.

Hayward, J., Millar, L. Petersen, S., Swinburn, B., & Lewis, A.J. (2014). "When Ignorance is Bliss: Weight Perception, Body Mass Index and Quality of Life in Adolescents." *International Journal of Obesity* (2014) 38, 1328–1334. http://www.nature.com/ijo/journal/v38/n10/full/ ijo201478a.html?WT.ec_id=IJO-201410.

Hirschmann, J.R. & Munter, C.H. (1988). *Overcoming Overeating.* New York, NY: Fawcett Columbine.

Hollis, J. (1985). *Fat is a Family Affair.* Center City, MN: Hazelden.

Hudson, J. I., Hiripi, E., Pope, H. G. Jr., & Kessler, R. C. (2007). "The Prevalence and Correlates of Eating Disorders in the National Comorbidity Survey Replication." *Biological Psychiatry, 61* (3), 348-358.

Jung, C.G. (1989). *Memories, Dreams, Reflections.* New York, NY: Vintage Books.

Katherine, A. (2004). *When Misery is Company: End Self-Sabotage and Become Content.* Center City, MN: Hazelden.

Kesey, K. (1962). *One Flew Over the Cuckoo's Nest.* New York, NY: Signet.

Kessler, D. (2009). *The End of Overeating: Taking Control of the Insatiable American Appetite.* New York, NY: Rodale.

Lair, J. (1975). *'I Ain't Well—But I Sure am Better': Mutual Need Therapy.* New York, NY: Fawcett Crest.

Lerner, H.G. (1989). *The Dance of Anger: A Woman's Guide to Changing the Patterns of Intimate Relationships.* New York, NY: Harper & Row.

Lowen, A. (1983). *Bioenergetics: The Revolutionary Therapy That Uses the Language of the Body to Heal the Problems of the Mind.* Markham, ON: Penguin.

Maslow, A.H. (1976). *The Farther Reaches of Human Nature.* Markham, ON: Penguin.

Maté, G. (2004). *When the Body Says No: The Cost of Hidden Stress.* Toronto, ON: Vintage Canada.

Maté, G. (2009). *In the Realm of Hungry Ghosts: Close Encounters with Addiction.* Toronto, ON: Vintage Canada.

McFarland, B. & Baker-Baumann, T.L. (1990). *Shame and Body Image: Culture and the Compulsive Eater.* Deerfield Beach, FL: Health Communications, Inc.

Moss, M. (2013). *Salt Sugar Fat: How the Food Giants Hooked Us.* Toronto: McClelland & Stewart.

Myss, C. (1996). *Anatomy of the Spirit: The Seven Stages of Power and Healing.* New York, NY: Three Rivers Press.

Myss, C. (2004). *Invisible Acts of Power: Personal Choices That Create Miracles.* New York, NY: Free Press.

Nair, S. G., Adams-Deutsch, T., Epstein D. H. & Shaham, Y. (2009). "The Neuropharmacology of Relapse to Food Seeking: Methodology, Main Findings, and Comparison with

Relapse to Drug Seeking". *Progress in Neurobiology 89*, 18–45.

Nevid, J.S., Greene, B., Johnson, P.A., & Taylor, S. (2009). *Essentials of Abnormal Psychology in a Changing World.* (2nd ed.) Toronto, ON: Pearson Education Canada.

National Eating Disorders Association (NEDA). USA. http://www.nationaleatingdisorders.org/.

National Eating Disorder Information Centre (NEDIC). Canada. http://www.nedic.ca.

National Initiative for Eating Disorders (NIED). Canada. http://nied.ca/.

National Institute of Mental Health (NIMH). USA. http://www.nimh.nih.gov/index.shtml.

Ontario Association of Consultants, Counsellors, Psychometrists and Psychotherapist (OACCPP). http://www.oaccpp.ca/.

Ontario College of Registered Psychotherapists (CRPO). http://www.crpo.ca/.

Orbach, Susie. (1978). *Fat is a Feminist Issue.* New York, NY: Berkley.

Peck, M.S. (1978). *The Road Less Traveled: A New psychology of Love, Traditional Values and Spiritual Growth.* New York, NY: Touchstone.

Perls, F. S., Hefferline, R.F., & Goodman, P. (1977). *Gestalt Therapy: Excitement and Growth in the Human Personality.* Toronto, ON: Bantam.

Pert, C.B. (1997). *Molecules of Emotion: The Science Behind Mind-Body Medicine.* New York, NY: Scribner.

Phelps, J.K. & Nourse, A.E. (1986). *The Hidden Addiction and How to Get Free*. Toronto, ON: Little, Brown.

Polster, E., & Polster, M. (1974). *Gestalt Therapy Integrated: Contours of Theory & Practice*. New York, NY: Vintage.

Roth, G. (1992). *When Food is Love: Exploring the Relationship Between Eating and Intimacy*. New York, NY: Plume.

Rubenstein, T. B., McGinn, A. P., Wildman, R. P., & Wylie-Rosett, J. (2010). "Disordered Eating in Adulthood is Associated with Reported Weight Loss Attempts in Childhood." *International Journal of Eating Disorders, 43*, 663–666.

Salinger, J.D. (1951). *Catcher in the Rye*. New York, NY: Little, Brown.

Secunda, V. (1990). *When You and Your Mother Can't Be Friends: Resolving the Most Complicated Relationship of Your Life*. New York, NY: Delta.

Secunda, V. (1992). *Women and their Fathers: The Sexual and Romantic Impact of the First Man in Your Life*. New York, NY: Delta.

Scanlon, J. (2009). "Sensationalist Literature or Expert Advice?" *Feminist Media Studies* 9 (1), 12.

Schenkel, S. (1984). *Giving Away success: Why Women Get Stuck and What to Do About It*. New York, NY: McGraw-Hill.

Shields, D. & Salerno, S. (2013). *Salinger*. New York, NY: Simon & Schuster.

Signell, K.A. (1990). *Wisdom of the Heart: Working with Women's Dreams*. Toronto, ON: Bantam.

Smith, M.J. (1975). *When I Say No, I Feel Guilty*. New York, NY: Bantam.

Trull, T.J. (2005). *Clinical Psychology*. Belmont, CA: Wadsworth, Cengage Learning.

University College London. (2014, Sept 10). " 'Fat Shaming' Doesn't Encourage Weight Loss." *ScienceDaily*. http://www.sciencedaily.com/releases/2014/09/140910214151.htm.

University College London. (2014, Aug 7). "Losing Weight Won't Necessarily Make You Happy, Researchers Say." *ScienceDaily*. http://www.sciencedaily.com/releases/2014/08/140807105430.htm.

University of Houston. (2015, April 6). "Stress and Obesity: Your Family Can Make You Fat." *ScienceDaily*. http://www.sciencedaily.com/releases/2015/04/150406133621.htm.

Weiner, S. (1998). "The Addiction of Overeating: Self-help Groups as Treatment Models." *Journal of Clinical Psychology, 54* (2), 163-167.

Wolf, N. (1990). *The Beauty Myth*. Toronto, ON: Vintage Books.

Williamson, D. A., White, M. A., York-Crowe, E., & Steward, T. M. (2004). "Cognitive-Behavioral Theories of Eating Disorders." *Behavior Modification, 28* (6), 711-738.

Yalom, I.D. (2003). *The Gift of Therapy: An Open Letter to a New Generation of Therapists and Their Patients*. New York, NY: Harper Perennial.

Yontef, G. (1993). "Gestalt Therapy: An Introduction." *Awareness, Dialogue, and Process*. The Gestalt Journal Press. http://www.gestalt.org/yontef.htm.

Zukav, G. & Francis, L. (2001). *The Heart of the Soul: Emotional Awareness*. Toronto, ON: Simon & Schuster.

ENDNOTES

Introduction

1. According to the fifth edition of the *Diagnostic and Statistical Manual of Mental Disorders* (*DSM-5*), binge eating disorder (BED) is defined as recurring episodes of eating significantly more food in a short period of time than most people would eat under similar circumstances, with episodes marked by feelings of lack of control. Someone with binge eating disorder may eat too quickly, even when he or she is not hungry. The person may have feelings of guilt, embarrassment, or disgust and may binge eat alone to hide the behavior. This disorder is associated with marked distress and occurs, on average, at least once a week over three months. Online at http://www.dsm5.org/documents/eating disorders fact sheet.pdf.

2. All Canadian citizens are entitled to copies of their medical records and need only pay the photocopying fee. In 2006, mine cost about $25.

3. Author and medical intuitive Carolyn Myss has written a number of best-selling books, including *Anatomy of the Spirit* (my favourite) and *Invisible Acts of Power*. Lots more information, including free downloads, can be found on her website http://www.myss.com.

4. The Clarke notes were arranged chronologically within categories (e.g., Progress Notes, Doctor's Orders, Social Work Reports, Psychological Reports, etc.). In 2013, I rearranged them strictly by timeline, which made a huge difference in terms of clarity and story-telling.

5. My inpatient stay: Mar 31,1967 - Jan 20, 1968. My outpatient visits: Jan 21,1968 - May 30,1969.

6. In 1990, Dr. Garfinkel, now a renowned expert on eating disorders, became President and Psychiatrist-in-Chief of the Clarke Institute, then served as the first President and Chief Executive Officer of the Centre for Addiction and Mental Health (CAMH) from 1997 to 2009. The letter's contents are discussed in Chapter 15.

Chapter 1: Appointment with Gilda

7. The *DSM-I*, published in 1952 by the American Psychiatric Association, was created to help treat soldiers (suffering from shell shock and other trauma-induced conditions) after WWII. It listed only 106 psychiatric disorders and was only 145 pages long. We're now up to the *DSM-5*, with almost 1000 pages. Online at http://www.turkpsikiyatri.org/arsiv/dsm-1952.pdf.

8. According to one of my psychology textbooks, *Essentials of Abnormal Psychology in a Changing World*, a loose association is now more commonly referred to as a "thought disorder" or "looseness of association" and signifies a lack of connectedness between the speaker's thoughts. The speaker may not be aware that he/she seems to be rambling. Nevid, J.S., Greene, B., Johnson, P.A., & Taylor, S. (2009). *Essentials of Abnormal Psychology in a Changing World*. (2nd ed.) Toronto, ON: Pearson Education Canada.

9. From the above same textbook: the Mental Status Exam helps assess a client's current state of mind and considers appearance, manner and approach, orientation, alertness and thought processes, mood and affect.

10. Once again, hallucinations are "Perceptions that occur in the absence of an external stimulus that are confused with reality."

11. "I am the Walrus," written by John Lennon and Paul McCartney is from the Beatles' *Magical Mystery Tour* album, released in November 1967 by Capitol Records (Publisher: Northern Songs Ltd., which was bought out by Michael Jackson). Online at http://www.rockmine.com/Beatles/ BeatleCo.html. More information is available at http://www.ascap.com.

12. The anti-fur movement didn't emerge until the 1970s and really took root in the 1980s. Online at http://www.ontheissuesmagazine.com/1998spring/sp98fur.php.

Chapter 2: The Gibble-Gabble

13. The award-winning film *One Flew over the Cuckoo's Nes*t was based on Ken Kesey's 1962 novel of the same name.

14. *Girl Interrupted*, the 1999 film starring Winona Ryder and Angelina Jolie, was based on the 1994 book by Susanna Kaysen. Online at http://www.imdb.com/title/tt0172493/?ref_=fn_al_tt_3.

Chapter 3: All in the Family

15. In one common Internet scam, fake Nigerian royalty send emails requesting financial loans to help them access their millions, currently withheld by bankers for various reasons. They pledge generous reimbursement.

16. According to Pulitzer Prize-winning author Michael Moss, sugar is "inherently loved by newborn babies" (p. 18). Moss explains that we are hard-wired to like the taste of sweetness by at least 10,000 sweetness receptors on our tongues, which in turn communicate with the pleasure zones in our brains. *Salt Sugar Fat: How the Food Giants Hooked Us*, McClelland & Stewart Ltd., 2013.

17. Shirley Temple was a child star during the Great Depression of the 1930s, who sang and danced her way into the hearts of moviegoers around the world. She died in 2014. Online at http://www.shirleytemple.com.

18. The Three Stooges: Curly, Larry and Moe. Curly waved his hand in front of Moe's face. Moe reacted by poking Curly in the eyes with two fingers.

19. To my great surprise, as I've discovered while writing this, eating disorders per se were not clearly recognized by the psychiatric community back the 1960s. In the 1952 *DSM-I*, the only version available when I was diagnosed in 1967, anorexia (then defined as loss of appetite) and bulimia (then defined as excessive appetite) were both placed in the broader category of "Psychophysiologic Gastrointestinal Reactions" and listed under "Supplementary terms of the digestive system." Only anorexia nervosa was mentioned in the *DSM-II*, published in 1968, and then under "Special Symptoms Not Elsewhere Classified" under the "Mental Disorders" heading (p. 48).

20. Eating disorders as such didn't appear until the 1980 *DSM-III*, which reclassified anorexia and bulimia based on a 1979 paper by psychiatrist Gerard Russell. The term "binge eating" didn't surface until the 1990s, as it began to be seen as distinct from

bulimia nervosa. Collier, D.A. and Treasure, J.L. "The Aetiology of Eating Disorders," British Journal of Psychiatry (2004), 185, pp. 363-365. And online at http://www.randomhistory.com.

21.   *The Caine Mutiny*, a film made in 1954, starred Humphrey Bogart as the paranoid navy Captain Queeg, who acted irrationally and grilled everyone on board the ship when some strawberries went missing. Online at http://www.imdb.com/title/tt0046816/?ref_=nv_sr_1.

22.   The line "No one's getting fat but Mama Cass" is from "Creeque Alley," written by John and Michelle Phillips of the Mamas and the Papas, and released as a single by RCA Victor in 1967 (Publisher: Universal Music Corporation). Online at http://www.creequealley.com, http://www.discogs.com/Mamas-The-Papas-Creeque-Alley/release/4926476. More information is available at http://www.ascap.com.

23.   The movie *The Snake Pit*, re-released on DVD in 2004, has influenced many writers. Online at http://www.imdb.com/title/tt0040806/?ref_=nm_flmg_act_27.

Chapter 4: Opening Night

24.   Film director Alan King made an award-winning film about Warrendale. Online at http://www.rogerebert.com/reviews/warrendale-1969; and http://www.browndale.net/id86.html.

25.   "Good controls for children," by Carol Dukoff. Brown Camps turned into Browndale. Online at http://www.browndale.net/id47.html.

26.   Three names in particular come to mind: Pat Capponi, Geoffrey Reaume, and David Reville. All have advocated for psychiatric survivors.

Capponi, in 1992, published *Upstairs in the Crazy House: The Life of a Psychiatric Survivor*. The book tells of her three-month stay on a hospital psychiatric ward, after which she was sent to room in a boarding house for the mentally ill, which she and others got closed down several years later. Now she successfully writes mystery novels. http://www.quillandquire.com/authors/profile.cfm?article_id=7114.

Reaume, an Associate Professor at York University (an admitted schizophrenic), has published 3 books since 2000 (most notably *Remembrance of Patients Past: Patient Life at the Toronto Hospital for the Insane, 1870-1940*) and co-founded the Psychiatric Survivor Archives in Toronto. http://www.mindfreedom.org/campaign/media/radio/mfradio/show/geoffrey-reaume

Reville was in 3 mental hospitals in the 1960s, but ultimately got elected as a Toronto Councillor and an MPP in Ontario (he has contributed to Mental illness and pathways into homelessness: annotated bibliography 1997). Both Reaume and Reville teach "Mad People's History" at university (Reaume at York and Reville at Ryerson). http://www.ryerson.ca/ds/for-faculty/index.html#Reville.

27. "Help," written by John Lennon and Paul McCartney, was from the Beatles' 1965 album of the same name released by Parlophone Records, and used to be part of my musical repertoire. BMI does not identify the publisher. Online at http://repertoire.bmi.com/Title.asp? blnWriter=true&blnPublisher=true&blnArtist =true&page=1&keyid=554585&ShowNbr =0&Sho wSeqNbr=0&querytype=WorkID and http://www.discogs.com/Beatles-Help/master/45895.

Chapter 5: Connections and Disconnections

28. Other family roles include the hero, mascot, caretaker (or enabler) and lost child. Curtis, O. (1999). *Chemical Dependency: A Family Affair.* Brooks Cole.

29. "The Great Pretender," was released as a single in 1955 by the Platters on the Mercury label. Written by manager Ram Buck (Publisher: Panther Music Corp.), it was the first #1 American R&B hit. Online at http://www.songfacts.com/detail.php?id=4073. More information is available at http://www.ascap.com.

30. Sugar triggers the same reward area in the brain as other addictive substances. Online at http://www.nydailynews.com/life-style/health/researcher-sugar-addictive-cocaine-obesity-diabetes-cancer-heart-disease-article-1.1054419#ixzz2qenpcInx; http://www.princeton.edu/main/news/archive/S22/88/56G31/index.xml?section=topstories;

http://www.ncbi.nlm.nih.gov/pubmed/18325546; and
http://www.ncbi.nlm.nih.gov/pubmed/12055324.

31. High-fructose corn syrup (HFC) wasn't discovered until the
     1970s, when increased cane and beet sugar costs fueled interest in
     this subsidized liquid ingredient, which made it cheaper and easier
     to use in processed foods. Moss, M. (2013). *Salt Sugar Fat: How
     the Food Giants Hooked Us.* Toronto, ON: McClelland & Stewart.

32. "50 Years of Pantyhose." *Smithsonian Magazine.* Online at
     http://www.smithsonianmag.com/arts-culture/50-Years-of-
     Pantyhose.

Chapter 6: Early in the Ninth

33. The Clarke Institute of Psychiatry officially opened on May 18,
     1966, but patients didn't arrive until a month later. "Suitable"
     (1966, May 19). *The Globe and Mail*; Toronto has new mental
     hospital. (1966, May 19). *Toronto Daily Star.*

34. "No strait-jackets at Clarke" headed a small paragraph in the
     Dateline Metro column in Section 2 of the *Toronto Daily Star*,
     June 14, 1966.

35. This is taken from Dr. Frayn's interview with Dr. Stauble. Frayn,
     D. H. (1996). *The Clarke and Its Founders: The Thirtieth
     Anniversary: A Retrospective Look at the Impossible Dream.*
     Toronto, ON: (p. 53).

36. Charles Kirk Clarke was the first head of the University of
     Toronto's Department of Psychiatry in 1908. He saw mental
     illness as a disease like other physical ailments. Online at
     http://www.biographi.ca/en/bio/clarke_charles_kirk_15E.html.

37. According to author David Goldbloom, the term lunatic came
     from a simplistic attempt to attribute different behaviour to lunar
     (moon) changes. David S. Goldbloom, *Building on History: The
     Centre for Addiction and Mental Health in the 21st Century.*

38. The eugenicists, including notables such as Alexander Graham
     Bell, wanted to improve the well-being of the population by either
     preventing "mental defectives" and non-Anglo-Saxon descendants
     (i.e., immigrants) from having children, or by encouraging those
     of superior breeding to mate and produce mentally healthy
     offspring.

39. CAMH in Toronto merged the former Addiction Research Foundation (ARF), the Donwood Institute (for alcohol and drug addiction), and the infamous Queen Street Mental Health Centre (also known as the Provincial Lunatic Asylum, Toronto Lunatic Asylum, 999 Queen Street, or just plain old 999).

40. Noted psychiatrist and psychoanalyst Douglas H. Frayn authored *The Clarke and its Founders: the Thirtieth Anniversary: A Retrospective Look at the Impossible Dream,* Clarke monograph series, No. 6. Toronto, ON (p. 53).

41. According to Dr. Frayn, the ninth, tenth and eleventh floors each had 34 beds (p. 30).

42. Largactil (or Largactyl), the trade name for chlorpromazine (along with Thorazine), is an antipsychotic drug in the phenothiazine category. Online at http://www.drugs.com/international/largactil.html and http://www.spiritus-temporis.com/chlorpromazine/adverse-effects.html.

43. Mania: "Exceptional Excitement." Nevid, J.S., Greene, B., Johnson, P.A., & Taylor, S. (2009). *Essentials of Abnormal Psychology in a Changing World.* (2nd ed.) Toronto, ON: Pearson Education Canada.

44. Cogentin (benzotropine). Online at http://www.drugs.com/mtm/cogentin.html.

45. Chloral hydrate. Online at http://www.drugs.com/mtm/chloralhydrate.html.

46. In 1976, Professor Sclafani published a paper showing that sugar cravings and the resultant obesity could be induced in rats by letting them eat as much sugar as they wanted – the first indication that compulsive overeating is linked to sugar addiction. Moss, M. (2013). *Salt Sugar Fat: How the Food Giants Hooked Us.* Toronto: ON: McClelland & Stewart (pp. 5-6); Avena, N., Rada, P. & Hoebel, B.G. (2008). *Evidence for sugar addiction: Behavioral and neurochemical effects of intermittent, excessive sugar intake. Neuroscience & Biobehavioral Review,* 32 (1), 20–39. Online at https://www.ncbi.nlm.nih.gov.

Chapter 7: O-Blah-Dee, O-Blah-Dah

47. This line is from "In My Life," written by John Lennon and Paul

McCartney for the Beatles' *Rubber Soul* album on Parlophone Records in 1965 (Publisher: Northern Songs Ltd). Online at http://www.lyricsdepot.com/the-beatles/in-my-life.html; https://www.ascap.com/Home/ace-title-search/index.aspx; and http://www.discogs.com/Beatles-Rubber-Soul/release/4816760.

48. "That's Life" was written by Dean. K. Thompson and Kelly L. Gordon for Frank Sinatra and released on Reprise Records in 1966. Online at http://www.oldielyrics.com/lyrics/frank_sinatra/thats_life.html and http://www.discogs.com/Frank-Sinatra-Thats-Life/master/144118.

49. George Gershwin wrote "Rhapsody in Blue" in 1924, for solo piano and jazz band. In the late 1950's, it was popularized by symphony conductor Leonard Bernstein. Online at http://www.last.fm/music; and http://www.discogs.com/Gershwin -Leonard-Bernstein-Rhapsody-In-Blue-An-American-In-Paris/master/112264.

50. If the name Greenspan sounds familiar, Lilly was the aunt of noted Canadian criminal defence attorneys, Brian and Ed.

51. The best summary of the Metrecal craze is featured in the obituary of creator, Joseph Genster. http://www.boston.com/bostonglobe/obituaries/articles/2010/08/28/c_joseph_genster_marketed_60s_diet_fad_metrecal_at_92/.

52. Ayds as a diet candy began in the late 1930s, peaked in the 1970s, but couldn't stay afloat despite a name change when the AIDS epidemic broke in the 1980s. http://www.yourememberthat.com/media/15018/Ayds_Diet_Candies/#.VFFbGhb4Jvp.

53. While "till death do us part" isn't part of a Jewish wedding ceremony, my parents married in a British registry office.

54. In 1994, after making his award-winning film *Schindler's List*, Director Seven Spielberg founded the Survivors of the Shoah Visual History Foundation at the University of Southern California, to record their stories. Online at http://sfi.usc.edu/about/institute#sthash.PcVMhQ1u.dpuf.

55. "Personality," written by Lloyd Price and Harold Logan, was recorded by Lloyd Price (Publisher: Irving Music). Following its 1959 release on the ABC-Paramount label, it became a crossover song, #2 on the pop chart and #1 on R&B. Online at

http://old.yoursonglyrics.com/personality-lloyd-price/;
http://repertoire.bmi.com/Title.asp? blnWriter=
true&blnPublisher=true&blnArtist=true&page=1&keyid=
1167927&ShowNbr=0&Sho wSeqNbr=0&querytype=WorkID;
http://www.discogs.com/Lloyd-Price-Mr-
Personality/master/575534.

56. Très bonne is the French feminine.

57. "Sentimental Journey" was written by Bud Green, Les Brown and
Ben Homer in 1944, and recorded by Doris Day. Online at
https://www.youtube.com/watch?v=PUw125JMVFI; "Cry Me a
River" was written by Arthur Hamilton in 1953, and recorded by
Julie London in 1955. Online at http://www.theguitarguy.com/
crymeari.htm. "Dear Hearts and Gentle People" was written by
Sammy Fain and Bob Hilliard in 1949, inspired by a phrase on a
scrap of paper left by Stephen Foster in 1864. Online at
https://en.wikipedia.org/wiki/Dear_Hearts_and_Gentle_People.

58. The song "26 Miles," sometimes known as "Santa Catalina,"
(Publisher: Beechwood Music Corporation) was written by Bruce
Belland and Glen Larson, two of The Four Preps who recorded it
in 1957 on the Capitol label. It rose to number 2 on the charts and
influenced Brian Wilson and Jimmy Buffett, among others. Online
at http://www.latimes.com/entertainment/la-ca-socal15jul15-
story.html.

59. Arthur Fields and Walter Donovan published "Aba Daba
Honeymoon" in 1914, but it became famous when Debbie
Reynolds and Carleton Carpenter recorded it as a single in 1950
for MGM Records. Online at https://www.youtube.com/watch?v
=VJHJAkhacGU; and http://www.discogs.com/Miss-Debbie-
Reynolds-And-C-Carpenter-With-MGM-Studio-Orchestra-Aba-
Daba-Honeymoon-Row-Row-Row/master/747857.

60. John Bradshaw, the noted author, TV personality, innovator,
counsellor, theologian, philosopher, public speaker and recovering
alcoholic, is a leading figure in addiction/recovery, family
systems, relationships, and spiritual and emotional growth who
introduced mainstream society to the phrases "inner child" and
"dysfunctional families." I videotaped all of his broadcasts on
PBS back in the 1980s. Online at http://www.johnbradshaw.com.

61. "You're Nobody Till Somebody Loves You," singer Dean

Martin's 1965 hit on Reprise Records, was written by Russ Morgan, Larry Stock and James Cavanaugh in 1944, and covered by many artists. Online at https://www.youtube.com/watch?v=DIAEAVKcKrs; and http://www.discogs.com/Dean-Martin-Youre-Nobody-Till-Somebody-Loves-You/master/637305.

62. When you eat too much processed sugar (not the natural sugar found in fruits and vegetables), your brain releases a lot of feel-good dopamine and endorphins, so you feel a mild euphoria or pleasure, along with a spike in your glucose level. There is scientific evidence that the more sugar you eat, the more you want to eat. However, once the eating stops, after a while, your blood sugar level plunges, creating a low or depression. William Dufty, in *Sugar Blues*, explains that when we eat sugar, most of it goes straight into the bloodstream, changing the fine balance between glucose and oxygen. The brain quickly registers this imbalance as a crisis, and releases hormones (e.g., insulin, adrenaline) to try to rebalance the blood's glucose and oxygen levels, often overshooting, causing a low blood glucose level. We feel up while eating the sugar, then down when the hormones rebalance.

63. Daytime talk show hosts included Gary Moore, Arthur Godfrey and Merv Griffin. In the evening, Jack Paar, Steve Allen, Dick Cavett and the beloved Johnny Carson reigned.

64. Line from "Hey Look Me Over," a song from the 1960 musical *Wildcat*, written by Cy Coleman and Carolyn Leigh and performed onstage by Lucille Ball. Online at https://www.youtube.com/watch?v=6Y1UEMU1gBk; and http://www.discogs.com/Michael-Kidd-And-N-Richard-Nash-Present-Lucille-Ball-Wildcat/release/5411902.

65. For young people, suicide was the third leading cause of death in the US in 2007 (ages 15-24), and the second in Canada since the 1970s. Online at http://www.cdc.gov/violenceprevention/pub/youth_suicide.html; http://www.canadiancrc.com/Youth_Suicide_in_Canada.aspx; and http://www.cmha.ca/mental_health/preventing-suicide/#.VcOam_nbwxI.

Chapter 8: Measuring the Marigolds

66. This is a line from the Frank Loesser song "Inch Worm," performed by Danny Kaye in the 1952 film *Hans Christian Anderson* (Publisher: Frank Music Corp) and released on an album by Decca Records that same year. The lyric describes how the inch worm measures the flowers without seeing their beauty. Online at https://www.youtube.com/watch?v=fXi3bjKowJU; http://bussongs.com/songs/inchworm.php and http://www.discogs.com/Danny-Kaye-Danny-Kaye-Sings-Selections-From-The-Samuel-Goldwyn-Technicolor-Production-Hans-Christian/release/4145803. More information is available at http://www.ascap.com.

67. British supermodel Twiggy is sometimes credited with starting the body image trend towards extreme thinness for the British working class.

68. The tests included the 1967 versions of the Wechsler Adult Intelligence Scale (WAIS), the 16 Personality Factors test (16PF), the Minnesota Multiphasic Personality Inventory (MMPI), a Sentence Completion Test, a Differential Diagnostic Test (DDT) and the Rorschach, a projective test that asks the person to describe inkblot-like pictures, and also requires the tester's subjective interpretation.

69. This series of drawings seemed like an early version of the Thematic Apperception Test (TAT).

Chapter 9: The Unwinding

70. HCG (human chorionic gonadatropin) is derived from a hormone produced by pregnant females. Mine may have come from the urine of pregnant mares. British Dr. A.T.W. Simmons invented HCG along with the HCG diet in the 1950s. It went out of fashion after the 1970s, then revived again in 2007, but with pills instead of injections. Online at http://hcgdietdrop.net/hcg-faqs.

71. My sister named my car Boris, as a tribute to Boris and Natasha, two characters from animated television series, *The Rocky and Bullwinkle Show*, which was produced by Jay Ward Productions.

72. The classic Gestalt book, *Gestalt Therapy: Excitement and Growth in the Human Personality,* was written by Fritz Perls, Ralph Hefferline, and Paul Goodman and published in 1951 by Julian Press. I have the 1971 paperback version by Bantam Press. Online at http://www.gestalt.org/phgintro.htm.

73. The song "I Whistle a Happy Tune," written by Richard Rodgers and Oscar Hammerstein (Publisher: Williamson Music Co.), is from their 1951 musical, *The King and I*, which was made into a movie in 1956. The music was released as an album that same year by Capitol Records. Online at http://www.cornel1801.com/videosong/The_King_and_I_I_Whistle_A_Happy_Tune/moviesong.html; http://www.imdb.com/title/tt0049408/?ref_=nv_sr_1 and http://www.discogs.com/Rodgers-And-Hammerstein-The-King-And-I/master/149896. More information is available at http://www.ascap.com.

74. *The Catcher in the Rye* was published in July 1951 by Little, Brown. After WWII, Salinger had a nervous breakdown and put himself into a mental hospital. Some say this book was about the war, while others say that the main character, Holden Caulfield, expressed the rage that J.D. couldn't. *Salinger*, by David Shields and Shane Salerno, Simon & Schuster, 2013.

75. James Joyce finally got *Ulysses* published in Paris in 1922, by friend Sylvia Beach. Online at http://jamesjoyce.ie/joyce/.

76. Herb Alpert's 1966 album, *What Now My Love*, recognizable by its cover, was #1 for nine weeks, and the title track won two Grammies. Online at http://www.tijuanabrass.com.

Chapter 10: Chez Clarke

77. In the 1960s, I attended the State University of New York at Buffalo, with the unwieldy acronym, SUNYAB.

78. *Girls*, the award-winning HBO TV series, was created in 2012 by Lena Dunham, its star. Online at http://www.imdb.com/title/tt1723816/?ref_=nm_flmg_wr_1.

79. Melanie Safka's album, *Leftover Wine*, was reissued on CD in 1993 by the Buddah label. Maybe you remember her pop hits: "I've Got a Brand New Pair of Roller Skates" and "What Have They Done To My Song Ma." Online at http://www.allmusic.com/album/leftover-wine-mw0000099945.

80. Cyanamid Canada closed the Niagara Falls plant in 1992. It had produced calcium cyanide, to help extract precious metal from ore. Online at http://www.niagarafallsreview.ca/2007/07/11/who-wants-some-cyanamid-soil-for-their-garden.

81. Brando played the Stanley Kowalski character in the 1951 movie version of Tennessee Williams' *Streetcar Named Desire*. Online at http://www.imdb.com/title/tt0044081/?ref_=nv_sr_1.

82. Edward Albee's original play, *Who's Afraid of Virginia Woolf?* appeared on Broadway in 1962. Mike Nichols directed the 1966 movie of the same name, starring Elizabeth Taylor and Richard Burton. Online at http://www.broadway.com/shows/whos-afraid-virginia-woolf/story/; and http://www.imdb.com/title/tt0061184/?ref_=fn_al_tt_1.

83. Ron Silver. Actor, Tony-award winner, political activist, 1946-2009. His IMDB biography describes his trademark "dark intense starting eyes." Online at http://www.imdb.com/name/nm0798779/bio? ref_=nm_ql_1.

84. Trull, T. J. (2005). *Clinical Psychology*. Belmont, CA: Wadsworth, Cengage Learning; and *The DSM Story*, online at http://articles.latimes.com/2010/feb/10/science/la-sci-dsmbox10-2010feb10.

Chapter 11: Plan B

85. The headline of his *New York Times* obituary read "John Treasure Jones, a Cunard Captain, 87." (May 17, 1993). Online at http://www.nytimes.com/1993/05/17/obituaries/john-treasure-jones-a-cunard-captain-87.html Note that Wikipedia incorrectly has the Captain not taking the *Mauritania*'s helm until December 1962. But he was Captain in the summer of 1962 when I was on board, although he may not have been there officially.

86. The company was called "Viner's of Sheffield."

87. Epstein, H. (1979). *Children of the Holocaust*. Bantam.

88. The Mansion House. Online at http://www.cityoflondon.gov.uk/about-the-city/the-lord-mayor/mansion-house/Pages/default.aspx.

Chapter 12: Reality Orientation

89. Riot and protest cities included: Boston, Newark, Tampa, Cincinnati, Cleveland, Minneapolis, Washington DC, Milwaukee, Durham NC, Memphis, and Detroit. In part, from memory, and in part, online at http://www.thepeoplehistory.com/1967.html.

90. Berton, P. (1997). *1967, The Last Great Year.* Toronto, ON: Doubleday.

91. Ibid.

92. *Your Pet Juliette*, the TV show, aired on the Canadian Broadcast Corporation (CBC) after *Hockey Night in Canada* from 1956-66. Online at http://www.thecanadianencyclopedia.ca/en/article/juliette/.

93. "Get a Job" was the 1958 doo-wop hit single by the Silhouettes, written by Earl Beal, Raymond Edwards, William Horton, and Richard Lewis and released by Ember Records (Publisher: EMI Longitude Music). Online at http://www.thesilhouettes.org; http://repertoire.bmi.com/Title.asp? blnWriter=true&blnPublisher=true&blnArtist=true&page=1&keyid=462391&ShowNbr=0&Sho wSeqNbr=0&querytype=WorkID; and http://www.discogs.com/Silhouettes-Get-A-Job-I-Am-Lonely/master/329084.

94. Excerpt from "Casey at the Bat," a poem by Ernest Lawrence Sayer, 1888. Online at http://www.poetryfoundation.org/poem/174665.

95. The Ontario Institute for Studies in Education (OISE) is now located several blocks west, along Bloor, between Bedford and St. George in Toronto.

96. Stelazine. Online at http://medical-dictionary.thefreedictionary.com/Stelazine.

97. Parnate is an MAO (Monoamine Oxidase) inhibitor that interferes with the amount of serotonin and other neurotransmitters in the central nervous system. Online at http://medical-dictionary.thefreedictionary.com/Parnate; http://www.drugs.com/pro/parnate.html.

98. Ryerson Polytechnic Institute. Ryerson didn't receive university accreditation until 1993, and became Ryerson University in 2001. Online at http://www.thecanadianencyclopedia.com/en/article/ryerson-university/.

99. Jewish Vocational Services (JVS) is still around, doing their good work.

100. Some information on distorted thinking by Aaron Beck and Albert Ellis became publicly available in the 1960s, although Albert Ellis's first book on Rational Emotional Behavior Therapy (REBT), *How to Live With a Neurotic*, was published in 1957. Beck's depression measurement scale, the *Beck Depression Inventory* (BDI), appeared in 1961, but his book, *Depression: Clinical Experimental and Theoretical Aspects*, wasn't published till 1967. Online at http://albertellis.org/ about-albert-ellis-phd/; http://www.goodtherapy.org/famous-psychologists/aaron-beck.html; and http://www.simplypsychology.org/cognitive-therapy.html.

Chapter 13: Leavings

101. British Ford made the Anglia, 1939-1967. Mine was a white 105E model. Online at http://car-from-uk.com/motors/anglia/; and http://www.fordanglia105eownersclub.co.uk/history/.

102. The Shaw Festival. Online at http://www.shawfest.com/history.

103. Calvin Rand. Online at http://vitacollections.ca/notlheritage/2771830/data.

104. Our host was probably Calvin Rand, Ibid, p. 14

105. Studio Arena Theatre. Online at http://theatre-costumes.com/studio_arena.html.

106. "A Moon for the Misbegotten," Eugene O'Neill's sequel to the award-winning "Long Day'sJourney into Night," was directed by Jose Quintero. Online at http://buffalo.com/2014/07/17/featured/throwback-theater-moon-misbegotten-studio-arena/; and http://www.digplanet.com/wiki/ Studio_Arena_Theater.

107. Dewhurst and Scott were married to and divorced from each other twice.

108. "She's Leaving Home" by John Lennon and Paul McCartney (Publisher: Sony/ATV Tunes LLC) was on the Beatles' 1967 album *Sgt. Pepper's Lonely Hearts Club Band* on the Parlophone label. Online at http://www.discogs.com/Beatles-Sgt-Peppers-Lonely-Hearts-Club-Band/master/23934. More information is available at http://www.ascap.com.

109. Elm Street runs east-west between Bay and Yonge Streets, two blocks north of Dundas.

110. Chuvalo lost this World Boxing Association fight in the 15th round to Ernie Terrell on November 1, 1965, at Maple Leaf Gardens. Online at http://georgechuvalo.ca/bio/; and http://www.imdb.com/ name/nm0161546/bio.

111. George Chuvalo and Floyd Patterson. You can see the fight online at https://www.youtube.com/watch? v=uhDntaI6XY8.

112. The Paddock Tavern is Toronto's third-oldest bar. Online at http://www.thepaddock.ca/history.

Chapter 14: Outpatient

113. This line is from Jimmy Webb's 1967 song "MacArthur Park," recorded as a single by Richard Harris in 1968 on the Dunhill label (Publisher: Universal Polygram International Publishing Inc.). It runs over 7 minutes. Online at http://www.songfacts.com/detail.php?id=1875; http:// www.discogs.com/Richard-Harris-Mac-Arthur-Park/master/216281. More information is available at http://www.ascap.com.

114. "I'd rather fight than switch" is the tagline from an old TV commercial for Tareyton cigarettes (yes, they actually advertised cigarettes on TV in the 1960s and '70s). The slogan appeared in radio, TV, print and billboard ads from 1963 to 1981. Online at https://en.wikipedia.org/wiki/Us_Tareyton_smokers_would_rather_fight_than_switch!.

115. TOPS was established as a non-profit organization in 1948. Online at http://www.tops.org.

116. The one-act play, *Chamber Music,* was written in 1962 by Arthur Kopit. The story takes place in 1938, as the women try to plan how to fend off an attack from the men's ward. I played the woman with the notebook, who thought she was author/poet

Gertrude Stein, and my lifelong friend Marilyn played suffragette activist Susan B. Anthony. Other characters include martyr Joan of Arc, politician Queen Isabella I of Spain, Constanze Mozart (the famed composer's wife), pilot Amelia Earhart, silent-film actress Pearl White, and explorer Osa Johnson. The play questions sanity and identity, suggesting that assertive women might be crazy. Online at https://en.wikipedia.org/wiki/Chamber_Music_ %28play%29 and http://blogcritics.org/theater-review-nyc-arthur-kopits- chamber/.

117. Now, a number of books have been written and countless studies done about the addictive qualities of sugar and fat, and how these foods are designed to create cravings.

118. "Lucy in the Sky with Diamonds," by John Lennon and Paul McCartney (Publisher: Northern Songs Ltd.), is on the Beatles' 1967 album, *Sgt. Pepper's Lonely Hearts Club Band* on the Parlophone label. Online at http://www.myrsten.nu/worldnet/ beatlesongs.htm; and http://www.discogs.com/ Beatles-Sgt-Peppers-Lonely-Hearts-Club-Band/master/23934. More information is available at http://www.ascap.com.

119. Jennifer Scanlon, examines the impact of Gurley Brown's book in her 2009 review "Sensationalist literature or expert advice?" published online in *Feminist Media Studies* 9 (1), 12. Online at http://www.tandfonline.com/doi/full/10.1080/ 14680770802619433.

120. Ibid. Gurley Brown took over the editorship of *Cosmopolitan* magazine in 1965.

121. Michael Jacot Productions was located just below Bloor on the east side of Jarvis or Sherbourne. Writer, actor and director Michael Jacot died in 2006 at the age of 82. When I met him, he was working on the 1970 film *The Last Act of Martin Weston*. Online at http://www.imdb.com/title/ tt0065965/?ref_=fn_al_tt_1.

122. Ten years later, Kit and Linda went on to make the award-winning *Degrassi TV* series. Online at https://en.wikipedia.org/wiki/ Degrassi_%28franchise%29.

123. I can find only one reference to a film Linda made about immigrant children, for the Toronto School Board. Online at http://en.wikipedia.org/wiki/Kit_Hood#cite_note-1. However, the article "Introducing Kit Hood and Linda Schuyler," refers to a

film by Schuyler called Between Two Worlds, which I haven't been able to track down yet. Online at http://cinemacanada.athabascau.ca/index.php/cinema/article/viewFile/2292/2342.

124. Dr. Jack Birnbaum wrote two books, *Cry Anger* and *The Pleasure Principle,* which used composite case studies of his clientele. He was a warm and kind-hearted person, who helped many of his clients.

Chapter 15: Up to the Bottom

125. Roger the Dodger's real name: Roger Palmer

126. The show was the pilot for a rather remarkable series called *Strange Paradise*, shot in May 1969 at CJOH-TV in Ottawa. This daily gothic drama aired throughout the US and on CBC in Canada. As the very first Canadian-American co-production of its kind, it focused on the supernatural, witchcraft, and voodoo, and starred Colin Fox and Dawn Greenhalgh, among a host of other notable Canadian talent. Online at http://www.strangeparadise.net.

127. This church has since been replaced by a retirement home, after it burned down in 1995. Online at https://en.wikipedia.org/wiki/St._Paul%27s-Avenue_Road_United_Church.

128. Mainstream acceptance of non-married members of the opposite sex living together wouldn't happen until the mid-1970s, when hit TV series *Three's Company* was okay enough to be broadcast. Then, the three major American TV networks (ABC, CBS and NBC), were the only game in town (there was no cable or satellite). They wouldn't risk airing a program if it didn't reflect some aspect or trend within conventional culture. The show featured one male and two female characters sharing an apartment as friends, and ran from 1976 to 1984. Online at http://www.imdb.com/title/tt0075596/?ref_=nv_sr_1.

129. American-born Doug Fetherling (now known as George Fetherling) is a prolific Canadian author, poet, scholar and editor. At the time I met him, he was working on a biography of Ben Hecht, a newspaperman he admired.

130. I met the late Ted Plantos, now known as "the people's poet," sometime between 1969 and 1971 at this event, which he may have started, since he is credited with founding or co-founding so

many important literary outlets for poetry and writing, especially in Toronto, and mentored many of today's successful poets. I was sad to learn of his passing, and remember him as a kind, good-natured and very funny man.

131. British Equity and the Alliance of Canadian Cinema, Television and Radio Artists (ACTRA) are unions for professional performers.

132. I worked for or with people like John Halas, of Halas & Batchelor, who wrote and animated the very first full-length version of George Orwell's *Animal Farm*. British comedian Spike Milligan, and jazz-blues singer George Melly.

133. Dr. Paul E. Garfinkel, whose major interest has been anorexia, became Chair of Psychiatry at University of Toronto in 1990, which automatically made him President and Psychiatrist-in-Chief at the Clarke. He ultimately served as President and CEO of CAMH for 12 years, from 1997 to 2009. Online at http://www.cihr-irsc.gc.ca/e/46618.html. He has written his own autobiography, *A Life in Psychiatry: Looking out, Looking in* (published by Barlow in 2014), which I have but can't read until I'm done with this.

134. Bulimia was the term used for binge eating with and without purging, but it didn't become an official eating disorder till 1980, when the *DSM-III* was released. Since Dr. Garfinkel had worked in this area, he probably had access to research on the topic. In addition, the *International Classification of Diseases (ICD-9)* published in 1975, listed bulimia (307.51) under "Other and unspecified disorders of eating." Online at http://historyofeating. umwblogs.org/history-of-eating-disorders/ and http://www.randomhistory.com/2008/08/08_eating.html.

135. EEG stands for Electroencephalograph. Electrodes are painlessly attached to your head at various places to measure your brain's electrical brainwave patterns which are fed into a computer. Certain patterns can indicate epilepsy, sleep disorders, or physical or mental problems in your brain.

136. According to the freedictionary.com, an hysterical personality disorder is characterized by "dramatic, reactive, and intensely exaggerated behavior, which is typically self-centred. It results in severe disturbance in interpersonal relationships that can lead to

psychosomatic disorders, depression, alcoholism, and drug dependency." Mosby's Medical Dictionary, 8th edition. Online at http:// medical-dictionary.thefreedictionary.com/ Hysterical+personality+disorder.

137. Dr. Garfinkel notes this tendency in his autobiography, *A Life in Psychiatry: Looking Out, Looking In*, published in 2014 by Barlow Book Publishing Inc., Toronto.

Chapter 16: A New Direction

138. This study, "Losing weight won't necessarily make you happy, researchers say," was conducted at University College London, and published by *ScienceDaily* on August 7, 2014. Online at http:// www.sciencedaily.com/releases/2014/08/ 140807105430.htm.

139. Online at https://www.brainyquote.com/quotes/authors/ g/gloria_steinem_3.html

140. *Alice in Wonderland* was written by Lewis Carroll in 1865.

141. See "The Hunch" in chapter 2.

142. Two recent books, both published by McClelland and Stewart, are worth mentioning. *Salt Sugar Fat: How the Food Giants Hooked Us*, by Michael Moss (2013), and *The End of Overeating: Taking Control of the Insatiable North American Appetite*, by David A. Kessler (2009).

143. William Dufty wrote *Sugar Blues* in the early 1970s, which included several pages on Dr. John Yudkin, a British professor and nutritionist who was highly discredited for his1972 book about the dangers of sugar, *Pure, White, and Deadly*. However, in an article in the British newspaper *The Telegraph*, writer Julia Lewin Smith describes how Yudkin's book was recently revived by Dr. Robert A. Lustig, and reissued in 2013 as *Pure, White, and Deadly: How Sugar is Killing Us and What We Can Do to Stop It*, with an introduction by Lustig. Also in 2013, research neuroscientist Dr. Nicole Avena, who has conducted original research on the addictive aspects of sugar for years, wrote *Why Diets Fail*." Online athttp://www.telegraph.co.uk/lifestyle/wellbeing/ diet/10634081/John-Yudkin-the-man-who-tried-to-warn-us-about-sugar.html and http://www.drnicoleavena.com.

144. More than fifty 12-step programs exist for alcoholism, drug addiction, eating, gambling, sex and sex addiction, other process addictions, depression, and other emotional issues. Online at http://www.12step.com/12stepprograms.html.

145. Rob Reiner directed the 1977 film *Oh, God!*, starring the late John Denver. Online at http://www.imdb.com/title/tt0076489/ ?ref_=nv_sr_3.

146. *The Twilight Zone*, created by Rod Serling, ran from 1959 to 1964. http://www.imdb.com/title/ tt0052520/.

147. Geneen Roth's first bestselling book, *Feeding the Hungry Heart*, was published in the early 1980s. I was influenced in the 1990's by one of her later hits, *When Food is Love. Exploring the Relationship Between Eating and Intimacy*, published by Plume in 1992.

148. Carl Gustav Jung, was a Swiss-born psychotherapist and psychiatrist whose work influenced many fields from anthropology and archeology to psychology, religion and spirituality, including Alcoholics Anonymous, online at http://www.cgjungcenter.org/welcome/who-is-carl-jung/.

149. See Organismic self-regulation in "Gestalt Therapy: An Introduction" by Gary Yontef, Ph.D.; "Gestalt Therapy" in the Encyclopedia of Mental Disorders. Online at http://www.gestalt.org/yontef.htm; http://www.minddisorders.com/Flu-Inv/Gestalt-therapy.html.

150. The Serenity Prayer, used by Alcoholics Anonymous and all 12-step programs, has generated some controversy over who wrote it. The daughter of theologian Reinhold Neibuhr claims he wrote it, according to a 2008 *New York Times* article. Online at http://www.nytimes.com/2008/07/11/us/ 11prayer.html?_r=0.

151. "Ontario Highway 401" reveals that the 401 has 16-18 lanes near Mississauga, the western outskirts of Toronto. Online at http://roadnow.com/canada/on/road_description.php?road=Ontario-Highway-401&id=r10000247#.VFUMFBb4Jvo.

152. The TV series *Leave it to Beaver* ran from 1957 to 1963. http://www.imdb.com/title/tt0050032/.

153. Back in the 1980s, The Gestalt Institute of Toronto only offered a three-year program. Now, it is a five-year program, thanks to the

requirements of the new College of Registered Psychotherapists of Ontario (CRPO), which officially accepted me as a Registered Psychotherapist as of April 1, 2015.

154. Starting from scratch at the age of 61, I was able to complete a four-year Honours B.A. program in Psychology at Ryerson University, Toronto, followed by a one-year Graduate Certificate in Addictions and Mental Health Counselling at Durham College, Oshawa.

155. In Ontario, the provincial health plan (OHIP) pays for everyone's physical treatment, but doesn't cover mental and emotional distress, including addiction, unless you can access a mental hospital like CAMH or find a psychiatrist who offers psychotherapy in addiction to medications.

156. In 1978, Susie Orbach wrote *Fat is a Feminist Issue*, which I devoured. In May 2013, I actually met her at a conference on eating disorders sponsored by NEDIC (National Eating Disorder Information Centre). I decided not to do the fan thing and to refrain from telling her how much that book meant to me. But as coincidence would have it, we bumped into each other while exiting/entering the ladies washroom. I burst into tears, and thanked her for that book, and she got teary-eyed, too. We had a moment.

157. Moss, Michael. (2013). *Salt Sugar Fat: How the Food Giants Hooked Us.* Toronto, ON: McLelland & Stewart.

158. I've borrowed and slightly altered this line from a poem by Ted Plantos called "Into Me," which is one of two he gave me, and which I recently discovered amongst my papers. The original line is: "without a sunlight of its own.

ABOUT THE AUTHOR

Natalie Gold is a Toronto-based Registered Psychotherapist in private practice since 2007. She specializes in binge eating and other disordered eating behaviours (food addiction, compulsive overeating and emotional eating), along with their accompanying weight and body image concerns. She has offered groups and workshops since 2002.

In her early years, after pursuing an international career as a blues/jazz singer, she spent almost three decades in market research as a focus group moderator and consultant, often for the Canadian government. Natalie has an Honours B.A. in Psychology from Ryerson University in Toronto, a graduate certificate in Addictions and Mental Health from Durham College in Oshawa, and after completing the four-year training program at the Gestalt Institute of Toronto, a post-grad certificate in Gestalt Therapy.

Natalie's expertise on binge-eating disorder is based on her education, as well as her personal life-long experience of the recovery process. She understands many of the struggles and issues of this complex, often misunderstood modern-day phenomenon. She integrates the experiential Gestalt approach with the latest results-oriented methods – Cognitive Behavioral Therapy (CBT), Dialectical Behavior Therapy (DBT) and Solution Focused Therapy – to meet her clients' needs.

Natalie still loves to sing (not just the blues), and also enjoys exploring Toronto's parks with her amazing rescue dog, Cassie.

Visit her website www.changehappens.ca, follow her on twitter @changehappensca, or email her at natalie@bingecrazy.com.

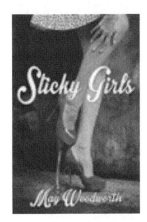

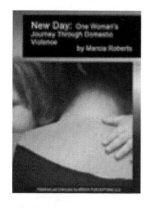

NEW DAY
*ONE WOMAN'S JOURNEY
THROUGH DOMESTIC
VIOLENCE (REVISED EDITION)*

By Marcia Roberts

"I am a survivor of domestic violence and abuse, but I am also a teacher, a mother and a writer. Because of all the great support I got during my four plus years of abuse, I would like to give back. I have compiled a story of my experience, based on current research and my own personal journals and emails that I kept for the last two years of the experience, as recommended by my counselors at a local abuse center. I am looking for a way to get my work out there so maybe other women can benefit, and not feel so alone or quite so hopeless. There is little out there on the topic that is autobiographical, and yet, as a former victim, I can tell you that that is the very thing that abused women or men need, to convince them to get out. This story needs to be told. It not just mine, but the story of so many other women and children. Their voices need to be heard. It is meant to be a mirror, too, that might reflect back reality to a victim who needs that clarity to be sure what to do next."

From Marcia Roberts's journal

Buy *New Day: One Woman's Journey Through Domestic Violence (Revised Edition)* at MyRomanceStory.com and wherever e-books are sold.

TOMORROWS

EMBRACING A HEALTHY FUTURE AFTER SURVIVING DOMESTIC ABUSE

By Marcia Roberts

Tomorrows: Embracing a Healthy Future After Surviving Domestic Abuse, is the continued story of a family struggling to do better than survive abuse at the hands of someone they love, it is their story of triumph over the greatest darkness to enter the life of a human being. Domestic abuse is so evil because it comes out of nowhere and is unpredictable, unprecedented, and seemingly, unstoppable. It forces the victims to choose sides and mount a defense against someone whom they would rather love. The family of *New Day* returns to their fight for safety in *Tomorrows* and to finally achieve peace, understanding, safety, and love. Led by a mother who only wants health, safety, and happiness for her children, and buoyed with protection from one who would later become step dad, the children of *Tomorrows* succeed.

Buy *Tomorrows: Embracing a Healthy Future After Surviving Domestic Abuse* at MyRomanceStory.com and wherever e-books are sold.

LARRY'S LEFT SIDE: A LIFE'S JOURNEY

By Laurence A. Cole

Laurence Cole was a medical student in England when he had a stroke and spent three months in a coma. He survived the coma only to find he had suffered severe brain damage and could not continue his medical education. This book takes us on the journey of his life as he struggled to retrain his brain (his "left side") build a family, fight being labeled "retarded", and ultimately achieve his doctorate in biochemistry. Dr. Cole went on to become one of the foremost cancer researchers in the United States and made major scientific evolutionary discoveries. He has several awards for research, was instrumental in numerous patents being awarded to Yale University, and has authored or co-authored more than 300 articles in peer-reviewed medical journals. He currently consults on hCG and gestational trophoblastic diseases all over the world through the USA hCG Reference Service.

Buy *Larry's Left Side: A Life's Journey* at MyRomanceStory.com and wherever e-books are sold.

BREAST HEALTH EXERCISES

By Renee Ridgeway

Easy, healthy and fun exercises that can be done at home at your own leisure. These instructional photos guide the viewer through step by step exercise-stretches. These exercises provide stress release, circulation and balance through the upper-mid body, breast and surrounding musculature.

Buy *Breast Health Exercises* at Amazon's Kindle Store, the Apple App Store and wherever e-books are sold.

Made in the USA
San Bernardino, CA
31 August 2016